Commentary on the Song of Songs and Other Writings

THE AUGUSTINIAN SERIES
VOLUME 10

Commentary
on the
Song of Songs
and Other Writings

❧

Giles of Rome, O.S.A.

with an introduction by
Roland E. Murphy, O. Carm.

edited by
John E. Rotelle, O.S.A.

Augustinian Press
1998

English translations:

Commentary on the Song of Songs: Mary Brennan (translator), Audrey Fellowes (editor).
Treatises: Dr. Michael Woodward
Sermons: The Three Vices of the World: Dr. Michael Woodward; other sermons: Gerard Deighan
Prayers: James Quinn, S.J.

Library of Congress Cataloging-in-Publication Data

Giles, of Rome, Archbishop of Bourges, ca. 1243-1316.
　　[De cantica canticorum. English]
　　Commentary on the Song of Songs and other writings / Giles of Rome ; with an introduction by Roland E. Murphy ; edited by John E. Rotelle.
　　　　p. cm. — (The Augustinian series ; v. 10)
　　Includes bibliographical references and index.
　　ISBN 0-941491-95-1 (alk. paper). — ISBN 0-941491-96-X
　　1. Bible. O.T. Song of Solomon—Commentaries. 2. Theology-Early works to 1800. 3. Sermons—Early works to 1800.
　　I. Rotelle, John E. II. Titles. III. Series.
　　BS1485.3G5513　　1997
　　230'.2—dc21　　　　　　　　　　　　　　　　　　　　　97-7353
　　　　　　　　　　　　　　　　　　　　　　　　　　　　　　CIP

Augustinian Press
P.O. Box 476
Villanova, PA 19085

To

Ansfried H. Hulsbosch, O.S.A.

❧

An Everlasting Tribute

Father Ansfridus Henricus Hulsbosch died suddenly of a heart-attack, while cycling through Amsterdam on 3 February 1973.

Born at Zandvoort, Holland, on 3 Mary 1912, he studied at Trinity College, Haarlem, and made first profession of vows on 21 September 1933. He was ordained a priest on 30 July 1938.

From 1938-1941 he studied theology at the Angelicum, Rome, and earned a doctorate in theology on 7 July 1941 with the thesis: *De Figura Christi patientis et resurgentis in epistulis S. Pauli.* After that he studied at the Biblicum, Rome, 1941-1944 and was awarded the degree doctor of biblical science on 8 January 1953 with his thesis: *Sagesse créatrice et éducatrice. Aspects de la théologie et de l'eschatologie des Livres Sapientiaux.* He was professor of New Testament at the Augustinian houses of studies in Holland (1945-1969) and Saint Monica's, Rome (1960-1965). He was member of the editorial board of the periodical *Tijdschrift voor Theologie,* coeditor of the Dutch translation of the New Testament, member of apologetical and ecumenical societies, and definitor of the Province of Holland (1958-1961). He was a prolific and profound scholar, who wrote numerous articles and books. His most famous book on *God's Creation* has been translated in several languages like his book on conversion. At the time of his death he was prior of Saint Augustine's in Amsterdam.

Contents

Foreword

Giles of Rome can definitely be classified as a person of our times. Like many famous people today he experienced difficulties and rejection early in his career as a philosopher and theologian. Rejected, he was then reinstated. Reinstated, he became one of the most famous thinkers of his day. Rejected by his peers, he was always supported by his confreres who entrusted to him their destiny in electing him prior general and the burden of head of The Augustinian School.

This man of contradictions, as it were, was appointed by the pope to help him in many tasks. He did so as a son of the Church. Finally, having been made an archbishop, he continued to serve his diocese; at the same time he lent his services to the Apostolic See of Rome.

In this book you will find the masterful work of Giles of Rome, Commentary on the Song of Songs and other works, which have been selected to emphasize the spirituality of the creative thinker.

Many time we acknowledge Giles as a philospher, theologian, etc. It is my intention, through the works here represented, to portray Giles as the man of faith, the friar of the Spirit, and the preacher of the good news.

I dedicate this work to a friar who opened up for me the power, force, and impact of the scriptures. Father Ansfried Hulsbosch, O.S.A., Province of Holland, taught me scripture at Collegio S. Monica, Rome. He was a soft-spoken professor, but his words and material were loud and clear. But there is more, his way of life was admirable: joy in the face of suffering through illness, acceptance in the face of rejection from his own. He supported all with inner peace, and this inner peace overflowed into his life, especially in his prayer and the celebration of the eucharist.

25 November 1997   John E. Rotelle, O.S.A.
Feast of Saint Thomas of Villanova

Biographical Introduction

Here lies
Giles of Rome,
of the
Order of Hermits of Saint Augustine,
princely dwelling of the virtues and purity of life
most discerning commentator on the matchless philosophy
of
Aristotle,
key and teacher of theology,
a lamp shedding light on difficulties,
Archbishop of Bourges
who died on 22 December 1316[1]

This is the epitaph that the friars of the Order of Saint Augustine placed on the tomb of Giles of Rome (Aegidius Romanus), and it sums up well the life and contribution of their fellow Augustinian. Giles died on 22 December 1316[2] at Avignon, France, which at that time was the seat of the papal court of Clement V. He was buried on Christmas eve in the Augustinian church in Avignon;[3] later his body was transferred to Paris and reinterred before the high altar of the monastery of the Grand Augustins, a place which was familiar to him and which had been given to him by Philip IV of France.

Early Life

There are no records which indicate the date and place of birth of Giles. Today scholars tend toward the year 1243 for the date of his birth.[4] This date is deduced from the requirement that a master of theology had to be thirty-five years of age before being appointed.[5] From the correspondence between Pope Honorius IV and Ralph d'Homblières, bishop of Paris, we learn that Giles was due to have been appointed master of theology in the university of Paris in 1278.[6] From this date it can safely be said that Giles was born no later than 1243.[7] Previous biographers certify the year of birth around 1247,[8] for it was said that Giles died at the age of sixty-nine.

Giles in most documents is referred to as Aegidius Romanus or Aegidius de Roma.[9] By the fact that Giles always had "of Rome" attached to his name, one assumes that he was born in Rome. Or it could be that he obtained the "of Rome" as his place of entrance into the Augustinian Order. Both customs prevailed. Jordan of Saxony (d.1380) in his celebrated work *The Life of the Brethren* claimed that Giles belonged to the celebrated Roman family of Colonna:

> Looking back as well as our knowledge allows on all the men of learning in this Order from the time of Saint Augustine up to our own generation, the foremost doctor of sacred theology was Brother Giles of Rome.[10]

Ambrose Massari of Cori, writing a half century later, asserts that Giles came from the Colonna section of Rome: "Among those who came after the Union we assign first place to that inspired man, Giles of Rome, from the Colonna region of Rome."[11] Trapè[12] and Mariani support this. As Mariani explains:

> These words lead us to think that Giles was not a descendant of the princely family, but rather had been born in the third region of Rome, which included the area bounded by the Campo Marzio, Saint Eustachia, Pigna, and Trevi quarters and was called "Colonna," not after the illustrious family of that name, who resided in the second or Trevi region, but after the Antonine Column that stood at its center.[13]

Scholars today are nearly unanimous in agreeing that Giles did not belong to the famous family.

In his will Giles mentions the monastery of Paris: "at whose breasts I was nourished from my youth,"[14] which would indicate that he was young when he was sent there. This phrase helps to ascertain Giles' time of entry into the Order of Saint Augustine. Gandolfo asserts that Giles "donned the Augustinian habit while in the flower of his youth," at the monastery of Santa Maria del Popolo in Rome.[15] Jordan of Saxony in the above-mentioned book states that Giles: "entered the Order as a very young man. His parents and friends tried to entice him back to the world by many allurements."[16] Whether Giles entered the Order against the wishes of his parents has never been ascertained or, to my knowledge, has appeared in other documents. However, from both of these accounts we can speculate that Giles probably entered the Order in 1257. After a year of novitiate he did some studies, the trivium, which would mean that he went to Paris to begin the academic year of September 1260. These years would coincide with the purchase of the house in Paris, situated at the Porte St. Eustache, the crossroads of the rue Montorgueil and rue Montmartre, from a widow named Theophania.[17] The prior general who sent Giles to Paris would have been Lanfranco of Milan (1256-1264);[18] he would have been the same who purchased the property in Paris.[19]

The conclusion of Mandonnet that Giles went to Paris in 1260 is reasonably accurate as indicated from the purchase of the property and from the statement in Giles' will.

Paris

What was once small schools or colleges or a collection of halls under a particular master turned into a flourishing university, the University of Paris, with an international faculty and student body, and with a faculty of arts and with the higher faculties of theology, medicine, and law. It is no wonder that when the mendicant orders, in their desire to serve the Church in many ways, entered the intellectual life, they began to establish themselves at the University of Paris: Dominicans and Franciscans, then Carmelites and Augustinians. For this reason the mendicant orders established houses in the city of Paris near the university.[20]

The arrival of the mendicants and their subsequent education and excellence at the University of Paris caused tensions, especially in the occupancy of the various chairs and of the office of regent masters. Initially, it had been the task of the canons of Notre Dame to teach theology. This arrangement was challenged by some well-educated diocesan clergy, some alumni of the university, who had become professional theologians and thus desired to teach in the higher faculty. It was these latter who wanted to teach and hold positions of authority, such as chairs and regent masters, before the arrival of the mendicants. They had banded together in a kind of union or guild of masters and became known as the *universitas magisterium*.[21]

The University of Paris was not without its conflicts, and these were settled from time to time by royal, papal, or diocesan intervention or a combination of all three. The university also had its glory. It was the leading university in France, a prestigious university in Europe, and the university of Paris. The faculty immersed itself in the problems of the day and offered opinions as to solutions and were asked by others for solutions to problems. In the theological world there was a lot of movement and interaction, for masters were putting forward new ideas and were also open to new ideas, new forms of expression. There were healthy exchanges between peers as well as differences of opinions between the University of Paris and other universities. There was no outright rejection of novel ideas which pervaded philosophy and theology and at times fostered bitter but healthy antagonism, intellectual debates, and numerous treatises.[22]

When the mendicants first joined the university, there was little difficulty. As the friars became educated and assumed positions of authority within the university structure and also within their own religious structure, there naturally arose conflict and jealousy between seculars and regulars. The friars were not only numerous and young but they had men of high intellectual caliber.

It was into this atmosphere of university life, intrigue, politics, and intellectualism that the young Giles was sent. He found himself outside of his country (the Papal States); he was thrust into an international environment in a famous center of learning; he mixed with young and old, students and masters, of various religious affiliations.

Education

As stated earlier, there is near unanimous agreement that Giles commenced studies in Paris in 1260. This date can also be deduced from the educational system of the times. Both Pierre Mandonnet and E. Esteban agree that 1260 is the starting year for Giles' study, but they reach this conclusion in different ways.

Giles, according to Mandonnet, began studies in the faculty of arts in 1260-1261 (academic year) and completed the first phase, three years, in 1263-1264, thus earning the degree of baccalarius artis. He then continued to the next phase, magister artis, in the same faculty of arts, and thus we come to the academic year 1266-1267. In 1267 he would then commence his theological studies which included five years of studies. So we are in the academic year 1271-1272 for completion of theological studies. After professional studies in theology he would have taken his first degree in the theological faculty and thus became baccalarius biblicus, most likely the academic year 1272-1273. Following this there was a two year course of study and exposition of the *Sentences* of Peter Lombard, at the end of which he would become baccalarius sententiarum, thus 1274-1275. As a baccalarius sententiarum he was obliged to teach as baccalarius formatus, and thus became eligible for the licentiatus in the academic year 1278-1279.[23] This year coincides with the above-mentioned letter between Honorarius IV and Bishop d'Homblières.

Esteban explains Giles' education in this way. In 1260-1261 Giles commenced studies for the degree of bachelor of arts, a course of three years; in 1264 he studied philosophy, a six year course, thus completing it in 1270. After two years of biblical studies, Giles began reading the *Sentences* in 1272, a three year course, and completed this in 1275. He then studied theology for four years, thus reaching 1279 as the year for being eligible for the licentiate.[24]

Under whom did Giles receive his education? There were no Augustinians at this time who held masterships in the University of Paris so it is presumed that Giles studied in the university for all courses because there was no studium generale in Paris as well where Giles could have studied the liberal arts as did the Dominican and Franciscan friars in their respective studia. We do not know if Giles had the freedom to select his own master or if the authorities of the Order in France imposed someone. Did he study under several? religious? secular? lay? There were probably fifteen regent masters of theology in 1269-1270; six were members of religious orders (including two Dominicans and one Franciscan).[25]

We do know that when Giles was studying at the university Thomas Aquinas, O.P., returned after an absence of ten years, so we can presume that between 1269 and 1272 Giles attended the lectures of Thomas Aquinas.[26]

Exile

On 18 January 1277 Pope John XXI (Magister Petrus Hispanus) wrote to Stephen Tempier, bishop of Paris, requesting him to make an investigation of the unrest and tensions at the university. The popes had repeatedly over the years taken an interest in the University of Paris.[27] Evidently word reached Rome about the novel ideas, especially the growing influence of Aristotle's works in philosophy and theology, and the wave of interest in eastern schol-

ars.[28] Already Tempier had condemned thirteen propositions in
1270.

Instead of reporting back to the pope as he was requested to do,
Tempier, after having consulted some theologians: "After receiving the advice of doctors of sacred theology and other prudent
men, we . . .,"[29] of whom Henry of Ghent was a member, issued a
condemnation of 219 propositions. This list was made public on 7
March 1277 and included, perhaps, in an oblique way, a condemnation of the teachings of Thomas Aquinas, Siger of Brabant,
Bonaventure, Roger Bacon, Henry of Ghent, Richard of Middle-
ton, and also Giles because of his alignment with the thought of
these masters.[30] The issuance of the 219 propositions brought to a
head the tensions generated by scholars in an attempt to fuse Aris-
totelianism and the subjects taught in the faculty of arts and in theology.

In England the archbishop of Canterbury, Robert Kilwardby,
followed suit, and on 18 March 1277 he condemned a group of
thirty propositions and also added a censure: "Anyone who person-
ally holds, teaches, or defends any of the foregoing propositions is
to be removed from his teaching office if he is a teacher; if he is a
bachelor, he is not to be promoted to the rank of master but is to
be expelled from the university."[31]

Although this controversy began long before Thomas Aquinas,
it flared up again during his second regency at the University of
Paris (1269-1272). Thomas and others opted for unicity of forms.
He maintained that "He would have formed the body to no purpose if, when breathing in the soul, he were to exclude the form he
had given it when forming it. Therefore the coming of the soul
does not remove all preceding forms."[32] Although principally a
philosophical question, it especially brought ramifications into the
theological sphere of thought.

The thought of Thomas Aquinas on the unicity of forms was not
condemned by the Tempier propositions of 1270 or 1277; it was,
however, included in the condemnations by the Dominican archbishop of Canterbury, Robert Kilwardby.

Giles at this time was preparing for the licentiate. Most likely he
was lecturing and writing. Already he had to his credit some note-
worthy works.[33] He was speaking out against the propositions and
publicly stating his views. Whether he was doing this to defend the
doctrine and reputation of his former teacher Thomas Aquinas
who had died in 1274 or because of his own involvement in the
intellectual milieu, we do not know. Most likely it was a combination of both. We have several reference points. Pope Honorius IV

shows that Giles was outspoken and freely and forcibly expressed his opinions: "He did not by any means retract but rather endeavored to confirm his views with various arguments."[34] There is also a report from the process on the life of Saint Thomas in which James of Viterbo, O.S.A., gives an account of Giles' support for Thomas Aquinas:

> The same James likewise told the witness that Giles of Rome, an Augustinian learned in sacred theology, had often said to him in conversation at the Paris residence: "Brother James, if the Friars Preachers had their way, they would be learned and intelligent, while we would be ordinary persons, and they would not have let us have the writings of Brother Thomas."[35]

Giles in his works speaks out against the Parisian propositions:

> I answer that the Paris article is concerned with this matter, for some articles claim that it is an error to say "make new species." I wish that those articles had been drawn up in the light of more mature advice, because they are not intelligible when they say God cannot make several of the same. But perhaps sounder counsel will be followed in regard to them later on.[36]

Writing on the creation of the soul, Giles says:

> Since this is an article condemned in Paris . . . Although it may be thought that none of those articles were rightly condemned (for we ourselves were in Paris at that time and attest that many of the articles passed not on the advice of the masters but due to the pigheadedness of a few), yet since the article is doubtful, it is not good to hold an eccentric position in such matters.[37]

Giles' strongest attacks come in his *Contra gradus et pluralitatem formarum,* written in 1277. He associated himself with others in support of Thomas Aquinas:[38]

> We shall therefore give it as our view . . . that to posit a plurality of forms contradicts the Catholic faith and contradicts the evidence of the senses. By positing a single form, then, we can better safeguard what the Catholic faith teaches.[39]

In the above Giles asserts rather emphatically that to maintain the plurality of forms was to hold an opinion contrary to the Catholic faith. He goes even further; he counsels silence on the part of those who hold to plurality of forms, for it is contrary to the teaching of the faith:

Let those who speak thus be silent. Let them not claim error if others maintain the contrary opinion of some doctors. They should realize that to speak out in this manner is simply to boast of their own weakness of intellect. For by believing that in this matter they are extolling themselves and not others, they show their own weakness, making it clear that they are unable to distinguish between definitions and sophisms, between a weak argument and a strong.[40]

Giles' utterances, writings, and positions caused Tempier, bishop of Paris, to refuse Giles the master's license and to send him away from the university. And thus Giles began his exile from the distinguished and his beloved University of Paris. But why did all this happen to Giles? Hissette affords us some insights:

They looked, then, for a quarrel with Giles of Rome. Why? Undoubtedly because this former student of Thomas Aquinas was defending, among other things, some theses of his master who was suspect at this time. For some teachings of Thomas had *certainly* been *attacked* in Tempier's great censure, even if the list as such does not, *perhaps*, include propositions drawn *directly* from his writings. Despite this latter fact, it seems certain, as Monsignor Delhaye insists, that Thomas was "aimed at, at least *indirectly*." According to Peckham, the thesis on the unicity of the substantial form even gave rise to an appeal to the Curia. Did this step originate with the legate, who supposedly referred to it in his interview with Henry of Ghent? This hypothesis is proposed by M. Hödl, but is excluded by M. Miethke for lack of cogent arguments. The circumstances surrounding the preparation of the 7 March decree are still very obscure, but one fact is certain: the thesis on the unicity of form is not among the 219 propositions censured, although it was considered by the legate, the bishop, and many theologians to be seriously heterodox. How is its omission to be explained? No other reason can be found but the esteem already attached to the memory of Thomas Aquinas.[41]

Italy

Giles left Paris most likely in 1278 or 1279. In 1279 Giles was at Perugia where the Roman province of the Order held its chapter; the chapter members elected Giles as definitor of the Roman province to the next general chapter.[42] In 1281 Giles participated as a definitor of the province of Rome in the general chapter held at Padua which opened on 15 August, feast of the Assumption. He is referred to as "Bacellarium Parisiensem."[43] In October of the same year (1281) Giles, bachelor of Paris, participated in the provincial chapter of the Roman province held at San Martino di Campiano. During this chapter financial provisions were made for three students at Paris, one of whom would later be Giles' successor at Paris, James of Viterbo.[44]

In May of 1283, the feast of Pentecost, Giles was present at the provincial chapter of the Roman province held in Cori and was designated as representative to the next provincial chapter of the Roman province to elect a prior provincial, definitors, and visitors: "The friars of this province agreed with complete unanimity on the venerable man, Giles of Rome, a bachelor of Paris, as an elector of the future prior provincial, definitors, and visitors, and in regard to everything else to be done at that coming chapter." Giles was also elected a discreet for the next general chapter.[45]

In May of 1284 Giles participated in the general chapter of Orvieto where he was again designated as "on behalf of our Roman province . . . Giles of Rome, bachelor of Paris."[46] In October of 1284, the feast of Saint Luke, Giles was a member of the provincial chapter of the Roman province which took place at Genazzano and again was designated as a representative: "All the friars agreed on the venerable Father, Giles of Rome, for all the official actions to be taken at the said chapter."[47] In May of 1285, on the feast of Pentecost, the provincial chapter of the Roman province took place at Tuscanella, and we find Giles present at it as vicar general for Clement of Osimo, prior general.[48] For the last time he was designated as bachelor. Yet in subsequent chapters, provincial and general, we do not find Giles among the membership: 1286 Roman provincial chapter (Città della Pieve), 1287 general chapter (Florence), 1287 Roman provincial chapter.[49] In 1288 at the provincial chapter of the Roman province we read: "For Giles of Rome, doctor of sacred theology, thirty gold florins."[50]

It is interesting to note that students and graduates of the University of Paris were held in high esteem, for they were given important positions of authority within their provinces, even students. Giles of Rome also enjoyed the esteem of his fellow province members as evidenced from the many times that they elected him a delegate to various chapters, provincial and general.

Return to Paris

As we have seen, when Giles left Paris he was occupied in Italy with the affairs of his own province, the Roman province, and of the Order of Saint Augustine. He was also writing, as we shall see in the chronology of his works; he was not teaching, for he was banned from doing this. Since his absence from Paris Bishop Stephen Tempier had died (1279), and Ralph d'Homblières, Parisian canon and master in theology, was appointed bishop of Paris.[51]

Why all of a sudden was there an interest on the part of Pope Honorius IV to reinstate Giles of Rome at Paris? The direct answer to the query is that we do not know. However, there is some background that will help us to unravel the mystery.

As indicated above, at a certain time in the history of the University of Paris the papacy took an interest in its affairs, and at times the papacy became overinvolved. Popes requested special considerations; at times popes took advantage of their position and privilege and examined a candidate and granted the license. Alexander IV (1254-1261) had the Cistercian Gui de l'Aumone examined by two cardinals and then conferred the license.[52] He almost had to take the same action for Thomas Aquinas, but the university acted before he had to intervene "before our letter arrived there."[53] Such interventions on the part of the papacy were not looked upon favorably, and such action also caused tension within the university faculties and also the mendicant orders.[54]

The intervention, however, of Pope Honorius IV was a little different than his predecessors. He does not ask the theology faculty to grant the license, nor does he grant it himself. He presents no threats. He requests that the chancellor and the theology masters convoke to discuss and decide Giles' case:

> To our esteemed brother bishop of Paris. It is a fact that our beloved son, Giles of Rome of the Order of Hermit Brothers of Saint Augustine, while studying at one time in Paris, said and wrote some things which your predecessor of happy memory, Stephen, bishop of Paris, thought should be withdrawn after he examined them himself and had them examined by the chancellor of Paris at that time and by other masters of the theological faculty. It is also the fact that Giles by no means withdrew them but rather tried to confirm them by various arguments. Recently, however, while at the Apostolic See, he humbly declared himself ready to withdraw, upon our request, what he had said or written that was judged should be withdrawn.
>
> We for our part have accepted this humble offer of his and have been moved by a spirit of compassion toward him. But because we thought it more fitting and profitable that the statements in question be deliberately withdrawn there where they were inadvisedly made orally and in writing, we thought he should be sent back to you. We therefore order your fraternity by this apostolic

document to assemble for this purpose our beloved son Nicholas, chancellor of Paris, and all the other masters of the theological faculty now resident in Paris, both those actually teaching and those not teaching. You are to proceed according to their advice in this matter. Once the friar in question has withdrawn, in the presence of all, whatever accusations against him you and the majority of the masters judge should be withdrawn and, in particular, whatever your said predecessor ordered withdrawn (as was said above), you are, by our authority, to see to it that he is freed of any burden and granted a license, according as you shall judge profitable, in God's sight and with the consent of the majority of the masters themselves, for the Catholic faith and for the good of the University of Paris.[55]

However, the last words of the letter, as Esteban points out, seem like a directive to the faculty of the university to promote Giles to the doctorate in theology: "see to it that he is freed of any burden and granted a license, according as you shall judge profitable, in God's sight and with the consent of the majority of the masters themselves, for the Catholic faith and the good of the University of Paris."[56]

Pope Honorius IV, as Cardinal Giacomo Savelli, was cardinal protector of the Augustinian and the Dominican orders. Conciliatory by nature, perhaps as pope he saw an opportunity to kill two birds with one stone: the rehabilitation of Giles would bring the rehabilitation of Thomas Aquinas whose teaching was affected by the 1277 condemnations and whose process for ecclesial recognition was stopped.[57]

Master of the University of Paris

The meeting requested by the pope must have taken place between May 1285, the date of the pope's letter, and December 1286, for on 22 December 1286 the faculty was meeting with the bishops to discuss Pope Martin IV's (1281-1285) decretal *Ad fructus uberes,* and it was during the course of that meeting that Godfrey of Fontaines mentioned that Giles was master. Giles' presence at the meeting cannot be determined, but most likely he was present.[58]

From the letter of Pope Honorius IV to Bishop Ralph d'Homblières we learn several things. There definitely was some type of formal retraction of the opinions which Giles said and wrote; however, there is no record of this document which would indicate specifics. The pope corroborates that the young bachelor in Paris did write and say things which irritated Bishop Tempier and other members of the university, that he did not revoke his opinions, and that he was censured for these opinions. Then the pope seems to indicate that Giles came before him to plead his case. Also, at this time, the papacy was very keen about the establishment of the Augustinian Order on a sure footing (the Great Union, 1256, was only twenty-nine years ago), especially in academic circles. This also could have been the wish of the former cardinals protector Richard Annibaldi (d.1276) and Giacomo Savelli (presently Honorius IV) who took an active interest in the development of the Order, and perhaps of the present prior general, Clement of Osimo.

The pope goes on to say that Giles was willing to adjust his previous statement in the form of a revocation. He concludes the letter with the request that Giles' case be reconsidered by the university faculty and that he be granted the degree.

Mandonnet does show that Giles had to withdraw some points of his teaching.[59] In the fifth *Quodlibet* (1290) Giles leaves as unsettled the question of the unity of forms in humans, a position which he had vigorously maintained in 1277.[60] In the second *Quodlibet* (1287), dealing with the question of how many angels there might be of the same species, Giles remarks that this is one of the issues included in the Paris condemnations and that it was not composed with due consideration. Nevertheless he feels himself bound to defend it and does so grudgingly and obviously without conviction.[61]

We are dealing with a young bachelor in 1277 on fire with knowledge and with admiration for his teachers, especially Thomas Aquinas. He was ready to tackle the world and defend positions without compromise. Giles must have been a person of exceptional ability; his writings at such an early stage in his career witness to this.

The Giles who petitioned the pope for special consideration, the Giles who returned to Paris in 1285 to assume the position of Master, was a changed person. Perhaps distance from the Paris scene, more reflection and writing may have pushed Giles' thought in another direction and precipitated his request to the pope.

Giles began his office of master in the academic year of 1 September 1285 and continued in office as regent master in Paris until 1293. During his tenure as regent master Giles gave six *Quodlibeta*.[62]

Several events occurred during his tenure. On 6 June 1286 Philip IV was crowned king at Rheims, and Giles was selected by the university to make the oration on behalf of the University of Paris.[63] It is interesting to note that Philip's education was entrusted to Giles.[64]

Another event which faced Giles was the conflict between seculars and regulars. We alluded to this earlier; it was a growing problem and came to a head in the university life in a conflict between the faculty of arts, which was mostly in the hands of the seculars, and the theology faculty which was principally in the hands of the regulars. Because of the increasing interest in Aristotle members of the faculty of arts found themselves in disagreement with the theology faculty and vice versa. The faculty of arts was not yet ready to endorse all the novel ideas which the theology professors held and expounded. Naturally the plurality of forms was one of the principal areas of contention, and Giles already had his difficulties with this.

Recourse was had to Rome, but Pope Martin IV was on his deathbed; a second recourse to Pope Honorius IV achieved no reply. The gathering of bishops and faculty in Paris in December 1286 was enveloped in a rather tense atmosphere. The bishops publicly condemned the mendicants, and this was followed by "determinations" in favor of the seculars by Henry of Ghent, Godfrey of Fontaines, and Gervase of Saint Eligius.[65]

Giles ("postea" the minutes say, which could mean some days or months) speaks to this point, and the relator (Godfrey of Fontaines) records this:

> Afterward, these points were disputed by Master Giles of the Augustinian Order, who is now regarded as the best in the entire city on all matters. He came to the conclusion that the bishops had by far the better side. Because of their novelty I have up to now been unable to obtain a copy of these decisions. If I am able to obtain one, I shall not delay in sending it.[66]

The phrase "who is now regarded as the best in the entire city on all matters" relates to us the high esteem in which Giles was held. It is interesting to note that here Giles supports the seculars; later he will be supporting the regulars in a similar case of exemption.

Another important episode which occurred during Giles' tenure as master in Paris was the decree of the Augustinian general chapter of Florence (May 1287) which stipulated that the doctrine of Giles be mandatory for teachers and students of the Order:

> Because the teaching of our esteemed Master Giles enlightens the entire world, we decree and command that all the lectors and students of our Order accept without any exception the present and future opinions and positions and sentences of the said Master. They are to assent to them and zealously defend his teaching with all possible care, so that being themselves enlightened they may be able to enlighten others.[67]

Because of Giles' designation as "master in the Augustinian Order" too, scholars were eager to know the exact date for the beginning of Giles' mastership in Paris. Certainly, the Augustinian Order would not recognize Giles' leadership if he were only a master of theology for several months. Also it is quite soon after being named master in Paris that this event occurred. Perhaps the Augustinians wanted a leader just as the Dominicans and Franciscans had their giants? Also, the decree was rather strict in terms of adherence to Giles' teaching, "the present and future opinions and positions and sentences of the said Master," which later was modified by Giles himself.[68] Putting aside the speculation, however, there was really no one else in the Augustinian Order who was as talented, well-known, and productive as Giles of Rome.

On Pentecost Sunday 1290 the general chapter of Regensburg (Ratisbon) opened. This was a very important chapter in the life of the Order, for it approved the Order's first constitutions. Clement of Osimo (d.1291) was the prior general. The *Constitutiones Ratisbonenses*, as they were commonly called, dealt with the whole life of the Order, and there was a section on studies. Giles was present at the chapter: "Giles of Rome, a doctor of sacred theology, was likewise there; he had active voice and decided everything as one of the definitors of the province of the Order."[69] Undoubtedly he had a hand in shaping the propositions on studies.[70] In addition Giles was given money for his expenses[71] and a role in the selection of students for Paris for reading the *Sentences*:

> We decree and entrust to Giles of Rome, our master, the authority to call bachelors to Paris to read the *Sentences*, as he shall think expedient for the good of the Order. We do so in view of his person, thinking he will act in such a way that no prejudice will be created against the Order on this account.[72]

Apart from the six *Quodlibeta*, Giles' writing suffered when he was master at Paris because of the administrative duties and also on account of his involvement in the adminstration of his Order. In August of 1290, some three months after the general chapter of Regensburg, Giles was present at the provincial chapter of his own province held at Santa Severa (Centocelle). He was awarded ten gold florins for his expenses,[73] and his room at Santa Maria del Popolo was reserved for him.[74] In September of 1291 he attended the provincial chapter at Viterbo and received money for his expenses.

The prior general, Clement of Osimo, died on 8 May 1291 at Orvieto, where the Roman curia was then living.[75] Paulus de Perusio, provincial of the Roman province, became the vicar general of the Order. In September of this year (1291), in accord with the *Constitutions* of the Order on the death of a prior general in office, the Roman province held its gathering of "definitors of the past year and of the provincial chapter held at Centocelle, in order that they may appoint electors (that is, a definitor and a discreet) of the next prior general, in the presence of Giles, our master and teacher."[76]

Students who studied theology in Paris normally spent four or five years there and then went to teach in the *studia generalia* of the Order and then returned to Paris to read the *Sentences.* However, these students would have to do an additional two years of auxiliary studies at Paris before reading the *Sentences.* Giles contended that, unlike the seculars, the Augustinian students had received experience in teaching in the houses of their Order, and thus requested that the Augustinians be dispensed from these two years of study before reading the *Sentences.* This was granted to the Augustinians and later, in 1355, it was extended to all regulars. This action is confirmed in two letters, one written by Giles and another by the cardinal of Porto.[77]

Prior General

On 6 January 1292 the general chapter of the Order of Saint Augustine convened at the monastery of Santa Maria del Popolo in Rome and unanimously elected Master Giles of Rome the ninth prior general of the Order.[78] The *Acts* of Giles' generalate have been lost; however from a circular letter which he sent to all priors provincial after his election we are able to get a glimpse of his program. Addressing the provincials he says:

> We ordain and command that you, the provincial, observe most diligently all that is set down in the *Constitutions* and that you see to it with anxious care that the other brothers in your province do the same. Moreover, as you make your way through your province, make it a point to go on foot and not on horseback . . . You will never have men who maintain regular observance in your province unless you, the provincial, observe it, and require that priors and also lectors observe it according to the manner set down in the *Constitutions*, for they are as it were the elders by whose example the younger brothers will be motivated to observance.[79]

From Giles' journeys, however, it is suspected that he traveled mounted or by carriage.

On 28 September 1292 Giles was in Cahors, in southern France, to establish an Augustinian monastery there;[80] in April of 1293 he was in Sainte Marie de Pontoise, northwest of Paris, where King Philip the Fair gave to the Augustinians a monastery which formerly belonged to the Friars of the Sack: "most especially as a favor to our beloved Giles of Rome, of the said Order, professor of sacred scripture."[81] Bishop Simon of Paris, who initially was against this provision, had recourse to the Holy See, as did Giles, but the bishop finally acquiesced on 29 December 1293.[82] Boniface VIII, on 13 September 1296, gave the property in perpetuum to the Augustinians.[83] In August 1294 he was again in Paris to receive permission from the king to sell the property in the Clos de Chardonnet which had been purchased, under the generalate of Clement of Osimo, from the chapter of Paris in 1285.[84] Previous to this the Augustinians were located near Sainte Eustache, purchased in 1259 by prior general Lanfranco.

The former monastery of the Friars of the Sack became the monastery of the Augustinian Friars, and the Augustinians held this monastery until 1790.[85] The only remnant of this monastery is the street which bears the name of Quai des Grands-Augustins.

In March of 1294 the Roman province held its chapter at Veroli. Roberto de Monte Rubiano was the vicar general of Giles for the chapter. From the *Acts* of the chapter we learn that Giles was in France, for they had to send someone (a runner) for confirmation of the provincial's election: "for a runner to go to Paris for confirmation of our elected provincial: 3 florins."[86] Even though prior general, Giles retained his mastership and the chair at Paris until 1293 when James of Viterbo became a master and replaced him.[87]

Archbishop of Bourges

On 25 April 1295 Giles of Rome, prior general of the Order of Saint Augustine, was appointed archbishop of Bourges, France, by Boniface VIII, who reigned from 1294 to 1303. Giles succeeded Simon de Beaulieu who had been transferred to Palestrina by Pope Celestine V (1294). It seems that with each new appointment Giles found difficulties, and his appointment as archbishop of Bourges was no exception.

Pope Celestine V had intended to appoint Jean de Savigny to the see, but Celestine resigned from the papacy, and Boniface wanted Giles. In a letter of 25 April 1295 the pope explains to the clergy and people of Bourges his reasons for the appointment:

The Apostolic Office to the venerable Giles, archbishop of Bourges. Due to the translation of our venerable brother Simon, bishop of Palestrina, formerly archbishop of Bourges, the church of Bourges has certainly been deprived of the solace given to it by its shepherd. Although our predecessor, Peter Murrone, at that time Celestine V, had intended to assign our beloved son, Master John of Savigny, to the church of Bourges, we have cancelled that provision for certain reasons which do not detract from the person of Master John, and our mind has settled on you, at that time prior general of the Order of Hermit Brothers of Saint Augustine. Give at the Lateran, 25 April of the first year of our pontificate.[88]

There were protests. Some resented the fact that a foreigner was appointed, even though Giles had spent much of his life in France. There were letters from nobility and clergy, but in the end there was acceptance, and acclaim came later.

The archdiocese of Bourges had a vast jurisdiction. In addition to being archbishop of Bourges, the archbishop assumed three kinds of jurisdiction: the title of primate of Aquitaine with jurisdiction as patriarch over the archdiocesan sees of Narbonne, Auth, Bordeaux, Toulouse, and Albi, and as metropolitan of the dioceses of Clermont, Limoges, Le Puy, Julle, and Saint Flour.[89]

On Pentecost Sunday, May 1295, the general chapter of the Augustinian Order gathered in Siena to elect a successor to Giles of Rome. Simon di Pistoia was unanimously elected. Giles, always the theologian and master, delivered a *Quodlibet*, and this became the practice for future chapters of the Order.[90] The *Acts* of the chapter report:

> At that time the venerable father, Giles of Rome, past prior general and recently appointed the new archbishop of Bourges, was present there and conducted general *Quodlibet* disputations. Peter, lector in Rome, supported him. Afterward he went to his archiepiscopal see for the first time.[91]

Shortly after Giles' installation in the see of Bourges, he convoked on Sunday, 22 January 1296, a provincial council in Clermont to which were invited all the prelates, ecclesiastical dignitaries, bishops, abbots, priors, deans, provosts, archdeacons, pastors, and holders of benefices. These were to convene on 5 March 1296 to correct abuses and to reform morals, especially among the clergy, by recalling into observance the ancient canons and statutes.[92]

Also in 1296 the papal bull *Clericis laicos* was promulgated by the Holy See. This papal document dealt with the problem of levying taxes on the clergy by the laity without the permission of the Holy See. Philip IV did not agree with the papal document, and thus decided to show his displeasure by retaliating. He forbade the sending of funds to Rome. Giles' support became very evident in this tense situation with Philip IV. Giles sided with the pope; however, it must have been difficult, for Philip IV and Giles had a close relationship.

Boniface VIII leaned heavily on Giles for advice, so much so that Giles was in Rome from 1297 (perhaps May?) to 1299. On account of his absence from his see, for this period Giles requested from the pope permission to appoint three vicars general who would be able to run the diocese and also other permissions for the efficient running of the archdiocese in his absence. Permissions were readily granted.[93]

In 1279 Nicholas III (d.1280) issued the papal bull *Exiit qui seminat* which decided the issue against the spirituals, a rift within the order of the Franciscan friars. It was Benedetto Gaetani, now Pope Boniface VIII, who was the principal author of the papal document. The powerful and famous Colonna family lent their support to the spirituals, so to show their displeasure to or to retaliate against Pope Boniface VIII the Colonna cardinals and others began to assert that Boniface VIII was not canonically elected because Celestine V had no power to resign from the papacy in 1294. Certainly, another schism could have again erupted within the Church. Giles, however, wrote his famous *De Renunciatione Papae* in which he clearly and vividly explained the nature of the papal offices and the entire process of Celestine's resignation, and thus Giles put to rest this explosive issue within the Church.[94] At the end of the year 1297 the canonization of King Louis IX of France took place.

In the autumn of 1298 the Colonna faction withdrew their objections and the final condemnation of the spirituals occurred. Giles remained in Rome until after August 1299.

In the autumn of 1299 Giles was back in his diocese of Bourges where he began to institute the feast of Saint Louis. He stayed in Bourges during the jubilee year of 1300, and was still receiving correspondence there from the pope at the end of 1301.[95]

In the autumn of 1302 Giles was back in Rome to participate in the council of the French hierarchy which was called by the pope to discuss his rapport with King Philip IV. It is at this meeting that Cardinal Matthew of Aquasparta, bishop of Porto, uttered his praise of Giles within the discussion of foreign bishops being appointed to French sees:

Likewise, the king cannot complain that foreigners are installed in his kingdom. It is quite true that our lord the supreme pontiff appointed Giles of the Augustinian Order. I do not dwell on praise of him, but you know the kind of cleric he is. He is a master of theology and was reared and educated in that realm.[96]

It was in this year (1302) that Giles completed perhaps his most famous work, *De ecclesiastica potestate*, in which he emphasizes papal authority in the conflict between Philip IV and Boniface VIII. Giles, with assistance from his confrere James of Viterbo, delineated the theological basis of the papal position. This work and the work of James of Viterbo, O.S.A., *De Regimine Christiano*, completed also in 1302, became the fundamental works for centuries for ecclesiological studies and treatises.[97]

At this time a very tense situation developed between Philip IV and Boniface VIII. Boniface issued the papal bull *Unam Sanctam*, the most famous medieval document on spiritual and temporal power. The bull resembled very much the theological positions of Giles in *De ecclesiastica potestate* and perhaps ideas had been culled from Giles' work, but the bull was essentially the work of Boniface VIII.[98] Theological in tone, it highlights the unity of the Church, a unity threatened when national hierarchies of bishops hesitated between allegiance to their king and obedience to the pope:

It is quite clear that Boniface VIII wished to make the Catholic conscience aware of the Roman Pontiff's prerogatives. The final formula, which represents the last word in his theology, refers to the conditions required for salvation and states that submission to the pope is an essential condition: "submission to the Roman Pontiff . . . is absolutely necessary for salvation." Now, the supernatural economy had been established by Christ, and at that time no one denied that it was concentrated in the Church. Consequently, the important thing was to bring out the role of the pope within the whole. Thus the bull *Unam Sanctam* is based on an entire theology of the Church and its mission, which constitutes the doctrinal framework in which the role of the supreme pontiff, the Church's head, has its place. The whole is linked to the divine level by the varied means which exegesis and philosophy offered to the minds of the age.[99]

From what we know, Giles stayed clear of the political events. Accusations between Philip and Boniface escalated; Boniface prepared a document of excommunication directed against Philip, but he never promulgated it. At Anagni the pope was harassed, especially by the Colonnas, and practically imprisoned. They wanted him to re-nounce the papacy. The townspeople turned the tide in Boniface's favor, and his enemies fled, but they left a sick man. He never recov-ered from a collapse and died in Rome on 11 October 1303.[100] One could imagine the feelings of Giles in all this: love for his pupil Philip IV and love for Boniface VIII, the man whom he assisted very often as cardinal and as pope with advice and who heeded his advice many times.

Giles most likely remained in Rome for the funeral and suffrages of Boniface VIII. Niccolo Boccasini (1240-1304) was elected pope on 22 October 1303 and received the necessary votes on the first ballot. He took the name of Benedict XI. He was a Dominican and a pas-toral pope who in his short reign managed to ease the tensions. He reconciled Philip IV to the papacy, mediated the papal bull *Clericis laicos*, and initiated the process of the principal perpetrators of Boni-face's days in Anagni, Nogaret, and Sciarra Colonna.[101] We find Giles in Rome again in March 1304 or most likely he remained there. On 17 January 1304 Giles assisted at the licentiate defense of his con-frere, Giacomo de Orto, at the Lateran palace at the request of Pope Benedict XI.[102] Giles returned to his diocese after a lengthy absence. Benedict XI died suddenly at Perugia on 7 July 1304.[103]

In 1305 Giles, now in his own diocese, became involved in a dispute concerning the primacy of Aquitaine.[104] Bertrand de Got (1260-1314), archbishop of Bordeaux since 1299, contended that his see and not Bourges held the primacy of Aquitaine. This debate was going on for centuries, but Bourges was considered to be the primatial see. The matter became complicated because Bordeaux lay in English territory and Bourges in French, and Giles upheld the primacy of his see in French territory. When Archbishop de Got showed no recognition, Giles excommunicated him and in-structed the bishop of Poitiers, Gauthier de Bruges, to publish the sentence in de Got's territory, which Gauthier did.[105]

To make matters worse, on 5 June 1305 Bertrand de Got was elected pope at Perugia by the cardinals who were split into parti-sans and opponents of Boniface VIII. His election, a victory for those against Boniface VIII, most likely was manipulated by Philip IV who wanted very much to get back at Boniface VIII. Clement was crowned at Lyons on 14 November 1305 in the presence of Philip IV.[106] Pope Clement V decreed shortly after his coronation that the archbishopric of Bordeaux was not dependent on Bourges.[107] To Gauthier de Bruges, who published Giles' excommunication, he deprived the bishopric of Poitiers and ordered him to a Franciscan monastery where he died in 1307.[108]

Clement kept the papal court in France and in his many trips pillaged cities ruthlessly:

> Pope Clement V stopped at Lyons and extorted a very large sum of money from the bishops and abbots of France who had business with the curia. But the king of France and his brothers and the French barons found him well-disposed and generous. He gave extensive privileges to French clerics. Around the feast of the Purification (2 February 1306) the said pope came to Cluny, where he levied many fines. At Bourges and Nevers he likewise demanded outrageous expenses. For these reasons, the churches of France, being forced to subsidize him, were heavily burdened.[109]

It would be safe to conjecture that Giles, archbishop of Bourges, did not have a permanent role in the papacy of Clement V. What is surprising is that more was not done to him. Perhaps his relationship with Philip IV (even though during the Boniface controversy this was somewhat strained), about which everyone knew, prompted the pope to respect this rapport if he wanted to have Philip's support.

As a result of the way Pope Clement V and his entourage acted in each city visited and of the pillage that took place, Giles, to have money to meet expenses, had to assume the role of a canon in order to acquire the stipend: "In order to receive daily distributions for the necessities of life, he was forced to attend the ecclesiastical hours as one of the simple canons."[110]

In 1306 the records indicated that Giles paid 300 Tours pounds to the Holy See; the records also show that Giles did not make the customary *ad limina* visit every two years. Some interpret the payment as a penalty.

> Giles, called "of Rome," a very well-known man and one of the outstanding lights of the company of those who want to be taken as "Augustinians." There is a noteworthy passage in the continuator of Nangius [volume, page 353], in which the following can be read regarding the journey of Clement V from Lyons to Bordeaux: Around the time of the feast of the Purification, Pope Clement . . . In a book of payments in the Vatican archive of Clement [appendix, page 284] it is recorded on the next-to-last day of July, 1306, that on 5 November he [Giles] paid 300 Tours pounds for each of the previous two-year periods, that is, for the years 1303 and 1305, on the occasion of the visit to the apostolic see which the archbishop of Bourges is obliged to make every two years.[111]

Since 1307 Philip had been plotting the suppression of the Knights Templars, but Clement V did not give in, for he was upset at the treatment of the Templars by Philip. However, Clement was not that independent from Philip, and the matter was submitted to the Council of Vienne which was convened by Clement V in October 1311 to discuss the Templars. Previous to this the bishops had received written information concerning this matter. However, before the bishops decided on this matter, Pope Clement V suppressed the Knights Templar on his own authority. In 1311 or 1312 Giles wrote his work *Contra exemptos* in which he elucidated the role of the regulars vis-à-vis the bishop:

> Consequently, if the student body in any house of studies is granted privileges so that they may study in a more advantageous way, this is done in order to prevent ignorance, for ignorance is the source of numerous evils. As Ambrose says: "You sin most seriously if you are ignorant." "Most seriously" means "most dangerously." And although ignorance excuses sin, according to the apostle's words: *I obtained mercy because I acted in ignorance,* yet one who sins through ignorance (even though that is to some degree an excuse) is placed in great danger by sinning in this fashion. For it would be better to suffer a serious illness and know its cause, so that a physician might apply treatment, than to suffer from a lesser illness and be ignorant of the cause, since then the physician would not be called to provide treatment. In order, then, that human beings may be rescued from this great danger and from becoming captives of the devil, it is good that by means of privileges and some indulgence men be induced to study. Thus it is that in some religious orders, for example, the orders of poverty, which are wholly devoted to study, exemptions and some privileges are granted, for it is as a result of study that ignorance is avoided both in students and in the simple folk who can be educated by the teaching of the students. And since ignorance is the most dangerous of sins, the supreme pontiff is to be praised for acting in this way, in view of the obvious advantages of this course of action both for avoiding ignorance and for defending the Catholic faith.[112]

From the above, one can see that Giles upheld exemptions only by way of exception, namely, for the good of the Church. In the very last chapter of the treatise Giles maintains that for religious who study and teach, exemption is to be tolerated: "for exemption is tolerated for those who are correctly taught and who give themselves to study."[113] Giles did not want the outright suppression of the Templars; he wanted them supervised more, With the suppression, however, the Templars' monastery in Bourges was granted to the Augustinian Hermits as a result of Giles' negotiations.

The next record that we have of Giles is the making of his will on 29 March 1315.[114] Then on 19 December 1316 he made a codicil to it.[115] On 8 September 1315 Giles held another provincial council at Bourges for the spiritual welfare of his people.[116]

In his will Giles bequeathed his property in the diocese of Soana and his library to the Augustinian monastery in Paris; his precious vessels and vestments for divine service went to the houses in Bourges and Rome.

Giles of Rome died in Avignon on 22 December 1316.

John E. Rotelle, O.S.A.

Notes

1. Luigi Torelli, *Secoli Agostiniani* (Bologna: Vaglierini poi Monte, 1659-1696), V (1280-1353) 347. See M. Anthony Hewson, *Giles of Rome and the Medieval Theory of Conception. A Study of the De formatione corporis humani in utero* (The Athlone Press, 1975) 3-37.

2. To my knowledge there is no doubt about the date of death. All of the earliest writers report this date: Ambrose of Cori, *Defensorium ordinis* (1481); Joseph Pamphilus, *Cronica Ordinis nostri* (Roma, 1581); Thomas Gratianus, *Anastasis Augustiniana* (Antwerp, 1613); Nicolaus Crusenius, *Monasticon Augustiniana* (Munich, 1623); Cornelius Curtius, *Virorum Illustrium ex ordine Eremitarum* (Antwerp, 1613); Thomas Herrera, *Alphabetum Augustinianum* (Salamanca, 1644); Philippus Elssius, *Encomiasticon Augustinianum* (Brussels, 1654); Luigi Torelli, *Secoli Agostiniani* (Bologna, 1680).

3. D. Gandolfo, *Dissertatio Historica* (Rome, 1704) 23.

4. Ugo Mariani, *Chiesa e Stato nei Teologi Agostiniani del Secolo XIV. Uomini e Dottrine*, 5 (Rome, 1957) 45-46.

5. P. Glorieux, Répertoire des maîtres en théologie de Paris au XIII siècle (Paris, 1933), I, 23 (hereafter Répetoire); H. Denifle and E. Chatelain, *Chatularium Universitatis Parisiensis*, 4 vols. (Paris, 1889-1897), I, 20, pages 78-80.

6. H. Denifle and E. Chatelain, *Chartularium*, I, 522, page 633.

7. P. Mandonnet, "La Carrière Scolaire de Gilles de Rome," *Révue des Sciences Philosophiques et Théologiques* 4 (Paris, 1910) 480-499. See also E. Esteban, "Antiquiores quae extant definitiones capitulorum generalium ordinis," *Analecta Augustiniana* II (1907-1908) 274-277 (hereafter Antiquiores); P. Glorieux, *Répertoire*, I, 15.

8. F. Lajard, "Gilles de Rome. Religieux, Augustinien, Théologien," *Histoire Littéraire de la France* (Paris, 1888) XXX, 421-566.

9. D. Perini, *Bibliographia Augustiniana* (Florence, 1929-1937) 237.

10. R. Arbesmann and W. Hümphner, *Jordani de Saxonia Ordinis Eremitarum S. Augustini Liber Vitasfratrum.* Cassaciacum, vol. I (American Series), New York, 1943, II, 22, page 236 (see English translation, *The Life of the Brethren* II, 22, page 237); see also page 472 where the authors cite two works which treated this problem: R. Scholz, *Aegidius Romanus, De ecclesiastica potestate,* Weimar, 1929, page ix, note 1, and A. Dyroff. "Aegidius von Colonne? Aegidius Conigiatus?" *Philosophisches Jahrbuch* 38 (1925) 18ff, and also note that at the time of Giles there were two other friars of the Roman province with the Columna name: "Paulus de Columpna Romanus" and "Jacobus de Columpna, Prov. Romanae," *Analecta Augustiniana* II, 439; III, 17.

11. Ambrogio Massari of Cori, *Chronicon Ordinis Eremitarum Sancti Augustini,* 1481, fol. x.

12. A. Trapè, "Egidio Romano," *Enciclopedia Italiana* V (Città del Vaticano, 1950) 138.

13. U. Mariani, *Chiesa e Stato nei Teologi Agostiniani del Secolo XIV* (Rome, 1957) 46-47. Most biographers, however, after Ambrose of Cori follow Jordan of Saxony rather than Ambrose and state that Giles belonged to the famous Colonna family.

14. National Archives of Paris, S.3634, 3; see Denifle, *Chartularium,* II, 716, page 172.

15. D. Gandolfo, *Dissertatio Historica de Ducentis Celeberrimis Augustinianis Scriptoribus* . . . (Roma: Typis Buagni, 1704), 20. Mandonnet, acknowledging the difficulty in ascertaining the age when Giles was sent to Paris, states: "Plusieurs biographes se sont essayés, ces derniers temps, à préciser les faits et gestes de Gilles de Rome. Néanmoins, on chercherait vainement, chez les uns et les autres, à part quelques données fragmentaires, une esquisse un peu ferme de la carrière scolaire de célèbre Ermite de Saint-Augustin," "La Carrière Scolaire de Gilles de Rome," in *Révue des Sciences Philosophiques et Théologiques* (Paris, 1910) 480.

16. R. Arbesmann, *Vitasfratrum,* 236.

17. H. Denifle and E. Chatelain, *Chartularium,* I, 358-359, page 405.

18. It is interesting to note that almost all the early Augustinian historians state that Clement of Osimo, prior general from 1271-1274 and then from 1284-1291, sent Giles to Paris. This would mean that the earliest Giles could have been sent to Paris would have been 1271. From the above we know that Giles most likely went to Paris in 1260 or thereafter, under the generalate of Lanfranco (1256-1264). Even if he went later, for example 1267, it still would not have been under the generalate of Clement of Osimo. Later historians continue this error. See E. Esteban, "Antiquiores," 275, note 1, which says: "Ex dictis non fuisset B. Clemens ab Auximo, Prior Generalis Ordinis, qui Aegidium Parisios misit, ut noster Lanteri affirmat (*Postrema Saecula rex Religionis Augustinianae,* I, pag. 48), quia B. Clemens primo ad Generalatum fuit

evectus anno 1269 (Lanteri, *ibid.* pag. 209); sed B. Lanfrancus, primus post unionem Generalis Ordinis Prior."

19. E. Ypma, *La Formation des Professeurs chez les Ermites de Saint-Augustin de 1256 à 1354* (Paris: Etudes Augustiniennes, 1956), 6-9. According to the deeds the Augustinians lived in Paris from December 1259. Ioannes de Eugubio was the vicar general. The whole plan was to organize the studies in the Order; it was not a case, as in some places in Italy, of finding a monastery for the hermits called from their hermitages. The following letter from prior general Lanfranco confirms the work of Ioannes de Eugubio:

> Noverint omnes, ad quos littere iste pervenerint, quod nos frater Lanfrancus, generalis prior fratrum heremitarum Ordinis sancti Augustini, de voluntate et consensu necnon auctoritate diffinitorum capituli generalis eiusdem Ordinis, et ipsum capitulum, approbamus et confirmamus omnia instrumenta et pacta, unum seu plura, facta inter dilectum nostrum fratrem Ioannes de Eugubio, Ordinis ipsius atque nostrum in Francia Vicarium, ex una parte, et reverendum patrem dominum ecclesie Parisiensis Episcopum, ex altera, pro loco nostro Parisius iuxta portam Montis Martirum sito. Promittentes nos, nostro et ipsius capituli seu ordinis nomine, sub ypoteca bonorum omnium predicti loci, quicquid per eos in hac parte factum est ratum in omnibus habituros. In huius autem rei testimonium, presentibus sigillum nostrum et ipsius capituli duximus apponenda.

Datum Cesene, in predicto capitulo, tercio nonas maii, pontificatus domini Alexandri pape quarti (anno sexto).

Paris National Archives, LL 7 (formerly 183), fol. xxvi.

20. E. Gilson, *La Philosophie au Moyen Age. Des origines patristiques à la fin du XIV siècle* (Paris: Payot, 1947) 391- 400 ("La fondation des Universités").

21. *Ibid.*, 394; see F. van Steenbergen. *La Philosophie au XIII siècle,* Philosophes Médiévaux, Tome IX (Paris: Bèatrice- Nauwelaerts, 1966) 104-106.

22. E. Gilson, *op. cit.*, 394-395.

23. P. Mandonnet, "La Carrière Scolaire de Gilles de Rome," *Révue des Sciences Philosophiques et Théologiques* (Paris, 1910) 482-483.

24. E. Esteban, "Antiquiores," *Analecta Augustiniana* II (1907-1908) 275, note 1.

25. P. Glorieux, "Répertoire"; see charts after page 328.

26. P. Mandonnet, *Siger de Brabant et L'Averroisme Latin au XIII Siècle,* vol. 1 (Louvain, 1911) 248: "il avait été le fidèle disciple de Thomas d'Aquin pendant le dernier séjour du saint docteur à Paris (1269-1272)."

27. E. Gilson, *op. cit.*, 396-397: "On comprend dès lors ce que signifient exactement et les reproches dont les papes accablent parfois l'Université de Paris et les louanges dont ils la comblent. Malgré les differences de détail qui tiennent à leurs conceptions individuelles et à leurs temperaments particuliers, ils s'accordent tous avec Innocent III pour voir dans Paris le centre intellectuel de toute la chrétienté. 'La science des écoles de Paris,' écrit Alexandre IV en 1255, est dans la sainte Église comme l'arbre de vie dans le paradis terrestre et comme la lampe resplendissante dans la maison du Seigneur. Comme une mère féconde d'érudition, elle fait abondamment jaillir des sources de la doctrine du salut les fleuves qui vont arroser la face stérile de la terre, elle réjouit partout la Cité de Dieu et subdivise les eaux de la science qu'elle fait couler sur les places publiques pour le rafraichissement des ames assoiffies de justice . . . C'est à Paris que le genre humain deforme par l'aveuglement de son ignorance originelle, recouvre sa vue et sa beauté par la connaissance de la lumière vraie qui rayonne de la science divine. Pourquoi Innocent IV presse-t-il les Cisterciens, en 1245, d'organizer et de développer un centre d'études près de l'Université de Paris? C'est que Paris est le creuset où l'or vient se fondre, où s'est construite la tour de David munie de ses ramparts et de laquelle viennent non seulement mille boucliers, mais l'armure presque entière des forts, puisqu'on en voit sortir continuellement les forts des forts, portant leurs glaives, et des hommes savants dans l'art de la guerre qui vont parcourir la terre entière. C'est pourquoi enfin, consacrant officiellement la prédominance de la cité des livres et des sciences, de la *Cariath Sepher*, Nicolas IV, en 1292, concèdera aux maîtres de l'Université de Paris le privilège d'enseigner par toute la terre sans avoir à subir de nouvel examen."

28. H. Denifle, *Chartularium* I, 471, page 541: "Episcopo Parisiensi. Relatio nimis implacida nostrum nuper turbavit auditum, amaricavit et animum, quod Parisius, ubi fons vivus sapientie salutaris habundanter huc usque scaturiit suos rivos limpidissimos fidem patefacientes catholicam usque ad terminos orbis terre diffundens, quidam errores in prejudicium ejusdem fidei de novo pullulasse dicuntur. Volumus itaque tibique auctoritate presentium districte precipiendo mandamus quatenus diligenter facias inspici vel inquiri, a quibus personis et in quibus locis errores hujusmodi dicti sunt sive scripti, et que didiceris sive inveneris, conscripta fideliter nobis per tuum nuntium transmittere quamcitius non omittas. Dat. Viterbii XV kal. Februarii, anno primo."

29. *Ibid.*, I, 473, page 543.

30. H. Denifle, *Chartularium* I, 473, pages 544-555.

31. *Ibid.*, I, 474, pages 558-560.

32. Thomas Aquinas, *Quaestiones Quodlibetales* I, q. 4, art. 1 (Marietti, 1956) 6.

33. See list of works in Appendix.

34. H. Denifle, *Chartularium* I, 533, page 633.

35. J. Bollandus and G. Henschenius, *Acta Sanctorum*, I Martii, ed. Carnandet, no. 82, page 712.

36. *Quodlibeta* II, q.8 (Venice 1502) fol. 14v.

37. *In secundum librum Sententiarum*, pars II, dist. XXXII, q. 2, art. 3 (Venice, 1580) 471.

38. P. Mandonnet, *Siger de Brabant et L'Averroisme Latin au XIII Siècle* (Louvain, 1911), 236-237: ". . . les disciples de Thomas d'Aquin ajouterent celle de leur activité scientifique et alors commença la publication de cette abondante littérature polémique qui ne devait plus cesser de longtemps." See also note 3.

39. *Contra gradus et pluralitatem formarum* (Venice, 1502), fol. 211v.

40. *Ibid.*, fol. 206v.

41. R. Hissette, "Etienne Tempier et ses condamnations," *Recherches de Théologie Ancienne et Médiévale XLVII* (1980) 246-247.

42. E. Esteban, "Capitula Antiqua Provinciae Romanae O.N.," *Analecta Augustiniana* 2 (1907-1908): 230 (hereafter "Capitula Antiqua"): "Item pro futuro capitulo Generalissimo Paduano pro dicta Romana provincia fecit (Discretos) fratrem Leonardum, lectorem, et fratrem Phylippum de Montelupone. Diffinitorem eligendum reservavit sibi, scilicet, prope Capitulum Generale: fecit fratrem Egidium Romanum, Bacellarium parisiensem."

43. *Ibid.*, page 245.

44. *Ibid.*, 246: "Item in eodem Capitulo provinciali imposita fuit et ordinata maxima collecta pro tribus studentibus, sive lectoribus novis, videlicet pro fratre Bernardino, fratre Iacobo de Columpna, Romano, et fratre Iacobo de Viterbio, pro quolibet preditorum provisio integra librorum, sicut preordinatum fuit in Capitulo Generali Paduano; et pro quolibet expense redditus eorum de parisius, scilicet, X floreni auri pro quolibet."

45. *Ibid.*, 246-247: "Diffinitur pro Generali Capitulo futuro fuit factus frater . . . et Discreti duo fuerunt facti pro eodum Capitulo Generali scilicet, frater Egidius Romanus, Bacellarius, et Prior provincialis." This last phrase does not mean that Giles was also prior provincial of the Roman province; see P. Glorieux, Repertoire, II, 400, page 293.

46. *Ibid.*, page 247.

47. *Ibid.*

48. *Ibid.*, 248: ". . . celebratum fuit provinciale Capitulum in loco de Tuscanella. Et vicarius Venerabilis fratris C[lementis], Generalis Prioris, fuit ibi frater Aegidius Romanus, Bacellarius."

49. *Ibid.*, 248-249. 270.

50. *Ibid.*, 272.

51. C. Eubel, *Hierarchia Catholica Medii Aevi* . . . 1198-1600, 391.

52. P. Glorieux, *Répertoire des Maîtres en Théologie de Paris au XIII Siècle* (Paris: J. Vrin 1933) 360, page 351: ". . . il fit ses études à Paris, mais c'est à la Curie qui'il réçut en 1256 (le 31 janvier) la licence en théologie."

53. Denifle, *Chartularium* I, 270, page 307.

54. E. Ypma, *La Formation des Professeurs chez les Ermites de Saint-Augustin de 1256 à 1354* (Paris: Études Augustiniennes, 1956) 113-119.

55. H. Denifle, *Chartularium* I, 522, page 633.

56. E. Esteban, "De tempore quo Aegidius Romanus promotus fuit ad S. Theologiae Magisterium," *Analecta Augustiniana* 2 (1907-1908) 280-281.

57. R. Wielockx, *Apologia. Aegidii Romani Opera Omnia* III.1 (Firenze: Leo S. Olschki, 1985) 220.

58. E. Esteban, *ibid.*, 279-280: H. Denifle. *Chartularium* II, 539, page 10: "Super his postea disputatum fuerat a magistro Egidio de Ordine Augustini, qui modo melior de tota villa in omnibus reputatur, et determinatum fuit ab eodem, quod episcopi essent in parte longius saniori. Quarum determinationem copiam propter novitatem habere ad presens non potui. Sed tamen si habere potuero, mittere non tardabo. Et ecce privilegia fratrum." See also notes 16 and 17 of this document in Denifle.

59. P. Mandonnet, "La Carrière Scolaire de Gilles de Rome," *Revue des Sciences Philosophiques et Théologiques* (Paris, 1910) 492-493.

60. *Quodlibet* V, q.19, fol. 65v.

61. *Quodlibet* II, q.8, fol. 14v.

62. P. Glorieux, *La littérature quodlibetique de 1260 à 1320* (Belgium: Le Saulchoir Kain, 1925) I, 140-148.

63. Paulus Aemilius, *De rebus gestis Francorum* (Paris, 1548) VIII, 337-340; see N. Mattioli, *Studio Critico sopra Egidio Romano Colonna*, Antologia Agostiniana I (Roma, 1896) 65-71.

64. D. Sainte-Marte (Sammarthani), *Gallia Christiana*, vol. II, *Ecclesia Bituricensis*, LXXV: Egidius, col. 76.

65. H. Denifle, *Chartularium* II, 539, pages 8-12; see also E. Esteban, "De tempore quo Aegidius Romanus promotus fuit a S. Theologiae Magisterium," *Analecta Augustiniana* II (1907-1908) 279. See also M. Anthony Hewson, *Giles of Rome and the Medieval Theory of Conception. A Study of the De formatione corporis humani in utero* (The Athlone Press, 1975) 3-37.

66. Denifle, *ibid.*, page 10.

67. Denifle, *Chartularium* II, 542, page 12; E. Esteban, "Antiquiores," 275.

68. See Denifle, *Chartularium* II, 567, page 42: Giles wrote this and toned it down.

69. E. Esteban, "Capitula Antiqua," 297.

70. Denifle, *Chartularium* II, 567, pages 40-42.

71. E. Esteban, "Antiquiores," page 296.

72. *Ibid.*; see Denifle, *Chartularium* II, 566, pages 39-40.

73. E. Esteban, "Capitula Antiqua," 298: "Imprimis pro fratre Egidio Romano, magistro nostro, pro sua provisione de gratia ordinata annuali x flor. auri."

74. E. Esteban, "Capitula Antiqua," 300: "Diffinimus quod in camera quam fecit fieri frater Egidius, Magister noster, in Dormitorio Sancte Marie de populo, mullus jacere debeat nisi de licentia Generalis prioris. Et si prior permiserit quod aliquis in ea jaceat, volumus quod subjaceat penitentie trium dierum in pane et aqua pro qualibet vice infra x dies." A very strange decision!

75. *Ibid.*, 323.

76. *Constitutiones Ordinis*, Cap. XL (Venice, 1508) fol. 35v: "Et idem prior provincialis (provinciae in qua Generalis obiit) per universas Ordinis provincias statum per suas litteras obitum dicti generalis notificare curabit, praecipiens eisdem termino eis supradictorum novem mensium assignato et [ut] in loco et tempore statuto et prefixo ad memoratum generale capitulum celebrandum debeant omnes qui electi fuerint ad prefatum capitulum sine prolongatione temporis convenire. Provincialibus prioribus nihilominus iniungens, ut quilibet ex eis, convocatis diffinitoribus proximi praeteriti provincialis capituli sue provincie una cum eis eligat diffinitores et discretos, si electi non fuerint, qui ad ipsum generale capitulum veniant ad terminum prenotatum."

77. H. Denifle, *Chartularium* II, 683, page 144: "Livre II des Contracts du grand convent de Paris de l'ordre des Freres Hermites de S. Augustin," fol. 23. Arch. nat. Paris. S.3640, fol. 3b. —Similia leguntur ibid, ad an. 1308(1309), Martii 17: "F. Gilles de Rome, archevesque de Bourges, de l'ordre Sainct Augustin, tesmoigne qu'estant regent dans ce convent de Paris, fust conclud dans l'assemblée tenue par l'Université dans Sainct Mathurin que les bacheliers de nostre Ordre ne demerureroyent pas si longtemps dans Paris que les autres, parce que apres avoir esté receus dans la faculté ils alloyent enseigner en d'autres convents. Also at the same entry: "Jean [Johannes de Murro, Ord. Min.], evesque de Parte et de Sainct Ruffine, le 30 juin 1310, a la requisition de F. Gilles de Rome, archevesque de Bourges, escrit d'Avignon a l'Université de Paris qu'estant bachelier il avoit ouy dire aux maistres de Paris, lorsqu'ils tratoient qu'il falloit avoir demeuré un certain temps dans Paris pour lire les Sentences, que ledict archevesque de Bourges respondit que c'estoit une chose indigne que les religieux Augustins qui avoyent enseigné en d'autres convents, apres avoir demeure quatre ou cinq ans dans Paris, revenant à Paris, feussent obliges d'y demeurer autant que les seculiers, mais qu'il falloit compter le temps qu'ils avoyent demeuré aux autres convents, à quoy tous les maistres consentirent." The letter of Giles, ibid., II, 715, page 172: "Huict docteurs en saincte theologie de la faculté de Paris con-

firment et ratifient ce que avoit este accordé aux Augustins du temps que
F. Gilles de Rome, archevesque de Bourges, estoit encore de la faculté de
Paris, scavoir est que les bacheliers de l'Ordre Saint Augustin ne seroyent
obligés de lire qu'un cours de Maistre des Sentences sans estre tenus de
lire un cours de philosophie." See also E. Ypma, *La Formation des Professeurs chez les Ermites de Saint-Augustin de 1256 a 1354* (Paris: Etudes
Augustiniennes, 1956) 85-86.

78. See *Catalogus Ordinis Sancti Augustini* (O.S.A.) iussu Rev.mi P. Martin Nolan eiusdem Ordinis Prioris Generalis editus (Romae: Curia Generalis Augustiniana, 1988) 796-797. In the listing of priors general the list
commences with the year 1244, the year of the founding of the Order,
and not 1256 which was the year of the Great Union. Hence priors general are listed from 1244 and not from 1256 as previously. For this reason
Giles of Rome is now the ninth prior general, and not the sixth as previously listed.

79. "Litterae prioris generalis ordinis Fr. Aegidii Romani," *Analecta
Augustiniana* IV (1911-1912) 202-204.

80. L. Torelli, *Secoli Agostiniani.* Tom. V, an. 1292, n. 9, page 133; see
also E. Esteban, "Capitula Antiqua," 366, footnote 1.

81. Denifle, *Chartularium* II, 583, page 61.

82. *Ibid.*, II, 586, pages 62-63; see "De possessione magni conventus
Parisiensis capta ab Aegidio Romano, priore generalis Ordine," *Analecta
Augustiniana* IV (1911-1912) 394.

83. G. Digard, M. Faucon, A. Thomas, and R. Fawtier, *Les Registres de
Boniface VIII. Recueil des Bulles de ce Pape publiés our analysées d'après les
manuscrits originaux des archives du Vatican* (Paris: E. De Boccard), 1907, I,
no. 1274, CCCLXXXV, col. 457-458 (hereafter "Les Registres de Boniface
VIII"): Anagni, 13 septembre 1296, approbatio concessionis cujusdam
(fol. 93) — Dilectis filiis priori et fratribus Heremitarum loci Parsiensis
ordinis sancti Augustini. Vestre religionis. Sane petitio vestra nobis expo-
sita continebat quod cla. me. Ludovicus rex Francorum, cupiens terrena
pro celestibus et transitoria pro eternis salubri commercio commutare,
quendam locum in civitate Parisiensi fratribus de Penitentia Jesu Christi
in puram contulit elemosinam intuitu pietatis. Eisdem vero fratribus locum ipsum deserentibus, arissimus in Christo filius noster Phylippus rex
Francorum illustris, nolens locum ipsum, qui dictorum contemplatione
fratrum deditus et attributus in pios usus fuerant, aliquatenus ad pro-
phanos reverti, ac habens ad vos specialem devotionis affectum, prefatum
locum cum juribus et pertinentiis suis vobis et successoribus in perpetuum regia liberalitate concessit. Hec concessio, jam ab episcopo
Parisiensi confirmata, a papa approbatur.

Dat. Anagnie, id. septembris, anno secundo.

84. Denifle, *Chartularium* II, 583, page 61: "Honorius IV venditionem cujusdam peciae terrae in loco qui dicitur Cardinetum sistae fratri Juvanli, Ord. Eremitarum S. Augustini vicario et procuratori, ad opus ipsorum fratrum Parisiis studentium, ab abbate et conventu monasterii S. Victoris factam confirmat." See also Denifle I, 358, page 405 and Nat. Arch. K.36b, no. 60.

85. D. Gutierrez, "De Antiquis Ordinis Eremitarum S. Augustini Bibliothecis," *Analecta Augustiniana* XXIII (1954) 231.

86. E. Esteban, "Capitula Antiqua," *Analecta Augustiniana* II (1907-1908) 366.

87. See E. Ypma, *La Formation des Professeurs chez les Ermites de Saint-Augustin de 1256 à 1354* (Paris: Etudes Augustinennes, 1956) 82-84; E. Esteban, "Capitula Antiqua," *Analecta Augustiniana* II (1907-1908) 272.324.341.346.365 in which it is stated that Giles, master in Paris, was given money for his expenses.

88. G. Digard, *Les Registres de Boniface* VIII, I, no. 70, col. 30.

89. Gaetano Moroni, *Dizionario di Erudizione Storico- Ecclesiastica da S. Pietro sino ai nostri giorni.* Vol. V (Venice: Emiliana, 1840) 79.

90. E. Esteban, "Capitula Antiqua," 368; see also footnote 2.

91. *Ibid.*

92. D. Sainte-Marthe (Sammarthani), *Gallia Christiana in Provincias Ecclesiasticas Distributas* . . . (Paris: Typographia Regia, 1720), vol. II, Ecclesia Bituricensis, LXXV: Egidius, col. 77 (hereafter *Gallia Christiana*).

93. G. Digard, *Le Registres de Boniface VIII*, no. 1138, CCLII, col. 406: Anagni 4 juillet 1296, licentia conferenci prebendas (fol. 62) — Venerabili fratri S. Archiepiscopo Bituricensi, Personam tuam — , Possit, non obstante contradictione, tres personas ydoneas in Bituricensi ecclesia, in qua receptio canonicorum et collatio prebendarum ad archiepiscopum et decanum ac capitulum ejusdem ecclesie noscitur communiter pertinere, in canonicos et in fratres recipere ac providere eorum singulis de singulis prebendis. Dat. Anagnie, v id. julii, anno secundo; no. 1139, CCLIII, col. 406: Anagni 11 juillet 1296, alia licentia (fol. 62) — Eidem. Dono scientie preditus-. Possit, quandiu apud sedem apostolicam morabitur, per ydoneos vicarios, unum vel plures, diocesim visitare et procurationes debitas in pecunia numerata per eos recipere. Dat. ut supra; no. 1798, CXLIII, col. 680: Vatican, 12 mars 1297, facultas (fol. 227v) — Venerabili fratri G. archiepiscopo "Bituricensi. De contractuum memoria-." Ut duabus ydoneis personis conferre possit tabellionatus officium. Dat. Rome apud Sanctum Petrum, IIII id. martii, anno tertio; no. 1863, CCVIII, col. 705: Orvieto, 23 juin 1297, notificatio dispensationis (fol. 242) — Dilecto filio . . . archdiacono Sigalonie in ecclesia Bituricensi et Jacobo Mathei Ursi de filiis Ursi, capellano nostro, Thesauriario Salamantino, ac . . . cantori Sancti Yterii de Aiis Bituricensis dioceses. Dono scientie.- Conceditur precibus E. archiepiscopi Bituriicensis in curia Romana

constituti ut ipse, quandiu apud sedem apostolicam morabitur, per vicarios
in diocesi sua visitationis officium exercere valeat; et eis injungitur ut execu-
tioni provideant. Dat. apud Urbemveterem, VIII, Kal. julii, anno tertio; no.
1864, CCVIIII, col. 705: Orvieto, 23 juin 1297, facultas (fol. 242v) — Venerabili fratris E. archiepiscopo Bituricensi. Dignum reputamus. — Ut violata
cimiterie et ecclesias ipse apud romanam ecclesiam moram trahens, per
ydoneas personas, reconciliari faciat. Dat. ut supra; no. 1893, CCXXXVIII,
col. 718-719: Orvieto, 14 juillet 1297, facultas (fol. 250v) — Venerabili fratri
E. Archiepiscopo Bituriicensi. Tue merita. Cum ei apud sedem apostolicam
morandi concessum fuerit quod possit per procuratores ydoneos, scilicet
archdiaconum Sigalonie in ecclesia Bituricensi, Jacobum Matheir Ursi capel-
lanum papae ac contorem Sancti Yterii de Aiis Bituricensis diocesis, diocesim
suam visitare, amplius ei conceditur ut per predictis a quacumque persona,
visitationis aut cujuscunque alie cause ratione, procurationes in pecunia numerata recipere valeat. Dat. apud Urbemveterem, II id. julii, anno tertio. I e.
m. tribus executoribus infra nominatis. Dat ut supra; no. 1936, CCLXXXI,
col. 740: Vatican, 4 mars 1297, indultum (fol. 261) — Venerabili fratri L.
archiepiscopo Bituricensi, Cum nos personan. Ut confessorem quem
voluerit eligere possit. Dat. Rome apud Sanctum Petrum, III non. martii,
anno tertio; no. 3162, CCLXXVIIII, col. 460: Anagni, 1 aout 1299, ut procurationes in pecunia per biennium recipere valeat (fol. 199) — Venerabili
fratri Egidio, archiepiscopo Bituricensi. Personam tuam. Dudum supra
scripto per Apostolicas litteras fuit indultum ut, quamdiu apud Sedem Apostolicam morari contingeret, procurationes a personis per ydoneum vicarium
visitatis et per alias litteras a quibuscumque quocumque modo debitas in
pecunia numerata recipere posset. Cum autem nunc, sicut proposuit in pre-
sentia domini pape constitutus, post moram quam apud dictam Sedem de
mandato Apostolico aliquamdiu contraxit, ad ecclesiam suam reverti cupiat,
indulgetur ei ut, postquam ad eam pervenerit ad biennum eadem gratia uti
valeat. Dat. Anagnie, Kal. augusti, anno quinto. In e. m. Sigalonie et . . . de
Sancoro archidiaconis, Bituricensis, et Jacobo Mathei Ursi, capellano nostro,
thesauriario Salamantine ecclesiarum. Dat. ut supra.

   94. See L. Torelli, *Secoli Agostiniani*, vol. V (1280-1353) 1295, 2, page
163. See Aegidius Romanus, *De Renunciatione Papal*, Text and Studies in
Religion 52, edited by John R. Eastman (The Edwin Mellon Press, 1992).

   95. G. Digard, *Registres Boniface VIII*, no. 4107, CLXXVII, col 110:
Anagni, 26 juillet 1301 — Conceditur E[gidio], archiepiscopo Bituricensi,
quod possit providere tam in cathedrali Bituricensi quam in singulis ecclesiis
collegialis Bituricensis civitatis ac diocesis hac vice de singulis personis
ydoneis (fol. 45) — Venerabili fratri E[gidio], archiepiscopo Bituricensi.
Personam tuam erga nos. Dat. Anagnie, vii Kal. augusti, anno septimo. See
M. Anthony Hewson, *Giles of Rome and the Medieval Theory of Conception.* A

Study of the De formatione corporis humani in utero (The Athlone Press, 1975) 3-37.

96. Bulaeus, *Historia Universitatis Parisiensis* (Paris, 1668) IV, 19.

97. U. Mariani, *Chiesa et Stato nei Teologi Agostiniani del Secolo XIV*. Uomini et Dottrine 5 (Roma, 1957) 162-172; see also J. Rivière, *Le Problème de l'Eglise et l'Etat au Temps de Philippe le Bel*, Spicilegium Sacrum Lovaniense, 8, 1926, 250-251.

98. J. Rivière, *op. cit.*, 404: "Rien ne prouve, en tout cas, et tout exclut que ce minutante ait ete Gilles de Rome en personne."

99. J. Rivière, *op. cit.*, 80.

100. G. Digard, *Philippe le Bel et le Saint-Siège de 1285 a 1304* (Paris, 1936) vol. II, 175-185.

101. G. Lizerand, *Clément V et Philippe IV le Bel* (Paris, 1910) 4-11.

102. Ch. Grandjean, *Les Registres de Benoit XI* (Paris: Ernest Thorin, 1883) 361, col. 254: "Au Lateran 17 janvier 1305: Jacobo de Orto ex ordine fratrum Heremitarum S. Augustini licentiam concedidt docendi, legendi, disputandi et determinandi Parisiis et ubique locorum in theologica facultate (no. 320, fol. 78) . . . tuque postmodum de mandato nostro sub venerabili fratre nostro Egidio, archiepiscopo Bituricensi, in aula nostri palatii Laterani in facultate predicta solenniter incepisti . . ."

103. G. Digard, *op. cit.*, vol. II, 207.

104. B. Hauréau, "Gauthier de Bruges," *Histoire Littéraire de la France XXV* (1869) 305.

105. D. Sainte-Marte (Sammarthani), *Gallia Christiana*, vol. II, Ecclesia Pictaviensis, LXV: Galterus, col. 1188.

106. G. Lizerand, *Clement V et Philippe le Bel* (Paris, 1910) 23-42, 47-48.

107. D. Sainte-Marthe (Sammarthani), *op. cit.*, vol. II, Ecclesia Burdigalensis, XLII: Betrandus II, col. 831.

108. *Ibid.*, LXV: Galterus, col 1186-1188.

109. S. Baluzius - G. Mollat, *Vitae Paparum Avenionensium*, vol. I (Paris, 1914) 3.

110. D. Sainte-Marthe (Sammarthani), *op. cit.*, vol. II, Ecclesia Bituricensis, LXXV: Egidius, col. 776.

111. S. Baluzius-G. Mollat, *op. cit.*, vol. II, 36.

112. Aegidius Romanus, *Contra Exemptos* I (Rome, 1555), fol. 1r.

113. *Ibid.*, XXVI, fol. 20r.

114. National Archives, Paris, S.3634, no. 3.

115. National Archives, Paris, S.3634, no. 4.

116. D. Gandolfo, *Dissertatio Historica de Ducentis Celeberrimis Augustinianis Scriptoribus* (Roma: Buagni, 1704) 22: "Provinciale Concilium celebravit sua in Bituricensi sede anno 1315 post Beatissimae Mariae Virginis Nativitatem, non sine summa spirituali utilitate Cleri, et Populi."

Biblical Introduction

The history of the interpretation of the Song of Songs is comparable to surveying the history of biblical exegesis from the third century to the Reformation (and even beyond). This period is dominated by the writings and approaches of the great exegete, Origen. His commentary on the Song of Songs was translated from Greek into Latin by Rufinus and of the original ten books there is extant only the prologue and commentary up to chapter 2, verse 15. After finishing the commentary he wrote several homilies and the Latin translation by Jerome has survived, up to chapter 2, verse 14. Despite the relatively modest size, these works set the tone for most of the later Christian understanding of the Song of Songs. While Origen did not neglect the historical meaning of the Song — he described it as a marriage song in the style of a drama — he did not find this approach profitable. He went on to analyze the Song in terms of God and God's people, that is, Christ and the Church, and he individualized this: Christ and the individual soul. Typical of Origen's approach to the text is his treatment of chapter 2, verses 10 and following, where the lover is described as leaping like a stag over mountains as he hastens to the home of his beloved. He utters the famous spring song: *Arise, my friend, my beautiful one, and come see, the winter is past. . . .*" Origen comments on this: "The statement that the flowers have appeared on the earth, and that the trees have budded, tells us further that the season of spring is now with us. Therefore he calls upon the bride, who has doubtless sat indoors all winter, to come forth as at a fitting time." After this dramatic reconstruction or "historical" reading of the text, Origen remarks: "But these things seem to me to afford no profit to the reader as far as the story goes. . . ." Hence he determines to give them a "spiritual" meaning.

Later writers, such as Gregory the Great, the Venerable Bede, and especially Bernard of Clairvaux developed the interpretation of the Song along these lines. Over a period of about eighteen years (1135-1153) Bernard composed eighty-six sermons for his community, and he never got beyond chapter 31! This is not a commentary, but reflections on the Song in the light of monastic experience, and he emphasizes the relationship between Christ and the individual soul. "Here love speaks everywhere!" he wrote, and he used this powerfully erotic language of the Song to proclaim boldly the love between Christ and the Christian. He does not rely on theory but on experience, the experience of divine love for which his followers had a taste. "I love, because I love; I love, that I may love," he wrote, and this flowed out into his sermons. The traditions of Origen and Bernard were carried on by later writers, such as the Spanish Carmelite, John of the Cross, who wrote his famous poem, the Spiritual Canticle, in the sixteenth century.

The author of the present commentary, Giles of Rome (1243-1316), was not a Cistercian, but an Augustinian, and is better known as a theologian and a bishop. He is reputed to be one of the last students to whom Thomas Aquinas lectured. In fact his study of the Song was published among some of the works of Aquinas. He also wrote on Ecclesiastes, Romans, and the gospel of Luke. But he did not specialize in the study of the bible. His interests lay in dogmatic theology and other practical aspects of church life in view of the offices he held (prior general of his Order, and later archbishop of Bourges). Neither could he escape the dominant trend in the medieval interpretation of the Song, but he does give it an interesting twist at times by citing Aristotle. In fact he was forced to interrupt his theological studies and leave Paris because of his defense of Aristotle. After a brief sojourn in Rome he returned to Paris to finish his theological studies, and even taught on the faculty of the University. His very active life supplied him with certain views which find expression in his commentary, for example, the distinction between the active and contemplative life, and his frequent reference to the works of Aristotle.

In this respect the study of Giles provides a striking contrast to the style of *lectio divina* that characterized the patristic and early medieval works. One might call it ponderous and theological, lacking the subjective and personal emphasis of love and experience that characterizes the monastic style. In identifying the female character he alternates between the Church and the individual soul, but most of the time it is the Church who is seen as the spouse in the Song. Giles makes this clear at the very beginning of the first lecture: "The principal aim of this work is to express the mutual desire felt by bride-groom and bride, or by Christ and the Church. And so because de-sires differ in different circumstances, we must divide this book to suit the various circumstances of the Church." Similarly, the raptur-ous statement in chapter 4, verse 10 (see also chapter 1, verses 2 and 4), *your breasts are better than wine*, is explained "that is, your teaching is superior to that of the philosophers, which is not adapted to its audience, but is based on a certain severity and excellence of expres-sion, abstaining from weighty judgments." (It is clear that Giles was commenting on the Vulgate text in one form or another — the cor-rect translation of the Hebrew is *your love is better than wine*).

But the reader of the Song may well ask: Are any of these tradi-tional interpretations of the Song valid? Especially today, in the light of the historical critical approach to the bible (and all ancient litera-ture), this kind of exegesis seems dated. Although dated, it is not outdated. The history of the exegesis of the Song bears witness to a remarkable fact: both Jewish and Christian exegesis agreed that the Song dealt with the relationship of God to God's people. For the Jew it is the story of the Lord and Israel (see the Targum). For the Chris-tian of course it is the story of Christ and the Church (including also the individual soul). It would never do to dismiss simply this stunning agreement between the two communities of faith that handed down the work to us. Moreover, there was already in the Bible some basis for this direction in interpretation. The covenant between the Lord and Israel came to be seen as a marriage, especially in the writings of the prophets (see Hosea 1–3; Isaiah 62:5), and Paul continues the marriage theme in the fifth chapter of Ephesians. Within the Song itself (8:6) there is the profound line about love:

> Strong as Death is love;
> intense as Sheol is ardor.
> Its shafts are shafts of fire;
> flames of Yah.

This translation (supported also by the New Jerusalem Bible) in-dicates not only the power of love, but also its association with God (Yah is the shortened form of the divine *yhwh*). The text does not tell us *how* love is connected with the Lord (in intensity? in origin?) but it affirms a connection. This association is lost in those translations that render the last line as "intense flame" (which is grammatically possible). Hence there is some real justification for the validity of the traditional interpretation.

These considerations make us realize that the Bible has several levels of meaning. I think that the historical critical meaning governs all later valid meanings which have been seen in the scriptures. It serves as a guide, as a guard against vagaries that can creep into interpretations over a long history. In the case of the Song of Songs one may be permitted to voice the regret that the historical critical meaning did not come into its own until the present century as far as Catholics were concerned. The Song was regarded as a textbook for mystics, as it were, and was not read by the average person as an inspired love song between a man and a woman. The attitude of the Church to human sexuality, to judge from the quirky pronouncements of the past theologians in this area, would have been quite different.

Roland E. Murphy, O. Carm.

Commentary on the Song of Songs

Prologue

Let me hear your voice, for your voice is sweet and your face is beautiful (Sg 2:14). At the beginning of any book, including the present one, there are two things we expect to be told. First, the title of the book. Second, the reasons for the work. However, in this case, it is from the second chapter that we obtain such information, variously interpreted though it has been. For if the words quoted above are spoken by the bridegroom to his bride, that is, by Christ to the Church, then they make the title of the book clear to us. If indeed they are understood as spoken by Christ, they clearly point to the reasons for the work. However, the book is entitled the Song of Songs, as can be seen from the gloss. All the same, the song we are taught in this book is not physical or sensual in meaning, but rather intellectual and spiritual. For we say that there are two kinds of words, the inward and the outward, or the sensuous and the intellectual, as Augustine explains in the *City of God*, Book XV, where he describes our thoughts themselves as the heart speaking. Therefore just as with outward speech, produced melodiously and in right proportion, the result is a sensuous song, so with inward speech directed to God also affectionately in right proportion and due order, the result is a kind of spiritual melody and intelligible song.

We must not confine the word song to sensuous singing alone. For in his work on *Music*, Boethius showed that there is somehow a musical proportion in all things, since each was created in accordance with a melody in a certain proportion, just as Augustine too in *Music*, chapter 6, applies musical rhythms in a wide sense to the actions of the soul. For he distinguishes five kinds of rhythms in chapter 5 of the work mentioned, as it is according to rhythms that are judicial, progressive, in actual occurrence, memorable, and harmonious that he guarantees the actions of the soul itself. In fact even normal usage allows a clear statement to be called a song, which is a customary mode of expression with geometricians: for when they wish to prove something geometrically they say that such and such a proposition "sings," if the point is clearly proven in that proposition.

Therefore because every heart lies open to God and every will speaks, and the thoughts and affections of the will do not depart from the melody and the proportions by means of and according to which we apply ourselves to the work of virtue, they can be called a kind of song. Such is the Song which is sung here. For here are expressed the proper feelings and the thoughts of any devout soul and even the whole Church, according to which the soul means to taste the divine sweetness and to enjoy the company of her spouse. And to speak metaphysically we can say that God has two ears, one of anger, the other of affection. With the ear of anger he hears cries of sorrow, as he said to Cain: *The voice of your brother's blood is crying out to me from the ground* (Gn 4:10). But with the ear of affection he is said to hear songs, that is, the feelings, thoughts, prayers, and longings of devout minds. And because it is pleasant for him, that is, for God, to hear such songs he takes the same delight in devout souls as a good father does in his good children. Therefore he invites the devout soul or the whole Church to sing in that way, saying: *Let me hear your voice,* and adds a reason, *for your voice is sweet and your face is beautiful.* For these are the two reasons why anyone is asked to sing: first on its own account because the singing is sweet and pleasant; secondly on account of the singer, who may have a handsome appearance: for anyone who likes the singer's face will probably take greater delight in the singing.

Christ indeed takes delight in the devout soul in both ways: because of the singing itself, in other words the goodness of feelings and thoughts, and because of its grace. For the grace of God existing in the soul's being makes the soul good, and its works pleasing to God. So it is clear that, if the above words are those of the bridegroom to his bride, they explain the title of this book, which is called the Song of Songs, because that is a way of showing the excellence of such a song as this. For a genitive plural was usually added to a nominative to indicate excellence, as in: king of kings, lord of lords. But if we prefer to explain the above words as the words of the Church speaking to Christ, they still tell us the reasons for the work, though the contents seem to exclude such an interpretation. All the same, to prevent any departure from the truth of the faith on that account, such an interpretation is not to be rejected. For in holy scripture we not only have to consider the literal meaning, which is there all the time, but also the mystical, which is not necessarily so. So let us say this, then, that the material and efficient cause is signified in the words: *Let me hear your voice.* The formal in: *for your voice is sweet,* the final is the addition: *and your face is beautiful.* The bridegroom and the bride, that is Christ and the Church, or Christ and the devout soul, is the matter of this book, as the gloss mentions. But if the bride says to the bridegroom, *Let me hear your voice,* we have the material as well as the efficient cause, because the bridegroom himself, who is the true God, as well as being the subject or matter of holy doctrine, is also principally the efficient cause of this knowledge. As for the instrumental cause, we are not concerned with it; for this kind of cause involves, with regard to doctrine, such things as instruments and a pen, as in that passage in the psalms: *My tongue is nimble as the pen of a skillful scribe* (Ps 45:2). Therefore just as it would be unnecessary, when inquiring about the author of some book, to ask with what kind of pen the book was written, so in a certain way it seems unnecessary for someone to be greatly anxious to examine the instrumental causes of holy scripture. For if it is accepted that the book is from the Holy Spirit, there should be no great anxiety to discover another author. But if someone still thinks we ought to do so, we can say that Solomon was such a cause of this book. He had three names, as the gloss mentions, and in accordance with the number of his names he wrote three books. For he was called Solomon, that is, the peacemaker; Idida, that is, the beloved (amiable to the Lord), and Ecclesiastes, that is, the preacher. For as peacemaker he wrote the book of Proverbs; as preacher, he wrote the book of Ecclesiastes. Then we have the formal cause in the next words: *Your voice is sweet.* In fact it was usual to divide this form into two, namely the form of actual treatment, which is the method of procedure, and the form of the matter treated, which is the arrangement of the chapters in relation to one another. However, the method of procedure in other sciences is by proof and refutation. But in sacred teaching, above all in the canon of scripture, it seems to be by inspiration, that is, revelation, because such a text depends more on revelation than on proof. In fact the method in this book seems to be especially concerned with affection, desire, and contemplation. Hence the gloss too considers that the method of this book shows with what desire the members cling to and strive to please the head, and with what affection the bridegroom loves the Church.

Hence the method of procedure in this book is appropriately signified by the kind of sweetness expressed in the words: *Your voice is sweet*, because pleasure, affection, and desire imply a certain sweetness in love. Hence also the form of the treatise can be known, which ought to be such as the method of procedure demands; in fact, because even the order of the chapters in relation to each other, if well understood, caresses and delights the soul, it is not inappropriate that the form of the treatise can be understood through its sweetness.

But we have the final cause in the next words: *Your face is beautiful.* Therefore the object of this book, as the gloss mentions, is the love in which the bride delights; and since this is principally because of the beauty of the bridegroom's appearance, such an object is appropriately hinted in the words: *Your face is beautiful.* Since love is the object in the whole of scripture, there might be some doubt as to how the love of God as object differs in this book from the rest of holy scripture, and as to whether, because knowledge as its object, it can be said to be practical knowledge. As a guide to such matters, it should be noted that in the whole of natural philosophy the object is to investigate the body susceptible to change insofar as it is susceptible to change, but in books dealing with constituent parts, such a purpose is restricted. For example, in the book of the *Physics,* the investigation of the body susceptible to change is not directed by any particular theory, but is a simple investigation of such a body without being restricted to this or that aspect of it; while in the book on *Coming into Being (De generatione)* such a limited investigation is concerned specifically with the body susceptible to change in its formal aspect, but in the book *On the Heavens (De coelo),* in its positional aspect; and so in other books the investigation of such a body is undertaken in a specialized manner.

In the same way also in the teaching of the Church, the love of God in general is sought after, in whatever way we are guided to such a love. But in particular books the way is specified, as for instance in Genesis, in according as we are led to it in contemplating the divine power, because there we are shown how God brought into being heaven and earth and all things from nothing. But in this book we are specifically guided to the love of God in contemplating the divine kindness, and meditating on the great affection with which Christ loves his bride, and with what great desire the devout soul must be moved to enjoy the divine sweetness.

If we have carefully noted these points, we shall find it not inappropriate to describe the love of God as the object of this book, even if it is the object of all sacred teaching; for this book calls us in a special way to the love of God and our neighbor. In answer to the second question it must be said that this is called loving or affectionate knowledge of God, as we have clearly proved in our examination of the book's first sentences. And if on this account someone wanted to call it practical, since loving is a kind of work, that person should repress the thought and be silent. For practical knowledge is principally directed toward external work: thus the political sciences are called practical; and policy, that is goodness, is dependent upon our works. For according to Aristotle: In that we do good we are good; and from like actions breed like habits. Goodness, however, is spiritual because it does not depend on external works, but on the contrary on the habit of love and its works. The holy scripture which is directed toward such goodness should not be called practical. Therefore just as the knowledge which is directed toward speculation is not called practical, even if to speculate is work of a certain kind, but receives its name from speculation and is called speculative, so also theology which is directed toward the affection or love or charity, because such works are not external, must get its specific name, theology, from them, and must be called affectionate or loving and not practical. With these observations in mind let us proceed to expound the text.

Lecture 1

Let him kiss me with the kisses of his mouth (Sg 1:2).

The principal aim of this work is to express the mutual desire felt by bridegroom and bride, or by Christ and the Church. And so because desires differ in different circumstances, we must divide this book to suit the various circumstances of the Church.

For we can look at the Church in three ways: first, regarding its original condition; secondly, regarding the position of the broken branch, for the Jews became blind and Gentiles were admitted, according to Romans 11:17: *You indeed* (that is, the Gentiles), *though a wild olive, were grafted on them* (that is, the branches of the good olive) *to share the root and the rich sap of the good olive tree.* Again it can be looked at with regard to its final condition, when the Jews will all be saved, because if by then the number of the children of Israel is as the sands of the sea the remnant will be saved.

And since there can be no extremes without a middle, then as well as a first and last state there must also be an intermediate one. Paul touches on these three states in a sense in Romans 11:25, when he says: *Blindness has come upon Israel in part,* referring to the original state, *until the Gentiles enter in full strength,* the intermediate state, as it means a gain for the Church, and almost all the Gentiles are converted. And he adds at the end: *and then all Israel will be saved,* referring to the final state when the Jews will be fully converted to Christ, which will be at the end of the world.

This book is divided into three parts according to these three states. First there is a description of the mutual desires of Christ and the Church, relating to the Church in its original state. Secondly, such desires are described in relation to the intermediate state. Thirdly, these desires are described in relation to the final state. The second part begins at: *Here comes Solomon's litter. Around it are sixty warriors* . . . just over halfway through the third chapter. The third part begins at: *I went down to the nut orchard,* near the end of the sixth chapter. The first part is divided into two, as the desires of the original Church can be differentiated in two ways, that is, relating to the attainment of good and the avoidance of evil. First, then, Solomon describes the desires of the bride, that is, of the Church or the devout soul as she desires to obtain divine delights and the enjoyment of Christ, her bridegroom. Secondly he sets out the particular desires he has to escape from external tribulations. The second part begins at: *I am black and lovely.*

The first part is divided into two, because the desire of the bride is placed first; in the second place, because the bride cannot suffice by herself to obtain what she desires, she invokes divine help. This second part begins at: *take me with you.* The first part is divided into three, because the bride's desire is given the first place. Secondly, the cause or reason for the desire is added. Thirdly, from the ascribed reason she concludes that her bridegroom is naturally desired. The second part begins at: *for better,* the third part at: *therefore the maidens.* But such is the desire of the Church that she desires *to be kissed with the kisses of God's mouth,* that is, to receive some of his sweetness and grace. So the words: *let him kiss,* should be read as a wish, that is, would that God the Father might kiss me *with the kisses of his mouth,* namely that God the Father might be the one who gives the kisses, the Son might be the mouth, and the Holy Spirit the kiss.

The Son is called the mouth of the Father as he is his word and his manifestation. The Holy Spirit is called the kiss, because just as in a kiss the bodily spirit or breath proceeds from the one giving the kiss through the mouth, so too the Holy Spirit proceeds also from the Father in proceeding from the Son, since it is from the Father that the Son has the power to breathe the Holy Spirit.

Therefore Augustine in the *Trinity* XV, 26, says that the Holy Spirit proceeds in the first place from the Father. Therefore the bride desires to taste the sweetness of grace, which is granted to the Holy Spirit, distributing his good gifts and his own grace.

For your breasts are better than wine, sweet-scented with the best oint-ments. Your name is like oil poured out: therefore the maidens love you.

The bride now defines the cause and reason for her desire. Be-fore we explain this passage, there are three doubts which occur to us about the words. First because this passage seems to be discon-nected. Although earlier the Church spoke in the third person, saying: *Let him kiss me . . .*, later in stating the cause, the Church has spoken to God in the second person, adding: *For your breasts are better.* Secondly, the passage also appears disconnected and the rea-soning inconsistent because, since the bride desired a kiss, if she wished to define the cause of her desire, she should have praised the lips which give the kiss, not the breasts. Thirdly, such a state-ment seems unsuitable because generally it is the brides, not the bridegrooms, who have breasts. Since, then, in the foregoing pas-sage the bride speaks to the bridegroom, it does not seem appro-priate that she should praise his breasts.

I must say in answer that the gloss has solved the first problem, in saying that the bride speaks in the manner of a lover, who is carried away by the ardor of her love, and so sometimes speaks of her beloved in the third person, and sometimes addresses him in the second. Or else we can say that at the beginning of her speech the bride speaks of him in the third person because at first she does not dare to address so great a lord in the second person. But once she has made her request, realizing that she cannot have such de-sires without divine grace, as we are told in 2 Corinthians 3:5: *Not that we are competent to think anything by ourselves, as if it came ourselves, but our competence comes from God,* so, trusting in God's help, she who at first had declared her desires to God in the third person, saying: *Let him kiss me . . .*, in specifying the reason for her desire addresses him in the second person, adding: *for your breasts are better . . .*

The second problem is solved as follows. According to Dionysius, in the first book of the *Divine Names,* intelligible things are incompre-hensible by the senses, and so although intelligible things are not fully explained by one sensible thing, yet many sensible things can give a clearer picture of one intelligible thing. Therefore it is to make it quite plain that the kiss sought by the bride was not carnal but spiritual (in which not only the goodness of the lips, but also of the breasts and of many other things perceptible to the senses is more than abundantly included) that in praising the aforesaid kiss the bride praises the breasts, not the lips.

The third problem is solved by the gloss as follows: that the bride attributes breasts to the bridegroom to show that she is speak-

ing figuratively. It can also be solved in another way: that in bodily
and spiritual marriage conditions are not the same. For in bodily
marriage the bride gives a dowry to the husband, but in a spiritual
marriage it is the opposite, because the bridegroom, that is Christ,
endows the soul, and therefore in this kind of marriage the breasts
are principally appropriate to the bridegroom. With these considerations in mind it should be noted that to specify a reason or cause
for which something is desired is to imply that it is good, for according to Aristotle, at the beginning of the book of *Ethics*, chapter 1,
and in the first book of *Rhetoric*, chapter 6, the good is what all
things strive after. And because spiritual goods are made known
through corporeal goods, so the bride in declaring the sweetness
of the bridegroom's kiss, or the goodness of divine sweetness,
proves it in three ways. First because it refreshes the taste, as indicated in the words: *For your breasts are better than wine.* Secondly because it revives the sense of smell, as indicated by the next words:
sweet-scented with the best ointments. Thirdly because it delights the
touch, as indicated in the words following this: *Your name is like oil
poured out.*

To understand the words it should be noted that the sweetness
which the Church, the bride of Christ, desires to attain is to be
found above all in the contemplative life. However, according to
what theologians, the apostles, philosophers, and Epicureans have
said of it, the contemplative life is not understood in a uniform
manner. For the philosophers consider the purpose of contemplation to be wisdom. Thus in *Ethics* 10, chapter 8, in the exposition of
happiness, it is shown that the effect produced by the act of contemplation is happiness of this kind. For according to the author
of the *Metaphysics*, the contemplation of wisdom is regarded by philosophers as the greatest happiness. Thus Aristotle in *Ethics* X, with
the aim of giving the highest praise to such happiness, shows it to
be supremely delightful, saying: "Philosophy seems to have marvel-
ously pure and constant delights." But contemplation, as the theologians speak of it, is based more on taste than theory, and more
on love and sweetness than on contemplation. And if the pursuit of
learning is sometimes found applicable to the contemplative life,
according to the theologians this is insofar as such employment
leads us to the love of God. If, then, anyone studies for the sake of
knowledge and not of edification and advancement in the love of
God, he must understand that he is living the contemplative life
according to the philosophers, and not according to the theologians. If, then, we choose to speak of these two kinds of contemplation by a certain comparison according to the senses, we may say

that the contemplative life of the philosophers refreshes hearing and sight, but the spiritual contemplation of the theologians refreshes taste, smell, and touch.

For though all the senses help us to acquire knowledge, it is hearing and sight that serve us best for this. For, according to Aristotle, all the knowledge that anyone has is acquired through either learning or discovery. Hearing, therefore, which is the sense through which we are teachable, according to Aristotle in the first book of *Metaphysics*, helps us toward the knowledge which is acquired through instruction, and we acquire knowledge through learning. But sight, which shows us the many differences between things (as is said in that same first book of the *Metaphysics*), helps us toward the knowledge which is acquired through discovery, and we gain knowledge in making discoveries. So philosophic contemplation, which is based on theory (taking the above matters into account), appears to refresh hearing and sight in particular. But spiritual contemplation, which is based on taste, and according to which we ourselves live, has to refresh taste, smell, and touch, which help us most in the needs of life. Hence since the happiness of the philosophers is based on the mind, but spiritual happiness is based completely and perfectly on the will, as can be explained in the proper place; and though the thoughts of the mind are called speeches and ideas, as Augustine says clearly in *The Trinity* V, 11, yet it is inaccurate to call them tastes, smells, and touches, because such things seem more to be concerned with the will.

Our proposition stated above seems good enough: that philosophic contemplation refreshes hearing and sight, but spiritual contemplation refreshes taste, smell, and touch. Therefore the bride means to commend spiritual, not philosophical, contemplation, when she says: *Your breasts are better than wine,* etc. In those words she touches upon three kinds of people in the Church, who in some way are refreshed by the divine sweetness. For insofar as the breasts of the bridegroom, that is, his sweet delight, are said to be better than wine, that is, than every physical taste, the perfect are made perfect who strive to taste such sweetness. Then just as such breasts are sweet-scented with the best ointments, that is, with all the perfumes perceptible by the senses, it refreshes those who are progressing toward such sweetness, drawn by their sense of smell. But as the name of Christ *is like oil poured out,* delighting the touch because of its softness and richness, it refreshes beginners more than anything else, those who have got no further than touch in their spiritual life. For just as a sense of touch is that by which perceptible life is restored in a sick person, because according to

Aristotle an animal is defined as such by its sense of touch, since without touch it is impossible for an animal to exist, hence beginners share in the spiritual life like sick persons, because they seem to possess only the sense of touch in accordance with such a life. But when they proceed to make progress through reason, they acquire the sense of smell as they move toward the odor of sweetness. When indeed they reach perfection, they delight entirely in Christ and taste his sweetness.

The next words: *therefore the maidens* infer that Christ the bridegroom is universally loved in the Church. And the text may be paraphrased as follows: Lord Jesus Christ, you who are all things, in every way adapting yourself to all persons, that is, to the perfect, to those making progress, and to beginners, bestowing your sweetness on all in the appropriate measure; and because you conform yourself thus to all, *therefore the maidens*, that is the beginners, *love you.* The bride, therefore, wishes to argue from the particular to the general. For if the maidens, that is the beginners, who seem to be a minority, love Christ, it follows that Christ is loved universally in the Church. And it should be noted that this conclusion: *therefore the maidens*, can be inferred in two ways: first what follows from all that has been said above, in the way shown just before that; secondly, what follows from what was said above that because the name of Christ *is like oil poured out*, it refreshes beginners, as explained, *Therefore the maidens*, meaning the beginners, *love you.* But the beginners are called maidens, as the gloss makes clear, because the maidens are old through sin but young through grace. Yet always it is concluded from the particular to the general that Christ is universally loved.

Lecture 2

Draw me after you (Sg 1:4).

After the bride has expressed her desire, namely, that she wishes to receive the sweetness of Christ, seeing that by herself she cannot obtain her desire, in this part she appeals for divine help. This part itself is divided into two. In asking for such help, the bride first puts in her request; secondly, there is the bridegroom's granting it, as appears from the words: *the king has brought me in.* Two points are made in the first part: first, the bride begs for divine help; secondly, she declares it is sweet and powerful. The first point is made in the words: *Draw me after you;* the second is in those following: *Let us run after the odor of your ointments.* It may, then, be interpreted as follows: Lord Jesus Christ, I see that I cannot come to you nor taste your sweetness by myself: therefore I beg for your help, asking you: *draw me after you.* For according to Christ's words in John 6:44: *No one can come to me unless the Father who sent me draws him.* And because the works of the Trinity are undivided, as Augustine says in Book I, 3 of *The Trinity,* and John of Damascus in Book III, chapter 18, therefore just as no one can come to Christ, the bridegroom, unless the Father draws him, so no can come to Christ, the bridegroom, unless Christ draws him. The bride, then, that is the Church, says rightly to her bridegroom, Christ, *Draw me after you. Let us run after the odor of your ointments.*

The bride declares that Christ's help is sweet and powerful. It may be interpreted as follows: it is not for foolish reasons that I say: *Draw me after you,* but because your attraction is sweet and powerful. For if you draw me, I shall not only move anyway, but even run *after the odor of your ointments;* that is, I shall move as fast as I can, just to smell the sweetness of your strength and your gifts. But it must be noted that when the bride says that she will run in the wake of Christ's attraction, she declares his attraction to be sweet, not violent, for to run is to move willingly. Again she declares that such an attraction is strong, because running implies a swiftness of movement which itself requires great strength. No wonder Christ draws sweetly and strongly, for Christ is God's strength and God's wisdom, according to Paul in 1 Corinthians 1:24. *And wisdom,* as we read in Wisdom 8:1, *reaches mightily from end to end and arranges everything well.*

It should also be noted that when the bride asks to be drawn, she speaks of herself in the singular, saying: *Draw me after you.* When she says that she responds to this attraction, she speaks of herself in the plural, saying: *Let us run after the odor,* etc. The reason for this is that God, as far as concerns himself, draws us in one way alone: for according to Dionysius, in chapter 4 of the *Divine Names,* God emits his intelligible rays in the same way as the sun its perceptible rays, without thought or choice. Yet we ourselves are not drawn in one way alone; for although God behaves in the same way toward all kinds of people, all do not behave uniformly toward him, because people react to the same influence in various ways. But I have explained elsewhere how this statement of Dionysius is to be understood, and how God treats all things in the same manner.

The king has brought me into his storerooms.

This describes the way in which the bridegroom responds to the requests of his bride. She has three things to say about it: first, that she has been introduced into the sweetness she had sought; secondly, she rejoices that she has obtained the good she had desired; thirdly, she declares that she was not deceived in regard to that good. The first is expressed in the words: *The king has brought me,* the second, in the addition: *we shall rejoice,* the third, in the words subjoined: *Remembering your breasts.* It may be interpreted as follows: I did not seek divine help in vain, because my bridegroom, who is Christ, king of kings and lord of lords, gave heed to my humble petition and *has brought me into his storerooms,* that is, into his sweetness, giving me his grace. But grace is called storerooms in the plural, because from it flow and are derived each of the spiritual virtues perfecting various powers, and according to the different virtues of the various powers we are glad and rejoice in the Lord in various ways. And being made perfect according to such virtues derived from grace, in a certain way we drink the wines of spiritual joy from different storerooms.

We shall rejoice and be glad in you.

This verse shows that the bride has obtained the good which she desired, that is, God himself. For according to the way of intelligence, we are first perfected according to divine grace, and after being perfected through grace we obtain him for whom grace has destined us, and therefore we have been led by grace to spiritual joy: we shall rejoice and be glad in you. But it should be noted that everyone in general longs for happiness, but all search for it in their own particular way. Some find happiness in love affairs, some in wealth, and in other such things in which there is no true happiness. For their delight is not centered on him who is the supreme and true good, but only on a tiny part of it, insofar as everything has a share in the beautiful and the good (*Ethics*, I, 8). But divine grace centers our happiness on the supreme and true good and no other. Thus the bride says expressly: *We shall rejoice and be glad in you*, who are the supreme and true good. Then she says next:

Remembering your breasts more than wine. The righteous love you.

She knows that she has not been deceived about the good which she had desired. As proof of this, it must be noted that this is the difference between perceptible and intellectual goods: that perceptible goods are thought to be great before they are possessed, but when possessed they lose their value, as can be inferred from Augustine in his book, *Teaching Christianity*, and from Aristotle in Book I of the *Ethics*. That is why people are disappointed when they acquire perceptible goods, because they do not find them as good as they anticipated after they have got them.

But in the case of intellectual goods, it is not the same, because their possession is regarded as greater and most important, and especially the supreme good which is God. The reason why perceptible goods give pleasure for a little time and are not found to be as good as they were believed to be can be attributed to the fact that goods of such kind are not enjoyable of themselves; and the fact that they give pleasure is due to the perverted desires of their possessors, because everyone thinks of what he should aim at in terms of his own character, as it is said in Book III of the *Ethics*, chapter 8. And because such desires accord with our changeable nature, it is easy for us to find things delightful at one moment and not so the next. Hence Aristotle says in Book I of the *Rhetoric* in the "Treatise on Debate" that change is pleasant, because change takes place in nature itself.

In the good things of God, or divine things, the case is otherwise; for such things are desirable in themselves, therefore delightful in themselves, because we desire them according to that within us which is highest and best. Hence also through our desire for them we are torn away from such inconstant fancies, because once we have possessions of this kind we never tire of them; on the contrary we are always finding them better than we thought before.

Therefore the words: *We remember your breasts,* may be interpreted in the following way, that is, remembering what we said of the breasts, that they are better than wine, we have not been deceived in such an opinion because the righteous, that is, those who understand rightly, love you more than wine. After she had been brought into the storerooms of the bridegroom and had tasted his sweetness, this bride might well have said the same as the queen of Sheba said to King Solomon (2 Chr 9:1-4), when after hearing of Solomon's fame she came to test him. And when she told him all that was on her mind, and after Solomon had answered all her questions, and there was nothing more for the king to explain, seeing the wisdom of Solomon she was amazed and humbled, saying to the king: *All that I heard of your accomplishments in my own country is true.*

It must be noted, however, that the bride first speaks in the singular, saying: *he has brought me into,* afterward in the plural, when she adds: *We shall rejoice and be glad in you, remembering your breasts* etc., words which we have explained above. Another explanation is also possible: that the bride who asked for one thing finds that it has been and is meant to be communicated to many people in many ways: rejoicing in this and for this, she says: *We shall rejoice and be glad* etc.

Lecture 3

I am black and beautiful, daughters of Jerusalem, like the tents of Kedar: like the curtains of Salma (Sg 1:5).

After the bride has stated her desire to receive divine sweetness or the good things of God, she now states her desire to avoid tribulation and evil. But to understand what she means, it must be noted that the bride of Christ is the Church. The Church, however, can be understood in two ways: first, as the whole congregation of the faithful; secondly, as the dignitaries of the Church, for when a name is applied to a whole society, it take its name from the higher part of the whole. Just as we see that this name "man" is the name of the whole combination of body and soul, yet because the intellective part in man is superior, we also call "man" that superior part which is called intellective, for what man does in accordance with the intellect he is said to do by himself. It is for this reason that Aristotle says, in Book IX of the *Ethics*, that man is more intellect than sense.

So too because the name "Church" is used of the whole assembly of the faithful, the clergy who hold the highest rank in the Church are called the Church. And what the dignitaries of the Church do is said to be what the Church does. Even the Lord says in connection with someone who refuses to listen to either one, two, or three, *Tell the Church* (Mt 18:17), that is, a church leader, according to one interpretation. So taking the Church in this way to mean the clergy themselves, we shall be able to interpret the contents of the text better.

In view of this it should be realized that, because of their responsibilities, the clergy are doubly beset: first, because of the outward

troubles they face; secondly, because of the troubles that sometimes so distract their minds that, when the trouble has passed and
they want to return to contemplation, they find it impossible to
recover the delight they had received from it before. Therefore
when Solomon describes the tribulations of the Church, that is, of
the clergy, he does so in two ways. First, he describes the outward
tribulations; secondly, their inward distraction at the beginning of
the third chapter, where he says: *On my bed at night I sought him whom
my soul loves.*

Regarding the first point, it must be noted that the early Church,
which is the subject of discussion here (as is clear from the text), was
beset by four kinds of tribulations. As far as two of them are concerned, they were the same as in the Church of today, whereas the
other two were different. For the Church of today, or the clergy of
these times, are doubly beset. First in the ministry of its children, for
it is not easy for administrators to be trouble-free, as can be seen from
2 Corinthians 11:25. They have trouble from heretics plotting
against them, for even today there are false Christians in power.

The early Church, however, had these two tribulations, for the
clergy of that time had the care of those placed under them, and
heretics plotted against them. The Church at that time was also
subject to two kinds of trouble which the Church of today is free of.
For at that time Christians, especially the clergy, were universally
attacked by Jews and Gentiles, which no longer happens. There is
no attack from the Gentiles, because the Gentiles have already entered the Church in full strength; there is no attack from the Jews,
because they have none of the authority over Christians which they
had at that time.

Solomon therefore makes two points. First, he describes the
troubles of the early Church differing from those of today; secondly, the things also which agree with those of today, as at the
beginning of the second chapter: *I am a rose of Sharon.*

The first part is itself divided into two parts, for the bride first
describes the kind of troubles referred to; secondly, she seeks the
help of Christ, in the words: *Tell me, you whom my soul loves.* But the
troubles afflicting the early Church, and differing from those of
today, were due to the goading of the Gentiles and the onslaughts
of the Jews. So she has two things to say on this subject: describing,
first, how the goading of the Gentiles troubles the Church; secondly, how the Church suffers from the onslaughts of the Jews, in
the passage beginning: *the sons of my mother.* The first part is divided
into two: first, the goading of the Gentiles is described; secondly, in
reply to that goading, an instruction to the children is added, in the

words: *do not look at me.* In connection with the first, it must be noted that it is to its goading that the Church owes its beauty: so that the story of the sufferings of the Church at the hands of the Gentiles is also the story of its beauty. The passage may be interpreted as follows: *Daughters of Jerusalem,* whom it is my duty to care for, I the Church your mother am black, like the tents of Kedar, but I am beautiful, like the curtains of Salma. Kedar was the second son of Ishmael (as we are told in Gn 25:9), and was a wanderer over the earth, like his father, Ishmael, of whom it had been said: *He will be a wild ass of a man, his hand against everyone and everyone's hand against him* (Gn 16:12). So Kedar, as if hateful to all men, refused to dwell among them, but camped outside in tents blackened by the rain. In the same way, since the Church was despised by the Gentiles it could not survive in their midst without trouble, as the gloss seems to indicate, noting the trouble the early Church had with the Gentiles. Yet though it was black from exterior troubles, on the inside: *I am beautiful like the curtains of Salma,* which were red, out of which he made the tabernacle, as the gloss mentions, or with which he covered the ark of the Lord, where beauty is noted as charity. Next she says:

Do not look at me because I am dark, for the sun has scorched me (Sg 1:6).

After the Church has described her distress, now she turns away from the distress that has come upon her to instruct her children and encourage them, saying: *Daughters of Jerusalem, do not look at me because I am dark, for the sun,* that is, Christ, *has scorched me,* that is, has blackened me. Christ is said to have blackened the early Church because he was the ultimate cause of its blackness, insofar as on account of Christ the Church had been blackened in suffering the troubles brought on it by the Gentiles. Therefore the Church uses such arguments in the endeavor to teach its children that their attention and main consideration should not be focused on anything leading to their goal, but on the goal itself; on the contrary, our troubles in the world are the means by which we come to Christ: Christ is our goal. Therefore when we find ourselves beset with troubles on account of Christ, we should not think or care about the troubles themselves, but our whole attention must be focused on Christ, for whose sake we are enduring such trials.

My mother's sons quarreled with me; they made me keeper of the vine-yards, my own vineyard I have neglected (Sg 1:6).

After the Church has told of her trouble with the Gentiles, she passes to her goading by the Jews. As evidence of this, it should be noted that it was owing to the persecution by the Jews of the apostles and Christians in Jerusalem that the said Christians turned to the Gentiles, according to the account in Acts 13:46: *We are now turning to the Gentiles.* And in turning to the Gentiles they became keepers of the vineyards, that is, of the Gentiles, because at least accidentally it was the Jews who made the early Church keeper of the vineyards of the Gentiles, by expelling it from Jerusalem. Therefore, while keeping watch over the Gentiles, the apostles were no longer guarding Jerusalem, which was, as it were, their own vineyard.

So in recounting the troubles with the Jews, the Church mentions three things. First, it names the people attacking it, in saying: *my mother's sons,* that is, the Jews, have quarrelled with me. For the synagogue was, as it were, our mother, because in a kind of way the Church proceeded from it. And because the Jews were the children of the synagogue, therefore the Church calls them her mother's sons. Secondly, she emphasizes the extent of the trouble, in adding: *they made me keeper of the vineyards;* for the trouble was so great that Christians were unable to remain in Jerusalem, and so they turned the Gentiles and became their keepers. Thirdly, she states the effect of the assault, in adding further: *my own vineyard I have neglected,* because the result was that they left Jerusalem.

Tell me, you whom my soul loves, where you graze your flock, and where you rest it at midday.

Seeing the Church involved in so many troubles, she seeks the help of Christ; and this is divided into two parts: first, there is the bride's request or question; secondly, there is added the reason for her question, with the words: *lest I begin to wander.* It may be interpreted in this way: O Lord Jesus Christ, my bridegroom, *you whom my soul loves,* you see me beset by so many troubles. Since, without you, I cannot escape from them, therefore: *tell me where you graze your flock, and where you rest it at midday.* The Church wanted to know where Christ's house was, because it is in a house that we eat and rest, and she knew that Christ was not a vagabond. On the contrary, anyone going to his house to seek him and have recourse to him in time of trouble knew that he would always find him ready and waiting. Therefore she said: *tell me where you rest your flock at midday.* Men lie down at night, but Christ lies down at midday and in full daylight, for he is the true God, that is, the true light, and in him there is no darkness.

Lest I begin to wander after the flocks of your companions (Sg 1:7).

She defines the reason for her question. In its troubles the Church has recourse to Christ, in case it begins to wander after the companions of Christ. But it is heretics who are called the companions of Christ, for they are unwilling to be imitators, but want to be his partners and companions, insofar as they are eager to teach their own doctrines and be masters, on the same level as Christ.

If you do not know yourself, O most beautiful of women (Sg 1:8).

Here is Christ's answer. As proof of this it must be realized that the bride was to be rebuked for two reasons. First because of her question: *tell me where you graze your flock*, implying that she wished to seek for an absent God, when she ought to have sought God within herself. So insofar as she had asked such a question, she was to be rebuked for ignorance. But in regard to the reason for her question, she was in some way to be rebuked for her lack of faith, for she seemed to doubt whether Christ was always present to help her, when she said: Lest I begin to wander.

Therefore this part is divided into two: because, first, Christ rebukes the bride for her ignorance; secondly, so that she may not lack faith, he tells her what evils will befall her as a result of such ignorance: *Go and follow*. And so he says: *O most beautiful of women*, therefore you seek me as absent, and you say: *Where do you graze your flock, where do you rest it?* — that is, because you do not know, for if you knew, you would seek me within yourself. It should be noted that Christ calls the Church fairest because God is to be sought in the soul, as the soul is his image. And since it is the soul he is rebuking for such ignorance, he calls her fairest, because as the image of God she is fairest.

Go and follow in the tracks of your own flock, and graze your kids beside the shepherds' tents (Sg 1:8).

He describes the evils which will befall her as the result of such ignorance, and mentions two: mental blindness and sensual wickedness. The passage may be interpreted in this way: if you, fairest of women, do not know: *Go and follow*, that is, you will go and follow *in the tracks of your own flock*, that is, the doctrines and example of heretics. For these are the same flocks which she had mentioned earlier: *Lest I begin to wander after the flocks of your companions,* that is, after the heretics, as was said, indicating willful ignorance; *and graze,* that is, you will graze *your kids,* that is, you will fulfill your carnal desires. For the young goat is a foul animal, and indicates the passions of the flesh. And so: *beside the shepherds' tents,* because you will follow your carnal desires as other worldly people do, these being understood as goat herds.

I have compared you, my love, to my horsemen pitted against the chariots of Pharaoh (Sg 1:9).

Because the bride appeared to lack faith, to prevent this and fill her with confidence in him, Christ mentions the gifts he has bestowed on her. These were of two kinds. First he mentions the gift he bestowed on her in trampling on her enemies. Secondly he mentions the gift he bestowed on her in the great beauty she acquired: *your cheeks are beautiful.* It may be interpreted in this way: *my love,* do not lack faith, because *I have compared you to my horsemen,* that is, to the people of Israel, who were my special people whom I possessed and ruled like a horse. Therefore I have compared you to that people *pitted against Pharaoh's chariots.* For just as Pharoah's chariots and his horsemen sank in the Red Sea, as we are told in Exodus 14, so I shall trample on and sink those demons that molest you, understood as Pharaoh's chariots.

Your cheeks are as beautiful as the turtle-dove's (Sg 1:10).

He mentions the good things he has bestowed on her, with which she could advance to greater heights, and enumerates the three most necessary good things he has bestowed on her: the first is charity; the second, faith, *your neck*; and the third, hope, golden ear-rings. It may be interpreted in this way: You ought to have faith in me not only because I have sunk your enemies to the bottom of the sea, but also because I have bestowed many good things on you to be deserved. I gave you the virtue of charity so that you might love me as shepherd and creator. He expressed this in the words: *your cheeks are beautiful,* that is, your nature is *like that of the turtle-dove.* The turtle-dove is a very loving animal, and when it loses its mate it rejects any other. In this is signified the ardor of charity.

Your neck is like jewels (Sg 1:10).

This shows that he has bestowed faith on her. It may be interpreted as follows: I have not only given you love, in making your cheeks like those of a turtle-dove, but I have also bestowed faith on you, in making your neck, that is, your faith, by which you are joined to me, the head, just as the head is joined to the body by the neck, in making your neck *like jewels*, that is, like an ornament that has no external covering, for you hold God purely and alone in your heart.

We shall make you golden earrings inlaid with silver (Sg 1:11).

He shows that he has bestowed hope on her. However, it is the hope of an eternal prize. But such a prize is twofold, namely, essential, as the joy of an uncreated good, and accidental, namely, of a created good. And he mentions both, saying: *we shall make you golden earrings*, that is, we shall fill you with the hope of an essential reward. For the essential reward is usually described as golden, just as the accidental is called gift. An ear-ring is called such a golden or essential reward, being a little chain of various colors connecting an ornament to the inside of the neck.

Therefore the essential reward is one God. Nevertheless according to the diversity of merits, not all will have equal joy in that God, as the Lord declares in John 14:2, *In my Father's house there are many rooms*. But this kind of golden ear-ring will be inlaid with silver on account of the addition of the accidental prize; for the accidental reward is as far outshone by the substantial as silver is by gold. However this kind of accidental reward is called inlaid on account of its diversity, for not all will possess the same accidental reward. But it should be noted that, when he speaks of the hope of a prize, he expressly says: *we shall make*, because hope refers to a time in the future.

While the king reclined on his couch, my spikenard gave out its scent (Sg 1:12).

This pictures the bride after correction. And because her rebuke had been twofold, that is, for ignorance and for lack of faith, her correction has two aspects. First the bride shows that she no longer lacks faith, but now has firm belief. Hence as if rebuked for lack of faith, she acknowledges the benefits bestowed on her. Secondly, as if rebuked for ignorance, she admits that she ought to seek not an absent but a present God, as appears from the words: *our bed is flourishing.*

In the first place it must be noted that, according to Aristotle in Book I of the *Rhetoric,* there is a difference between correction and vengeance. For correction, or punishment, is inflicted in the interest of the sufferer, to reform him; but vengeance in the interest of the one who inflicts it, for his own personal satisfaction. Therefore when someone is corrected, if he improves as a result of correction and finds comfort in his corrector, he must be commended and praised so as to remain steadfast in his amended ways.

This part is therefore divided into two: first, the bride's correction in regard to her lack of faith; secondly, her commendation, in the words: *How beautiful you are, my love.* The bride's correction in regard to her lack of faith occurs in her recognition of the gifts she has received, for she acknowledges the help given to her. But such help, as was said, came in four ways, remarkably prophetic of Christ. For instance, the overthrow of her enemies can be applied to the incarnation. For although the prince of this world was cast out through the passion, this was only because the man who suffered was God, and because God was made man in the incarnation. Therefore it is not inconsistent to apply the overthrow of her enemies to the incarnation. But the gift of love can be applied to the passion, because no one has *greater love than one who lays down his life for his friends* (Jn 15:13). Then the gift of faith can be applied to the resurrection. For after Christ's passion all the apostles were in suspense; but in rising again Christ confirmed them in the faith, because after his passion he appeared to them in his own living presence on many occasions for forty days, speaking of the kingdom of God, as we are told in Acts 1. Again hope can be applied to the ascension, and to the sending of the Holy Spirit: because at his ascension Christ sent his Church the Holy Spirit, whom in receiving they possess as a pledge of their eternal inheritance, because it strengthened their hope regarding eternal rewards. Therefore the bride celebrates four events in the four gifts she acknowledges. For first she acknowledges the incarnation, through which her enemies are overthrown. Secondly, the passion, by which the love of Christ is made known. Thirdly, the resurrection, through which our faith is confirmed. Fourthly and lastly, she acknowledges the sending of the Holy Spirit, through which our hope is strengthened.

The second part begins at: *a bunch of myrrh;* the third at: *a cluster of Cyprus;* the fourth at: *from the vineyards of Engedi.* Therefore the bride says: *while the king reclined on his couch,* that is, in the bosom of the Father where he rests, *my spikenard,* that is, my humility, etc. For spikenard is a small and fragrant plant, and symbolizes the humility which poured forth its fragrance when, reflecting on the humility of his Church, the Son became man.

My beloved is for me a bunch of myrrh, he will lie between my breasts (Sg 1:13).

She acknowledges the passion, in saying: *my beloved is for me a bunch of myrrh.* Myrrh, according to the gloss, is a tree of Arabia, five cubits high, which secretes a green and bitter substance, and hence symbolizes the passion of Christ. But this passion was *a bunch of myrrh.* A bunch means something gathered, and a diminutive noun. Thus Christ was thought to be diminished by his passion. Isaiah 53:2: *He had no beauty or charm.* With the consequence: *And so neither did we think anything of him.* Again there was a gathering of myrrh, that is, of bitterness, within him, on account of the many sufferings and insults that he endured. And in the passion he was literally given wine mixed with myrrh. And because Christ bestowed such great gifts on his bride as to be willing to suffer and die for her, in recognition of this the bride adds that her beloved was such that he would lie between her breasts, that is, between the mind and the will, because she wants to know nothing that would displease him, and love nothing that he would abhor.

My beloved is for me a cluster of cyprus (Sg 1:14).

She acknowledges the resurrection, in saying: *My beloved is for me a cluster of cyprus,* that is, very sweet, delightful, and pleasant. Cyprus is an island, the clusters of grapes of which make the best wine. And because wine gladdens the heart of man, so the resurrection is understood here; for when the Lord was seen after the resurrection, the disciples rejoiced (John 20).

In the vineyards of Engedi.

She acknowledges the sending of the Holy Spirit. This may be interpreted as follows: You, my beloved, are not only a cluster of cyprus, gladdening the soul through the resurrection, but you are also for me a cluster of grapes in the vineyards of Engedi, that is, you are for me a cluster of balsam. For according to the gloss, there are in Engedi balsam trees growing like vines; hence it symbolizes the sending of the Holy Spirit, because we receive the gifts of the

Holy Spirit through the anointing with chrism, which is made of balsam and oil.

How beautiful you are, my love: how beautiful: you have the eyes of doves (Sg 1:15).

Praise is given to the bride. And it is divided into two parts, because first Christ praises the bride; secondly, because all our good is from Christ and the bride recognizes this, she refers and directs this praise to Christ, saying of him: *How beautiful you are.* Christ's words may be interpreted thus: All your beauty is due to my influence over you, which you willingly accept. And he says: *how beautiful you are,* twice, to show that she is beautiful both inwardly and outwardly, in action and intention. Therefore he adds: *you have the eyes of doves.* For my two eyes are action and intention. The dove in fact is a fertile and simple creature, and we have the eyes of doves when our action is fertile through goodness and our intention is simple through righteousness.

How handsome and graceful you are, my beloved (Sg 1:16).

The bride attributes her own beauty to Christ. It may be interpreted as follows: You, my beloved, said to me: *How beautiful you are, my love, how beautiful.* So because I have nothing that I have not received from you, I do not wish to boast as if I had not received it. I acknowledge that all my beauty comes from your beauty. Therefore that twofold beauty, which you said is in me, is more abundantly and completely preserved in you, for which reason, *my beloved, how handsome and graceful you are.*

Our bed is flourishing.

The bride shows that she has been rebuked for her ignorance, and confesses her belief in a present not an absent God. For the bride had asked Christ where he fed and where he rested, showing herself to be doubly ignorant. So she makes two points: first, she acknowledges that he feeds within herself; secondly, that he rests within herself, where she says: *The beams of our house.* It may be interpreted as follows: Like someone ignorant, I was asking where you fed, my beloved, but now I know that you feed within myself. For you feed among flowers, according to the words quoted below: *who feeds among lilies. Since our bed is flourishing,* therefore you feed in my bed, that is, in my mind or my conscience.

The beams of our house are of cedar, our rafters of cypress.

She acknowledges that he rests in herself. For Christ's rest is where the gifts and powers of the Holy Spirit are. So it may be interpreted as follows: I confess, my beloved, not only that you feed in me, because our bed is flourishing, but that you rest in me, for *the beams of our house*, that is, of our mind and conscience or powers, *are of cedar*, owing to the powers of the Holy Spirit, and *our rafters of cypress*, owing to the gifts of the Holy Spirit. For the long pieces of wood joined at the top are called the beams of a house, and symbolize the powers of the Holy Spirit, which though of many kinds are joined at the top, insofar as they flow from divine grace which is in the essence of the soul in which such powers are rooted. Also these powers are described as of cedar for their incorruptibility. But the pieces of wood connecting the actual beams are called rafters, since the rafters adhere more closely to the sides from which the roof of a house rises, than the actual beams could. So they are called rafters, and signify the gifts of the Holy Spirit, through which the Holy Spirit inspires us. For in accordance with such inspiration the virtues remain in us more firmly. Such rafters are indeed of cypress because of their fragrance, for their fragrance is wafted continually to the Holy Spirit.

Lecture 4

I am a rose of Sharon (Sg 2:1).

After a description of the troubles of the early Church which differed from those of the Church of today, there now follows a description of those which were similar. Such troubles are in fact twofold, the ministry of the children and the snares of heretics. So this part is also divided into two. First, the imitation of Christ is laid down, as he invites the Church to produce or take care of the flowers and arrest the heretics. Secondly it lays down the submission of the bride, who is ready to obey Christ, where she says: *my beloved is mine.*

The first part is divided into two, because in the first Christ invites the Church to look after her children; secondly, to arrest the heretics, where it says: *catch the little foxes.* First he invites the Church to undertake a duty; secondly to carry out the duty, where she says: *the voice of my beloved.*

In the first place it should be noted that, first, Christ invites the Church to minister to the children and take care of them. Secondly, the bride sees it is no good rejecting the advice of the bridegroom and so does not answer the bridegroom, implying that she assents to his advice. She turns to the children, explaining how the duty undertaken is to be understood, where she says: *like an apple tree.* Thirdly Christ confirms such an explanation, saying: *I charge you,* etc. The first part is divided into three, as he invites the Church to minister to the children and take care of them in three ways. He first invites the Church to do this by means of example; secondly, by means of reward, where he says: *like a lily;* thirdly, by means of merit, where he says: *like a lily among thorns.* It may be interpreted

81

as follows: You, my love, are troubled by the Gentiles, because you are very dark like the tents of Kedar; you are also troubled by the Jews, because your mother's sons quarrelled with you. But besides this you have to endure tribulation for the ministry of your children, to which you must be persuaded by my own example, because I am the rose of Sharon. I am not a rose growing in an out-of-the-way place, but in Sharon, and *I have laid down my life for my sheep* (Jn 10:17). So you too must follow my example and do the same.

And a lily of the valleys.

This points to: by means of reward. It may be interpreted as follows: Not only, my love, must you lay down your life for your children in your care of them, so as to be a rose of Sharon like myself, but you must also do this in the knowledge that I am a lily of the valleys, or the beauty and reward of the humble. Therefore if you humble yourself to do this, you will have a recompense and a reward from me.

Like a lily among thorns is my love among the daughters (Sg 2:2).

This points to: by means of merit. For it is a way of speaking, if anyone wanted to have someone as a friend and said in his hearing: If anyone wants to be my friend he must be as good as gold. The other, if he was at all intelligent, would then understand he would have to be such a person if he wished to be his friend. Christ speaks to the Church in the same way, when he says: *like a lily among thorns is my love among the daughters.* Therefore you, my bride, if you want to be my love you must expose yourself to thorns, that is, to tribulation, for the sake of your children, and be purified or distressed on account of such thorns, because this will be to your merit. In saying this he invites her to undertake her duties by means of merit.

Like an apple tree among the trees of the wood is my beloved among the sons. I sat in the shadow of him whom I desired, and his fruit was sweet to my taste (Sg 2:3).

The Church explains to its children how they ought to behave in undertaking a duty. It wishes to show that it must first attend to itself, and after that to others. And this it shows on two grounds. First because of the difference between the active and contemplative life. Secondly because of the natural order of love. The first argument runs as follows: The contemplative life is better than the active life, according to the Lord's saying to Mary that she had chosen *the best part* (Lk 10:42), because she had chosen the contemplative life. But the greater good must have first attention. Therefore since a church leader pays more attention to himself in the contemplative life, but seems to pay more attention to those under him in the active life he ought to attend to himself before those subject to him. The second argument is inferred from the natural order of love. For love leads straight to good. And because any good keeps better where it is whole rather than where it is partial, so our good keeps better in God where it is whole, rather than where it is partial. Also anything keeps better in itself than in its likeness, so we must love God more than ourselves, and ourselves more than our neighbor. Therefore according to the natural order of love the church leader must first love and pay attention to the good for himself before he does so for those subject to him.

In setting out these arguments the Church proceeds as follows: first she explains the means or virtues of these arguments. Secondly she argues from the means themselves, where she says: *support me with flowers*. The first part is divided into two, as she explains the two means. For first she considers the means of contemplation with all its delight; secondly, that of the ordering of love, where she says: *the king took me into the vinery*. The first means, then, is implicit in the fact that the bridegroom is supremely good, and that she sat in his, that is her bridegroom's, shadow, and tasted his fruit in which she found great sweetness. Therefore she says that he is *like an apple tree among the trees of the wood,* that is, growing wild, not because he himself is growing wild, but by comparison. Just as all things are dry and he alone is green, so all the trees are growing wild and he alone is cultivated and supremely good, supremely delightful and desirable. *Thus is my beloved among the sons;* that is, among other righteous men he is supremely desirable, because all holy men are almost alien to God in comparison with Christ, because they are not natural sons as he is. And because such is her bridegroom she therefore adds: *I sat in his shadow,* that is, my bridegroom's, whose shadow I longed for. *And his fruit was sweet to my taste.* For we sit in Christ's shadow when we are not consumed by the fires of lust. And his fruit is sweet to our taste when we abandon earthly cares to delight in divine grace.

The king took me into the vinery, and taught me the order of love (Sg 2:4).

She considers the second means, that of the ordering of love, saying: *the king,* that is, Christ, *took me into the vinery,* that is, into the richness of spiritual joy which is symbolized by wine, *and taught me the order of love*, that is, endowed me with the right order of love.

Support me with flowers, surround me with apples, for I am faint with love (Sg 2:5).

The Church has proved by the above-mentioned means that a church leader must attend to himself before others; and she makes two points, as two means were assigned. So she first argues from the first means, secondly from the second, where she says: *his left arm,* etc. It may be interpreted in this way: it was said that the sweetness of my beloved is most delightful and so to be sought first. Therefore, daughters of Jerusalem, I must attend to myself before you: *Support me with flowers, surround me with apples*. In other words: you must allow me to be supported with flowers, letting nothing impede the delight I receive from Christ, who is the rose of Sharon. You must also allow me to be surrounded with apples, letting nothing impede the sweetness I receive from my beloved, who is an apple tree. And she adds her reason: *for I am faint with love*. Also it must be noted that, above, Christ was called *rose of Sharon* and *apple tree* in the singular, whereas here the Church speaks of him in the plural, saying: *Support me with flowers, surround me with apples*. The fact is that goodness and sweetness are each unique in Christ. However, when they are transmitted to us, each is increased and diversified according to the various gifts of grace. Also it should be noted that one is said to act because one allows something or does not prevent it from happening. And in that way the Church tells her children to provide her with flowers and surround her with apples, that is, put branches of apple trees round her; for she is asking them to allow her to be thus surrounded and supported without impediment, since for the delight of the smell, or the sweetness of contemplation, she must attend to herself before the other children.

His left arm will be under my head and his right arm will embrace me (Sg 2:6).

She comes to this conclusion too by the second means, and it may be understood as follows. Just as for the sweetness of contemplation, so for the right ordering of love, I must attend to myself through the contemplative life before attending to you through the active life; therefore *his left arm*, that is, the left arm of Christ, which signifies the active life, will be *under my head*, that is, receive minor attention. *And his right arm*, that is, the life of contemplation through which I attend to myself, *will embrace me,* that is, will be above my head, because it will be what I shall attend to first. For I shall attend first to myself and afterward to you.

I charge you, daughters of Jerusalem, by the gazelles and the deer of the field, not to wake and not to disturb my love until she is ready (Sg 2:7).

This confirms the former explanation. For the bride had explained the duty she had undertaken, and how she wished to attend to herself first, with Christ's right arm above her, and after that her children, with his left arm under her head, and did not wish her children to prevent her from enjoying the sweetness of contemplation. So wishing to confirm this, Christ says: *Daughters of Jerusalem,* who are under the rule of my bride, *I charge,* that is, I beg and beseech you, for although I may command, I want to beg *you, by the gazelles and the deer of the field,* that is, for the sake of the clergy or the doctors of the Church, who are the gazelles, and ought to understand exactly what is good for those subject to them, and are the deer of the field, who must run to the rescue of their faulty subjects; for the sake of such clergy, for the sake of my bride, I beg you, *not to wake and not to disturb* her, *my love,* from her contemplative sleep *until she is ready,* because she must first attend to herself and to divine sweetness and afterward to your actions.

Lecture 5

The voice of my beloved! Look, he comes bounding on the mountains, leaping across the hills (Sg 2:8).

After inviting the Church to undertake a duty, care for her children, in this part the bridegroom invites her to carry out that duty. He does this in two stages. For Christ first invites the Church to carry out such a duty; secondly, he explains how to do it, where he says: *rise up, my love, my beautiful one.*

The first part is divided into three, as Christ invites the Church to carry out the aforesaid duty in three ways: first he invites her on his own behalf; secondly on behalf of her pupils, where she says: *my beloved;* thirdly on behalf of her helpers, where she says: *the voice of the turtle-dove.* Concerning the first, it should be noted that in carrying out the duty entrusted to him (for the present) the church leader must do three things. For first, he must hasten with all speed to rectify the faults of those under him; secondly, he must be clear-sighted and ardent in his endeavor to get to grips with such faults; thirdly, he must be diligent in his instruction of those under him. And because Christ does all these things, so on behalf of Christ himself and inspired by his example, the church leader must treat those under him in the same way.

Therefore we might formulate the argument thus: Every action of Christ is an instruction for the clergy; even despite the fact that it is an instruction for all Christians, it is particularly an instruction for the clergy. But Christ hastens swiftly to the help of his children; he has clearly and lovingly observed their faults and instructed them faithfully. Therefore you also, Church, you, my bride, you, church leader, who are symbolized by the bride and the Church, must do the same. And this is the only argument that verifies the means. Thus this part is divided into three, according to the means dealt with. First it is shown that Christ hastens swiftly to help us; secondly, that he has observed our faults clearly and lovingly, where the Church says: *my beloved is like,* thirdly that he has faithfully and usefully instructed us, where she says: *look, he stands.* Therefore she says first: *The voice of my beloved,* implying *is heard in me.* For she heard the voice of her beloved within herself, as in the words of the psalm: *I shall listen to what the Lord God says in me* (Ps 85:9). And because interior speech can be called a kind of vision (as Augustine says in *The Trinity* XV, 2), therefore if the bride heard her beloved within herself, in a certain way she saw him, and seeing him, amazed at his swiftness and his care, she said: *Look, he comes bounding on the mountains, leaping across the hills,* that is, the angels, patriarchs, kings, and prophets, of whom Christ was the offspring. This signifies the great and careful swiftness of Christ in coming to our help. Passing over the angels, he came into the world as the offspring of the patriarchs, kings, and prophets to help correct our faults. But why the angels can be called mountains, the patriarchs and kings hills, is easy to see if we think of the height of angels, patriarchs, and kings.

My beloved is like a gazelle or a young stag.

This shows how Christ observes our faults lovingly and sharp-sightedly. It may be interpreted as follows: I have not only heard my beloved speaking within me, and by listening to him have seen as well that he leaped across the angels, patriarchs, and kings and came to us; but I have also seen that *my beloved is like a gazelle* in subtly observing our faults, because according to the gloss a gazelle has keen sight. Again *he is like a young stag* in subtly observing our faults. For according to the gloss a young stag runs quickly, and can therefore symbolize the excellence of Christ's love. For it is by love that we are carried wherever we are carried, according to Augustine's saying in the *Confessions* XIII, 9, 10: "My weight is my love: by that I am carried wherever I am carried." And if there is much love, we are carried actively and swiftly.

See, he stands behind our wall, looking through the windows, gazing through the lattice. My beloved speaks to me and says: Rise up, be quick, my love, my dove, my beautiful one, and come away (Sg 2:9-10).

It is shown that Christ has faithfully and usefully instructed us. Hence these words are still the words of the bride, who sees that

Christ *stands behind our wall,* that is, behind our flesh, ready to teach us faithfully and usefully. He is both *standing behind our wall and looking through the windows,* that is, through the words of the prophets, explaining them to us. For the sayings of the prophets are more obscure than those written in the law; therefore such words are indicated by: *through the lattice.* But the commands of the law, which are plainer, are indicated by *through the windows.* And then a reason has to be understood: you, the bride, can see what I, your beloved, have done, and what diligent care I have taken of the children; and so, inspired by my example, you yourself must diligently carry out the duty entrusted to you on behalf of the pupils. And in this regard she makes two points. First she tells of Christ's delightful intention; secondly, she adds the reason for the visitation, where she says: *For now the winter is past.* For the bride says: *My beloved speaks to me* and says: *Rise up, be quick, my love,* for love; *my dove,* for simplicity; *my beautiful one,* for the splendor of the divine image; *be quick,* that is, *and come away,* by carrying out the duty entrusted to you, by taking care of your children.

For now the winter is past, the rain is over and gone (Sg 2:11).

He explains how this refers to the pupils and implies the following reason: When the material is available, then is the time to go to work and get it into the right shapes. Well, your pupils and children are now available to listen to your advice; so you must rise up and be quick, and carry out the duty you have been entrusted with in regard to them. To prove his point he uses only one means, namely, the pupils are available, dividing it into two, as availability can be understood and considered in two ways. For he shows first that the pupils have been put into the right disposition through the application of contradiction. Secondly, by the inducement of proposals, where he says: *the flowers have appeared.* It may be interpreted as follows: I am right in saying that you must rise up and minister to your children, because *now the winter is past,* that is, the frost of infidelity, which according to the gloss is meant by winter, is over and gone from your children, thanks to which your children have acquired the disposition to obey. *The rain is over and gone,* that is, the wickedness of intemperance and sensual pleasure is over and gone, thanks to which your children have acquired the disposition to obey your instructions. For by rain, which is damp, sensual pleasure is meant. For just as dampness spreads everywhere, with nothing to stop it, so the sensualists pursue every passion, unhampered by rational judgment to act as a brake and bring them to a stop.

*The flowers have appeared in our land, the time for pruning has
come* (Sg 2:12).

He shows that the pupils are well disposed toward the proposed
conditions. And it may be interpreted as follows: I am right in saying
that you must rise up, for your pupils and children are not only well
disposed, because they are prepared to forgo or have even forgone
injurious conditions, but we also see appropriate and harmonious
conditions already becoming visible in them. Hence *the flowers*, that
is, the beginnings of good works, as the gloss explains, *have appeared
in our land*, that is, in our children, whom like the land we must till
and cultivate. *The time for pruning has come*, because they are obviously
in the mood for joy, or growth. It should be noted that the Lord calls
us, his children, his land, because what is done to one of the least of
us he considers will have been done to himself. This symbolizes his
great kindness.

The voice of the turtle-dove is heard in our land.

He adduces the reason for the many helps. He also implies the
following reason: Man must rise up to work as soon as he sees there
are many sources of help at hand, which will enable him to reach
his aim. And because you, my bride, have many sources of help
assisting you to minister to your children, you must rise up and
minister to them by carrying out the duty entrusted to you. But in
regard to this reason, he explains only the virtue of the means, noting the sources of help which the Church has. And concerning this
he makes three points, as there are three such helps, namely, divine and human help, human help being twofold, that is, the help
of both Gentiles and Jews. For some of the Jews had been converted
and were prepared to help the Church; and other converts came
from the Gentiles, who were prepared to do the same. Therefore
he first mentions divine help, when he says: *the voice of the turtle-dove*,
that is, the voice of the Holy Spirit, as the gloss explains, *is heard in
our land.* For the Holy Spirit himself intercedes for us with inde-
scribable groans, as it is said in Romans 8. And because you have so
much help, you must not be slow to rise up.

The fig tree has produced its green figs (Sg 2:13).

He makes the same point regarding the help of the Jews. And it
may be interpreted as follows: I am right in saying that you must
rise up, because the fig tree, that is, the synagogue, which is used to

being a fig tree because of the sweetness of its divine worship, *has produced its green figs,* that is, it has produced its figs which, although they are not completely ripe, but are hard, are still ready and prepared to help you. This can also be read in another way, but then with a different meaning, explaining "to produce" as "to throw out" and "throw away." Thus: the synagogue *has produced,* that is, thrown out *its figs,* that is, its unripe figs, because it already has some ripe figs ready to ripen fully. For the fig can also be called hard fruit, for these appear on the fig tree before they are ripe.

The blossoming vines have spread their fragrance.

Thirdly he makes the same point regarding the Gentiles. For the Church must rise up and carry out the duty entrusted to it, because *the blossoming vines have spread their fragrance,* and because some of the Gentiles are already prepared to help you. Therefore you are left with no excuse for not rising up and taking diligent care of your children.

Rise up, my love, my beautiful one; and come, my dove, in the clefts of the rock, in the hollow of the wall (Sg 2:14).

Christ explains to the Church the kind of duty she had to carry out. And he makes two points. For he shows first to what end the Church must carry out the duty entrusted to her, and to what end she must lead her children. Secondly, he shows how she must lead her children to that end, where he says: *show me your face.* Therefore he says: *you, my love,* for love; *my beautiful one,* for simplicity of heart; *rise up, and come, in the clefts of the rock,* that is, in the wounds of Christ, for according to Paul in 1 Corinthians 10: *But the rock was Christ.* For we come within the clefts of the rock when we lead our pupils to a contemplation on the passion of Christ. The Church must also come *in the hollow of the wall,* because she must lead her its children to the truth of the faith. According to the gloss, the wall is a pile of stones heaped up on top of each other without mortar. In the same way our faith consists of articles and judgments, without the mortar of reason, and therefore it cannot cement the matter. Nevertheless all the articles are gathered into one, because they refer either to the divinity or to the humanity of Christ. Divinity and humanity were both fully present in the one hypostasis of Christ. Therefore he says in the singular: *in the hollow of the wall.* The hollow symbolizes the lowest position, deep down; for we must humbly accept the truth of the faith, and hold our mind prisoner in obedience to Christ. Therefore it is clear that the Church must undertake the care of its children for two reasons. First in order to lead them a contemplation on the passion of Christ, about which Chrysostom says, in a sermon on Christ's passion, that the cross of Christ is the philosophy of Christians. So, in remembering the bitterness of Christ's passion, they will refrain from pursuing their own desires, and thereby prove that their feelings are good. Secondly, the Church must lead them to the truth of the faith, to keep them from pursuing the way of error, and thereby prove that their thoughts are good.

Show me your face, let me hear your voice. For your voice is sweet, and your face is lovely.

Christ shows how the Church or church leaders can lead their children to the things that have been mentioned. As a guide to this, it should be noted that the church leader must lead those under him to the good in two ways, that is, by example and by word, as it says in Acts 1: *Jesus began to do and, after that, to teach.* And to the extent that the church leader gives a good example to those under him, he leads them to the good and to the sense of good or the clefts of the rock, because he leads them to contemplate the passion of Christ, and so they refrain from pursuing evil inclinations. Saint Paul made the same point in 1 Corinthians 11:1: *Follow my example as I follow Christ's.* But to the extent that he preaches to them, he leads them to the truth of the faith, or to the hollow of the wall, because he shows them what to believe and what not to believe. For although anyone is led by the word to good conduct, this is to the extent that preaching presupposes the good life of the preacher; for, as Gregory says: "He whose life is despised is bound to have his preaching despised." Hence it is clear that these statements agree with what he had said earlier. The Lord says to the Church herself or to the church leaders: *Show me your face,* that is, show your face to my children, whom I have entrusted to you, that is, show them the good example of your own good life. But the good example itself is called the face. For just as the face is visible to all, so the good works of the clergy must be visible to all, so that they may lead their children to good, according to the passage in Matthew 5:16: *Let your light shine so brightly before all, that they may see your good works and glorify your Father who is in heaven.* And he adds: *Let me hear your voice,* that is, let my children entrusted to your care hear you preaching. For whatever the Church does for its children entrusted to it, Christ regards as done to himself. But he adds the reason for what he had said, saying: *For your voice is sweet,* when you preach to my children, *and your face is lovely,* when you give them good example.

Catch for us the little foxes which destroy the vines. For our vineyard is in bloom (Sg 2:15).

Christ invites the Church to root out heretics, and mentions four points. First he says that heretics must be arrested, when he says: *catch for us the foxes,* for fraudulence, because they secretly undermine sound doctrine. Secondly he appoints a time for the arrest, when he says: *little,* because when heretics begin to sprout up and are young, that is the right moment to arrest them, that is, to refute them by sound doctrine, because after they have become confirmed in their error, they are not so easy to convert. Or they must be literally arrested, for they must be put out of the way, to prevent them destroying the Church. And so, thirdly, he adds the reason for arresting them, when he says: *which destroy the vines.* For they must be arrested because of the damage they cause, for they are destroying the Church. Fourthly he adds the opportunity for causing damage, in adding: *for our vineyard is in bloom.* For this is the reason why the heretics have the opportunity to cause damage, because the vineyard, that is, the Church, is in flower; and this was particularly true in the early Church, about which Solomon is speaking. It might even still be time with regard to those who are not strongly rooted in the faith.

My beloved is mine, and I am his (Sg 2:16).

After the various ways of imitating Christ have been described, here (as was said) the service of the Church is described. And this part is divided into three. First the service of the Church is described; secondly the reason for the service, where the Church says: *who feeds among the lilies;* thirdly, to prevent the Church from failing in such service, she implores the help of Christ, where she says: *Return, be like.* It may be interpreted as follows: *My beloved is mine,* understand, she says, so that I may minister to my children and arrest heretics; *and I am his,* implying, I am ready to obey, and thus indicating her service.

Who feeds among the lilies, until the day dawns and the shadows depart (Sg 2:17).

The Church indicates the reason for her service, which is to obey Christ. Those who obey him are lilies that are characterized by the dazzling whiteness of purity. And it may be interpreted as follows: I wish to obey my bridegroom, for it is he *who feeds among the lilies*, that is, among the pure minds that serve him. Therefore, in order to be pure, I wish to obey him always, *until the shadows depart*, that is, until the obscure knowledge, which is all we have in this life, ceases; and *the day*, namely of eternity, *breaks*, that is, dawns. In this she indicates that whoever desires to be always pure must always obey Christ. For if we always feed among lilies and love pure minds as long as the present life lasts, we want to do so far more in the life to come; thus the *until* above must be read inclusively, and not exclusively.

Return, my beloved; be like a gazelle or a young stag on the mountains of Bethel.

The Church begs Christ's help and assistance to enable her to serve him constantly. And it may be interpreted as follows: You, my beloved, *who dwell on the mountains of Bethel*, that is, above the angels. Bethel means "house of God," or "abode of God." Hence the mountains of Bethel symbolize those who hold high rank in the house of God. But, my beloved, you who are above them, *return*; that is, if I have carelessly happened to stray away from you, still return to me, helping me to come back to you and remain with you. And *be like a gazelle*, which possesses sharp sight, looking mercifully upon our failings. And also *be like a young stag*, which moves swiftly. So run quickly to the help of my failings, before they get worse.

Lecture 6

On my bed at night I sought the one whom my soul loves. I sought him, but could not find him (Sg 3:1).

As was said above, the Church has two worries concerning her children: first with regard to external troubles; secondly with regard to internal discord. She has come to the end of the part dealing with external troubles, and now proceeds to consider the internal discord. And this part is divided into three: first she describes the kind of discord; secondly she adds Christ's compassion, where he says: *I adjure you*; thirdly she brings this treatise on the character of the early Church to an end; hence there is added a commendation of the said Church, in the words: *Who is this?*

The discord of the Church, or of the church leader, is of the following kind: that the very same external anxieties in which the care of her children involve her are so demanding that, when she wishes to return to contemplation, she often finds herself wanting in the sweetness that she had before; hence, on her bed, she seeks Christ and cannot find him. And whenever this happens to her, she has to rise up and look for him in the streets and marketplaces of the city, that is, in all her desires and actions, to see if any of them might have displeased Christ and make her feel there is no peace in her heart. And in this unhappy state, the city watchmen, that is, vain thoughts, come upon her which she has to get rid of, because Christ is not to be found in such thoughts. And as soon as these have gone, she does find Christ. And because these events take place in order, therefore this part is divided into four: first, we have a description of the return to contemplation; secondly, the search for Christ (*I shall rise and go about*); thirdly, the preoccupation with

95

various wandering thoughts (*the watchmen found me*); fourthly, the finding of Christ (*a little while after parting from them*).

It may be interpreted as follows: I, the church leader, or the Church, after the ministry and the active life, wishing to return to the sweetness of contemplation, *on my bed*, that is, in my conscience, *sought him at night*, meaning at a suitable time, namely, a time of silence, for such is the nighttime. *I sought the one whom my soul loves: I sought him, but could not find him*, because I found myself frustrated and troubled in my conscience on account of external concerns. This deals with the return to contemplation: how the church leader returns from the active to the contemplative life to find Christ there.

I shall rise and go about the city: in the streets and marketplaces I shall seek the one whom my soul loves (Sg 3:2).

This describes the bride's search to find him. And it may be interpreted as follows: returning to contemplation I sought Christ but could not find him. Hence in order to find him, I must make a new search for him: *I shall rise and go about the city*, that is, I shall examine my conscience with assiduous contemplation. *And in the narrow streets and marketplaces*, that is, examining all the words, desires, and actions which I have done, said and been tempted by, I shall see whether I have done anything to displease him, and in so doing *I shall seek the one whom my soul loves*, that is, Christ. For if anyone cannot return to the sweetness of contemplation after a spell of action, he cannot help thinking that he may have done something wrong which prevents him feeling the customary sweetness. And so he has to search through the whole city, that is, his conscience. But it should be noted that conscience is the bed on which Christ rests; for the bed is too narrow for more than one person to lie on it, that is, Christ or the devil: *For the bed is too narrow for more than one to lie on, and the blanket too small to cover two* (Is 28:20). But if we examine our conscience and our heart for the kind of sins we may find there, we discover there is the same difference between the major and minor sins as there is in a city between the streets and the marketplaces.

I sought him, but could not find him. The watchmen, going their rounds in the city, found me. I said: Have you seen the one whom my soul loves? (Sg 3:3).

This describes the concern with vain thoughts. It may be interpreted as follows: I returned to contemplation; I sought Christ in the streets and marketplaces. *I sought him but could not find him*, and the reason why I could not find him is that *the city watchmen, that is, vain thoughts, going their rounds in the city, found me.* So being occupied with these I could not find Christ, because we can hardly say a single "Our Father" without vain thoughts coming upon us. Therefore such thoughts are called the watchmen of the city, because they are always ready to catch us and take up our time. But when such watchmen or thoughts do take up our time, we must get rid of them: because Christ cannot be found in such thoughts. So there is irony in saying to such watchmen: *Have you seen* Christ, *the one whom my soul loves?*

A little while after parting from them, I found the one whom my soul loves (Sg 3:4).

First she describes the finding of Christ; secondly the seizing of him, where she says: *I held him.* It may be interpreted as follows: Thus vain thoughts, or the city watchmen, found me. But after parting from them, that is, by getting rid of them, *I found* Christ, *the one whom my soul loves.* Anyone can be sure that, if he returns to contemplation and diligently examines his conscience, renouncing vain thoughts, after doing all this, he will find Christ.

I held him, and will not let him go until I bring him to my mother's house, and to the bedchamber of her who bore me.

She describes the seizing of Christ. And first she makes clear that she has seized him firmly, in saying: *I held him,* as if to say: I did not take him just anyhow, but seized him with a firm grip. Secondly she shows that her grip would be a lasting one, in adding: *and will not let him go,* as if to say, I shall hold him forever. Thirdly, she implies that she has seized him for a purpose, in adding: *until I bring him to my mother's house,* referring to the older children, *and to the bedchamber of her who bore me,* referring to the younger ones.

Thus the Church must behave like a good mother, for after she has found Christ, she must hold on to him, and not let him go until she brings him to the hearts of the older children, who are the house of their mother, that is, the house of grace, for grace is the mother of all, since it gives us spiritual being. The older children of the Church are called the house of grace, because they possess more of grace. So the Church must also bring Christ to the hearts of the younger children, who are called the bedchamber of her who bore them, that is, the bedchamber of grace, because they possess less of grace. A bedchamber is a small house. But it should be noted that the Church does not aim to bring Christ to the older and younger children as if they did not possess Christ, for in that case they would not be the house and dwelling of grace, but so as to rejoice in the contemplation of the gifts of grace of the older and younger. It can also be understood in the way that, as they are led to either place, so some become the house of grace, and thus the older, and others become the dwelling, and thus the younger.

I adjure you, daughters of Jerusalem, by the gazelles and the deer of the field, not to wake and not to disturb my love until she is ready (Sg 3:5).

This shows Christ's compassion. For Christ sees that the Church or the church leader is sometimes disturbed in contemplation by external affairs, and says with sympathy for him: *I adjure you*, that is, I beseech you, *daughters of Jerusalem*, whom the church leader has in his care, *by the gazelles and the deer of the field*, that is, by the clergy themselves, as was explained above, *not to wake*, from the sleep of contemplation, *and not to disturb*, in the quiet of her delight, *my love*, the Church, *until she is ready*. But it should be noted that he has twice entreated the daughters of Jerusalem not to disturb their mother, the Church, in her sleep of contemplation, because there are two ways in which those under him may err with regard to the church leader's care of them. First if they thought that the clergy's first duty was to attend to them, rather than themselves; hence the first words: *I adjure*. Secondly, if they thought that, after beginning to attend to them, the cleric ought not to return to contemplation, paying attention to himself; hence Christ's second entreaty to the daughters of Jerusalem to allow their mother to persist in contemplation.

Who is she ascending through the desert, like a column of smoke, fragrant with myrrh and frankincense, with all the powders of the perfumer? (Sg 3:6).

About to end this treatise describing the state of the early Church, and because praise makes the best end to a song, he ends his treatise by commending the early Church in five ways. First for her ascension, for ascending is praiseworthy, and in admiration of this, he says: *Who is she ascending?* Secondly he commends the Church for her place of ascent, in adding: *through the desert.* If ascent is praiseworthy for its own sake, yet ascent through the desert is more so, with its thorny ways and many obstructions, since it is the highest praise to live a good life in the midst of a vicious and perverse people. Thirdly he commends her for her way of ascent, in saying: *like a column of smoke.* The column of smoke is the Church, quick to ascend, even though she is very dark and obscure. Thus the early Church was dark on the outside, yet quick and upright within. Fourthly he commends her for the mortification of the body, in saying: *fragrant with myrrh.* For myrrh is bitter, and symbolizes mortification of the body, as the gloss says. Therefore the smoke, to which the Church is compared, rises fragrant with myrrh, because she tries to please God with the mortification of the body: *Those who belong to Christ have crucified their flesh with its vices and lusts* (Gal 5:24). Fifthly, he commends her for her devotion to prayer and all her virtues, in saying: *and frankincense, with all the powders of the perfumer,* as the gloss explains. So that the scent of frankincense represents prayer, but all the powders of the perfumer represent all the virtues.

Lecture 7

Look, sixty of the bravest men in Israel surround Solomon's bed (Sg 3:7).

The treatise defining the essence of the early Church having come to an end, here we have the beginning of a treatise defining the essence of the present-day Church. And just as the first treatise began with a description of the early Church and ended with praise for the Church, saying: *Who is she ascending,* so in this part the state of the present-day Church will first be described, and the treatise will end with praise for the Church, saying: *Who is she appearing,* near the end of chapter 6.

The first part is divided into two: first the present-day Church is described with regard to her diversity, secondly with regard to her truth, where he says: *you are beautiful, my love,* near the beginning of the sixth chapter. The first part is divided into two: first the state of the Church is described with regard to the contemplative life, secondly with regard to the active life, where she says: *I am asleep but my heart keeps watch.* The first part is divided into two. The conditions required for contemplation are described first. Secondly, the Church sees that she cannot keep them on her own, and implores Christ's help, where she says: *May my beloved come,* at the beginning of Chapter 5. However there are three conditions for the contemplative life: first there must be conversion to God; secondly, abandonment of the world; thirdly, patient endurance of temptation. So this part is divided into three: the first part shows the Church's conversion to Christ; the second her decision to forsake the world, where he says: *How beautiful you are,* at the beginning of the fourth chapter; and the third part shows her consent to endure temptation, where he says: *how beautiful are your breasts,* just over halfway through the chapter mentioned. For the first, it should be noted that everything good in the Church concerning the beginners, those progressing and those fully instructed, is due to Christ, and so it is proper that we should be converted to him from whom we have received such good things. Therefore the argument can be formulated as follows: Anyone should be converted to one from whom he has received all the good things he has; but the Church has received all the good things she has from Christ, therefore she must be converted to him. This particular argument runs as follows: first it shows.that Christ has bestowed all his good things on the Church for the daughters of Jerusalem; secondly, it therefore concludes that the daughters of Zion themselves should be converted to Christ, in the words: *Come out, daughters of Zion, and see.* The first part is divided into three: for first it is shown that the good things given to the beginners are from Christ, in the symbol of the bed, where it says: *Solomon's bed*; secondly it shows that the good things given to those progressing are from him, in the symbol of the litter, where it says: *He made himself a litter*; thirdly it shows that the good things given to those fully instructed are from him, in the metaphor of the golden headrest, where it says: *its headrest of gold.*

It should be noted that the beginners in the Church are particularly in need of guardians, to prevent the devil and evil temptations attacking and overcoming them as if they were helpless. Therefore Christ shows his infinite kindness and his great care for the good of the beginners by the fact that he is willing to give them guardians. And because there are three kinds of such guardians, so this part is divided into three: first it shows that such beginners are protected by those who proclaim the true doctrine, where it says: *They all have swords*; secondly by those who proclaim true justice, where it says: *the sword of each.* It may be interpreted as follows: The early Church had many troubles, but we see that in the present-day Church calmness reigns. For *look*, we see that those who appear to be of no importance are *the bed of Solomon*, for Christ rests in them. And it is such a bed that *sixty of the bravest men in Israel surround*, that is, guard, proclaiming true life. For those who intend to preach on morals must become strong not weak through temptation.

It should be noted that the number of those guardians, that is, the number sixty, well suits their duty. For the number sixty is six times ten, which means a true life in the following way: that we live truly and rightly if, throughout the six days which we have to work, that is, throughout our whole life, which the number six means, being the perfect number, we keep the ten commandments of the decalogue. But it should be clearly noted that in beginning his treatise on the present-day Church, Solomon begins it from his bed, that is, from the quiet, because persecution has now ceased.

They all have swords, and are expert in war (Sg 3:8).

He shows that such beginners are protected by those proclaiming true doctrine, and it may be interpreted as follows: Such brave men are not only sixty in number, as they proclaim true life, but *all are expert in war and have swords*, as they proclaim true holy doctrine, according to Ephesians 6:17: *And the sword of the Spirit which is the word of God.*

The sword of each on his thigh because of the terrors at night.

He shows that the beginners are protected by those who proclaim true justice. It is not enough for anyone to preach the faith by proclaiming true doctrine, but he must proclaim it to be true justice, so that he does what he says and believes what he teaches; for it is right and proper that someone should be in himself the same as he preaches the other ought to be. Therefore the preachers who have to protect Solomon's bed, or the beginners, must have a sword not merely in their mouth, so as to speak without doing anything, but *the sword of each must be on his thigh,* by restraining his thighs, living a chaste life and practicing what he preaches. But he adds the reason why Christ wants his bed to be protected so carefully; *because of the terrors at night,* that is, because of the assaults of the devil and other evil temptations.

King Solomon made himself a litter of wood of Libanus. He made its poles of silver (Sg 3:9).

He shows that the good of those progressing is from Christ. As proof of this it should be noted that the beginners are called a bed, because Christ is at rest in them; yet they are not a litter, because they do not bring Christ to others, by begetting him in the hearts of others. But those progressing are a litter, that is, a carriage, because they carry and bring Christ to others. Three good things possessed by those progressing are mentioned. The first of these is presumably ordained for God, which is indicated when he says: *King Solomon made himself a litter,* that is, ordained it for himself, who is the true God. Secondly, the good is mentioned which those progressing possess ordained for themselves, when he adds: *of wood of Lebanon,* that is, of white wood, because they must be pure in themselves. Thirdly the good is mentioned which they possess ordained for their neighbors, when he adds: *He made the poles of silver.* Because those who are progressing must have silver poles, supporting others and proclaiming the truth to them: this is signified by silver, which is a sonorous metal.

The headrest of gold, the step of purple: the center he paved with love, for the daughters of Jerusalem.

He describes the fully instructed. As proof of this it should be noted that a litter gets its name from the fact that it carries something, and is described as a carriage because it brings someone who is at rest. The headrest, however, is the top part of the seat, against which the seated person leans his head and rests; hence the headrest symbolizes the fully-instructed, who hold the highest rank in the Church. Their good is described in three ways: first with reference to the position they hold, in that it is high and shining or splendid; this is indicated when it is called *a headrest of gold.* Secondly it is described with reference to the way by which they rise to such a position, when it is said *the step of purple.* For purple is made from the blood of a fish. Hence the gloss on Chapter 8 says: When cut with a knife some shellfish emit drops of a purple color, which are collected and made into a purple dye. Hence they prefigure the passion of Christ by reason of the bloodshed. This passion is the way that leads to the perfect state, for those entering by it acquire a state of perfection. Thirdly the good of the fully-instructed is described with reference to the virtue by which they have moved toward such a position, when he says: *The center he paved with love,* because love is the central virtue by which a resting-place of this kind is paved or constructed, insofar as it is by virtue of love that the fully-instructed rise to such a position. He also adds the reason why there is such an order in the Church, when he says: *for the daughters of Jerusalem,* because Christ wished to suffer for us, and he set his Church in order and endowed it with various perfections.

Come out, daughters of Zion, and see King Solomon wearing the diadem with which his mother has crowned him on his wedding-day, the day of his heart's delight (Sg 3:11).

It is inferred from the conditions that those who are in the Church, and particularly the clergy, must be converted to Christ. For if Christ brought such great benefits to the Church on account of its members, it is fitting that those who are in the Church should be converted to him. Therefore he says: *Come out, daughters of Zion, and see King Solomon wearing the diadem with which his mother has crowned him,* that is, be converted to Christ, and contemplate his passion, not only in your mind, but in your own feelings: the passion, that is, in which his mother, namely, the synagogue, crowned him with a diadem, for the Jews literally crowned Christ in his passion with a crown of thorns. And although it was because of their false accusation that this was placed on Christ to shame him, nevertheless the symbol is true in proclaiming the dignity of majesty, because *for this God raised him up,* etc. So the inscription: *King of the Jews* was nailed to the cross (Jn 19:19). This was on his, that is, Christ's, wedding-day, because in his passion he united the Church to himself, giving his blood as the price and bringing the thief into paradise (Lk 23:41). *And on the day of his heart's delight,* that is, the synagogue's, because literally the Jews and the synagogue were glad and rejoiced at Christ's passion.

Lecture 8

How beautiful you are, my love, how beautiful you are (Sg 4:1).

After it has been shown that those in the Church must be converted to Christ, here he shows that they must abandon the world. Nor is there any perversion of order because of this; for although in the general way abandoning the world would precede adherence to God, yet by the way of perfection and fulfillment adherence to God comes first. Thus it is more essential for the good to be converted to God. But this part is divided into three, as it is shown that the Church has to abandon the world in three ways. This is shown first from the Church's position; secondly from her purpose: *you will be crowned from the top*; thirdly from the love that Christ has for her: *you have wounded my heart*.

In the first part he considers the following argument: One whose position requires absolute excellence must avoid impurity, so as to incur no defilement to discredit his position. The position of the Church, however, requires absolute excellence. Therefore she must avoid the world, where there is impurity, so as not to be defiled. This argument proceeds as follows: first he shows that the Church, with regard to all her possessions, must have excellence. Secondly he infers from this that the position of the Church requires absolute excellence, where he says: *I shall go to the mountain of myrrh*. Thirdly he shows that as a result the Church must withdraw from the world, where he says *Come from Libanus*. First, it must be noted that in everything three factors are necessary, that is: substance, power, and effect. Indeed in showing that the position of the Church must require excellence in every respect, he makes three points: first he commends this, and proves it concerning sub-

stance; secondly concerning power, where he says: *your eyes*; thirdly
concerning effect, where he says: *your hair.* Therefore he says: *how
beautiful you are, my love,* with respect to the inward substance, re-
peating: *how beautiful you are,* with respect to the outward, for in
everyone there is a twofold person, the outward and the inward, a
twofold substance, spiritual and material.

The early Church was beautiful inwardly, but very dark outwardly;
hence in contrast with that Church, the present-day Church is called
beautiful inwardly and outwardly, because the persecutions by Gentiles and Jews have ceased.

Your eyes are like those of doves, apart from what is hidden within.

He shows that the Church needs excellence with regard to virtue or with regard to powers. Hence he says: *Your eyes,* that is, the
intellect and the emotions, are *like those of doves,* that is, containing
simplicity and righteousness like doves, *apart from what is hidden
within,* that is, apart from the activities of intellect and emotion,
which are hidden within because they are not being transformed
into external matter. He means that for the excellence of activities,
which he will discuss next, the Church has the excellence of the
eyes, that is, of powers or virtues. For the powers or virtues of the
soul, such as the intellect and emotions, are called its eyes, because
the eye is that by means of which we direct our aim at something as
a goal. The motivating force may be either the intellect or emotions, the intellect in the case of a purpose, the emotions in the
case of an inclination. But such eyes are the eyes of doves when the
intellect is simple and righteous, that is, without a particle of sin,
and the emotions are without a shred of malice.

Your hair is like flocks of she-goats, coming up from Mount Gilead.

He proves she has excellence with regard to effect. And he
makes two points: first he shows this with regard to the effect of
emotion; secondly with regard to the effect of intellect, where he
says: *your teeth.* So he says: *your hair,* that is, your affections, which
are called hair because they are rooted in the uppermost part of
the soul, are *like flocks of she-goats that have come up from Mount Gilead.*
Here he has three things to say. First that the affections have to be
flocks because they must be gathered together, not scattered in the
same way as evil emotions, which prey on good things that are scattered and individual. Secondly they have to be flocks of she-goats,
that is, they must be elevated, as she-goats make for upland pastures. Thirdly they have to come up from Mount Gilead, which may

be interpreted as the hill of testimony, because literally the present-day Church and all devout souls who are the subject here ascend in their thoughts to Mount Gilead, that is, to the hill of testimony, to the examples of the past, and to the sublime testimony of the scriptures.

Your teeth are like a flock of shorn (ewes) which have come up from the washing. All have twins, and not one of them is barren (Sg 4:2).

He describes the beauty of intellectual activities, and makes five points as such activities may be studied in five ways. First he shows what kind of activities these must be as they are in the intellect. Secondly what kind they must be as they are symbolized in words, where he says: *like a scarlet headband.* Thirdly, as they are fulfilled in works, where he says: *like a piece.* Fourthly as they are directed to the confusion of opponents, where he says: *like a tower.* Fifthly, as they are directed to the teaching of the very young, where he says: *your two breasts.* So he says: *your teeth,* that is, the thoughts of the intellect. They are called teeth because, just as the teeth break up something which is whole into pieces, so the human being uses the intellect by means of many concepts to break up what is understood as one concept into others. Hence in chapter 25 of *Ecclesiastical Hierarchy,* Dionysius calls angels upper teeth, because what they understand by a single concept they divide into subordinate ones by means of many concepts. But such teeth, or concepts, must be *like a flock of shorn ewes, which have come up from the washing,* for they must be shorn of their earthly wool and must come up from the washing for their moral purity; and they must be the sort of concepts that *have twins,* for giving counsel and instruction. Among those conceptions there must be none that is barren, because they must be worthy of some fruit.

Your lips are like a scarlet headband, and your speech is sweet (Sg 4:3).

He shows what speech must be like which expresses such thoughts, and mentions the two qualities that speech must have. First it must be restrained, and in regard to this he says: *your lips are like a scarlet headband;* for just as a headband keeps our hair in place, so temperate speech makes us keep to the truth. But this headband has to be scarlet because it is a red dye, and contemplative discourse must be particularly concerned with the passion of Christ. Secondly speech must be orderly and calm; and with regard to his words: *your speech is sweet,* according to Proverbs 16:24. Calm words are like a honeycomb.

Your cheeks are like a piece of pomegranate, apart from what is hidden within.

He shows what the effects of the intellect must be as they are fulfilled in works. For our actions must be in harmony with our interior and exterior emotions, because our sanctity must not be a fiction. So he says: *your cheeks,* that is, your actions, which are unconcealed like cheeks, are *like a piece of pomegranate,* that is, like a broken pomegranate. When broken it shows itself to be just the same outside as inside. So our actions must show us as we really are. But a pomegranate is like an orange, and when broken discloses many reddish seeds. So also many good works must proceed from the single virtue of charity. And so because interior beauty must be present at the same time as exterior beauty, it is added: *apart from what is hidden within.*

Your neck is like the tower of David which was built with bulwarks. A thousand shields hang on it, all of them the armor of warriors (Sg 4:4).

He shows the right kind of concepts required for resisting opponents, saying: *your neck,* that is, your teaching and your good concepts by which you are joined to my head, just as the head is joined to the body by the neck. But it is such a neck: *like the tower of David, which was built with bulwarks,* that it is enough to repel all the onslaughts of opponents. Therefore he adds: *a thousand shields,* that is, the perfect number of the scriptures, *hang on it, and all the armor of warriors.* For our faith is fortified by the scriptures and the articles of the faith; we are, as it were, recognized by certain shields in the divine light, which illuminates: *all the armor of warriors.* For whatever virtue there is in every intellect, it is preserved more abundantly and more perfectly in the divine light.

Your two breasts are like the twin fawns of a roe, that feed among the lilies, until the day dawns and the shadows depart (Sg 4:5).

He defines the operations of the intellect as they are directed toward the instruction of the very young, and makes four points. The activities of the intellect, or the teaching, must first be proportionate to the very young pupils. Therefore he says: *your two breasts,* because the very young being unable to chew anything hard suck the breasts, as in that passage in 1 Corinthians 3:2: *As infants in Christ, I gave you milk, not solid food.* And he says: *two breasts for the two testaments,* or for the literal meaning signified by the words, and the mystical meaning signified by the matter. Secondly, this teaching must be charitable, because the teacher must teach with ardor. Therefore he adds: *like the twin fawns of a roe*, which symbolizes the twofold aspect of charity. Thirdly, the teacher must teach orthodox doctrine, for he must teach according to the tenets of holy scripture. Therefore he adds: *which feed among the lilies*, that is, in the clear light of the holy scriptures, because we must teach others what we are taught in the holy scriptures. Fourthly, with perseverance; therefore he adds: *until the shadows depart*, that is, until the darkness comes to an end, in which the whole of our present life is passed. *And the day dawns*, that is, of eternity, which will be in the life to come, when we shall have no need of the teaching which we need now.

I shall go to the mountain of myrrh and the hill of frankincense. You are all beautiful, my love, and there is no flaw in you (Sg 4:6).

He concludes from the conditions that the state of the Church requires such beauty, and it may be interpreted as follows: I have said, Church, that you are beautiful in all your ways. Therefore *I shall go to the mountain of myrrh*, that is, to you who are a mountain of myrrh, for the mortification of the body, *and to the hill of frankincense*, that is, to you who are a hill of frankincense, for assiduous and manifold prayer; and (supply: let me say) *you are all beautiful, my love, and there is no flaw in you*. For if the Church requires beauty in all its ways, its beauty must be total. But it should be carefully noted that the aforesaid beauty of the Church must not be referred to its present activity as such, but to the state not as it is but as it ought to be, so that it must always be progressing, for which it must abandon the world.

Come from Lebanon, my bride, come from Lebanon, come (Sg 4:8).

From these circumstances he infers that she must abandon the world, and it may be interpreted as follows: It is a fact that your position requires total beauty, my bride; therefore to prevent you from being corrupted by the world, *come from Lebanon*, that is, come from the world, and withdraw from the world, *come from Lebanon, come*. He also says *come* three times for faith in the Trinity, to which she must lead others, as the gloss says. Or rather, because she must abandon the world unless the Father leads her out of it by his own power, as it says in the psalm: *He brought Israel out of the midst of it with a powerful hand and outstretched arm* (Ps 126:12). And unless the Son guides her with his wisdom, Wisdom 10: Wisdom delivered him, that is, Adam, together with all who were to be saved, from his sin, from which no one can be delivered unless brought out of the world, James 4:4: *Anyone who chooses to be a friend of the world will become an enemy of God.* And unless the Holy Spirit attracts him to himself by his own goodness and mercy, Isaiah 63:14: *The spirit of the Lord was his guide.* Or else he says *come* three times, because just as we sin in thought, word, and deed, so we must go to Christ by these three. Then the world is called Lebanon, that is, bright, by contrast, for there is no brightness in it. Just as a wood gets its name from its lack of light, and a fishpond from its lack of fish, so the world gets its name from its lack of purity.

You will be crowned if you come from the top of Amana, from the summit of Senir and Hermon, from the lions' dens, from the leopards' mountains (Sg 4:8).

He proves his point by arguing from the conclusion, as follows: You must abandon that for which, when you have abandoned it, you may obtain your crown and reach your goal; but if you abandon the world, you will be crowned; therefore you must abandon the world. With this argument he asserts only that if you abandon the world you will be crowned. So for a full appreciation of what he means, it should be noted that the world corrupts in four ways. First it corrupts the irascible person through the opportunity to frighten others; secondly it corrupts the lustful through intemperance and filthiness; thirdly it corrupts the will through injustice; fourthly it corrupts the speculative mind through paganism. Therefore he says: *you will be crowned if you come from the top of Amana,* that is, from the world, by abandoning timidity which corrupts the irascible person. Amana is interpreted as hemmed in, and symbolizes the world, which confines and constrains itself. Again *you will be crowned if you come from the summit of Senir,* that is, from filthiness and intemperance, by abandoning it, because it corrupts the lustful. Senir, according to the gloss, equals a stench. Again *you will be crowned if you come from the summit of Hermon,* that is, from injustice, by abandoning it because it corrupts the appetite of the intellect, or the will. For Hermon is interpreted as anathematizing or separation from God, which mostly comes about through injustice, and particularly as it is a common fault. Again *you will be crowned* if you come *from the lions' dens,* that is, if you abandon imprudence which corrupts practical intelligence. For human beings differ from savage beasts, because they are political animals through the tameness which has not been acquired by savage beasts, understood by the lions, which do not restrain their emotions through prudence, as humans do. Again *you will be crowned if you come from the leopards' mountains*, that is, from paganism, which corrupts the speculative intellect. For heretics and infidels lie in wait like leopards, and it is to be understood that by abandoning this you will completely abandon the world. And since you will not be crowned unless you abandon these things, you must abandon the world completely in order to be crowned.

You have wounded my heart, my sisters, my bride, you have wounded my heart with one of your eyes and with one curl on your neck (Sg 4:9).

He makes a third point in arguing from divine love. It is certainly right that we should love those who love us, and because Christ loves us in the highest degree we must love him. Therefore since we cannot remain true to his love unless we abandon the world, we must abandon the world. He only gives the middle term of this argument, namely, that Christ loves us in the highest degree. Therefore this is what I want from you, *my sister*, by the likeness of our nature, *my bride*, by faith. *You have wounded my heart* with the arrow of love *in one of your eyes*, that is, in the unity of your thoughts, *and with one curl on your neck*, that is, in the unity of your affections. By the eyes through which we observe, we must understand the activities of the intellect, because they please God when they are united by faith. *By the hair*, as was said above, we must understand the emotions, which please God when they are united by love and by other perfect feelings; and because we cannot possess such unity unless we abandon the world, we must abandon the world.

Lecture 9

How beautiful are your breasts, my sisters, my bride. Your breasts are more beautiful than wine, and the fragrance of your ointments more than any perfume (Sg 4:10).

It was earlier shown that the Church, especially from the point of view of contemplatives, must turn toward Christ because of the goodness received from him, and must abandon the world to avoid being infected with its filth. Here the writer shows that the Church must endure temptations in order to attain its goal and merit a larger share of goodness. And so he implies the following argument: Anyone who can easily endure any trouble, if it can help him pursue his goal and make him a better person, must suffer willingly in order to attain those ends. But the Church, particularly as regards the contemplative state, can easily endure temptations, and since it is through these that she merits her goal and increases in goodness, she must endure them patiently.

This argument proceeds as follows. First he shows that the contemplatives can easily overcome every temptation. Secondly he thus concludes that the Church wants to allow them to be tempted, so that thus they may attain their end and glory, where he says: *awake, north wind.* The first part is divided into two: for first he shows that the contemplatives overcome temptation; secondly he shows that they can do this easily, where he says: *your plants.* The first part is divided into two, for first he shows that there is no kind of temptation which they cannot overcome; secondly he thus concludes that, as regards the contemplatives, the Church can overcome every temptation without exception, where he says: *My sister is a locked garden.* The first part is divided into three, as there are

115

three kinds of temptations. For first he shows that the Church can overcome the temptations of the devil; secondly he shows it can overcome the temptations of the world, where he says: *distill sweetness like a honeycomb*; thirdly he says that she can overcome the temptations of the body, where he says: *and the scent of your garments.* Concerning the first it should be noted that the devil overpowers us in two ways: first by deceiving us, when he transforms himself into an angel of light. And against this it is doctrine that prevails, which the contemplatives possess most of all, because having no contact with the world they have a greater perception of the divine influence. In his book, *Good Fortune*, Aristotle points out that some simple people are very fortunate, because being cut off from the world of the senses they have a better perception of immaterial substances and of God through their understanding, just as the blind, who cannot rely on sight, have better memories. And with regard to this he says: *My sister, my bride, how beautiful are your breasts,* that is, how beautiful is your teaching, which is called nipples and breasts because it is adapted to its audience. And so he adds: *your breasts are more beautiful than wine,* that is, your teaching is superior to that of the philosophers, which is not adapted to its audience, but is based on a certain severity and excellence of expression, abstaining from weighty judgments. So teaching of such kind is called wine, not milk, because it lacks sweetness. Secondly the devil overcomes us if he finds us stripped of virtues, and with regard to this it is added: *and the fragrance of your ointments,* that is, your reputation for spiritual virtues, as the gloss explains, *is more beautiful than any perfume,* that is, it surpasses all human knowledge, and for that reason you need not be afraid of the devil overcoming you by deception.

Your lips distill sweetness like a honeycomb, my bride, honey and milk are under your tongue. And the scent of your garments is like the scent of frankincense (Sg 4:11).

He shows that the Church overcomes the assaults of the world. For the world is divided between the faithful and the faithless, and we overcome it best of all if we pour out doctrine to the faithful and conceal it from the faithless, to prevent them catching us out in an argument. Therefore he says: *your lips distill sweetness like a honeycomb,* with reference to the faithless, to whom you must not communicate the sweetness of sacred doctrine, but keep it beneath your tongue. *The scent of your garments,* that is, the scent of the body, for the body is as it were a kind of garment for the soul, and its scent is: *like the scent of frankincense.* For when frankincense is burnt on a fire it emits a scent. So when the body of contemplatives is goaded by temptations, they overcome it with continence, they give forth a fragrance and earn merit. From this it can be shown that, in regard to the contemplative life, the Church can overcome the temptations of the body.

My sister, my bride, is a locked garden; a locked garden, a sealed fountain (Sg 4:12).

He infers that all temptations without exception can be overcome, and it may be interpreted as follows: You, Church, as has been shown, can overcome all the temptations of the devil, the world, and the body; therefore you are: *a locked garden, my sister, my bride, you are a locked garden.* And he says a locked garden twice to emphasis that neither the temptations of the world nor of the body can gain entrance to her. He adds that she is also: *a sealed fountain,* because she is also immune to the temptations of the devil. The Church, then, is a locked garden, as she contains fruit that is free from the filth of the body. She is a locked garden, as she contains true fruit, not that which has been adulterated by the vanities of the world. She is a sealed fountain; she contains sweet waters not made bitter by the wiles of the devil.

Your plants are a garden of pomegranates with the choicest fruits (Sg 4:13).

He shows that, as regards the contemplatives, the Church can easily overcome every temptation. For very little grace is enough to overcome any temptation. So whoever possesses superabundant grace will overcome them easily. Superabundant grace is recognized to the extent that it leads others to grace, for everything is perfect when it can beget its own likeness. Therefore to show that the Church can easily overcome every temptation is to show that the overflowing of grace, as it flows from the Church to her children, is enough to overcome every temptation.

The gifts of divine grace overflow from the more perfect to the imperfect, not that the perfect are the cause of grace itself; on the contrary grace itself is caused by God alone. But because, through preaching, good works, and example, the perfect lead the imperfect to receive grace, and sometimes through their prayers obtain grace for the future, and by administering the sacraments, they produce some effect on the Church, by which, unless anyone objects, the Church receives grace.

So he makes two points. First he shows that any kind of temptation can be overcome by such overflowings; secondly he concludes from this that the Church can overcome all temptations without exception, where he says: *a garden fountain.* Concerning the first he makes three points. First he shows that the temptations of the world can be overcome by such overflowing; secondly, those of the devil, where he says: *with henna and nard;* thirdly those of the body, where he says: *myrrh and aloes.* So he says: *your plants,* that is, the gifts of grace overflowing from you to others are *a garden of pomegranates,* that is, of those trees *with the choicest fruits,* that is, with the fruit of the trees mentioned. For the fruit of pomegranates has a rough surface, but inside it has reddish seeds, and they symbolize the Church's teaching, whose meaning is entrusted to those who are within her. To those outside, the Church shows only her surface. Hence this part answers to what was said above: *your lips distill sweetness; honey and milk are under your tongue.* Therefore just as it was shown by those words that the Church can overcome the assaults of the world, so by these it is shown that by the gifts of grace overflowing from the Church to her children, they can overcome others.

Henna with spikenard, spikenard and saffron, cassia and cinnamon with all the trees of Lebanon (Sg 4:14).

He shows that it is possible to overcome the temptations of the devil by such plants. So it is read as follows: *Your plants* are not only a garden of pomegranates, but the plants are also of such kind as: *henna.* For, according to the gloss, henna is an aromatic shrub with a white seed; and so it can symbolize the perfection of the speculative intellect, because an intellect of this kind shines brightly, becoming illuminated by the light of faith or by the light of the active intellect. (From this it is clear that this name, cypress, is equivalent to an island and a tree.) And plants of this kind are *spikenard,* for spikenard is a fragrant, glowing herb. Hence it can symbolize perfection of the emotions because it makes us understand charity, as the gloss says. Plants of such kind include not only spikenard, but also *saffron,* for saffron is a golden color and can symbolize prudence to which good counsel is devoted, whose concern is to give clear and pure advice. Prudence, however, is found in the practical intelligence. Hence it symbolizes the perfection of the practical intelligence.

Plants of this kind are also *cassia and cinnamon,* which indicate the perfection of the irascible and the lustful. For cinnamon has its strength outside on the bark and signifies the perfection of the irascible, which is achieved by the strength which consists in making attacks. But wild cassia has its goodness inside and signifies the perfection of the lustful, which is achieved by continence; its goodness appears to exist inwardly, because goodness consists more in withdrawing than in attacking, for in a sense its way is the reverse of strength. And hence it is that indifference, which is called a defect, is less opposed to moderation than is want of moderation; and daring, which is called excess, is less opposed to courage than is timidity, as it is said in 2 *Ethics*. And plants of this kind are with all the trees of Lebanon, that is, with all the other perfections symbolized by the trees of Lebanon, by reason of their whiteness and purity. And those who have perfected their speculative and practical intellect, their irascibility and lustfulness, and have other due perfections, are able to resist the devil. Therefore through what has just been said it is also understood that the plants of the bride can also overcome the temptations of the devil. Hence this part is in agreement with the earlier part, that the breasts of the bride were more beautiful than wine, referring to the intellect. And the fragrance of the ointments was more beautiful than any perfume, by reason of the virtues relating to other powers. Nevertheless, through those themselves, namely, the henna and spikenard, we are able to understand the perfection of the powers by which we overcome the devil.

Myrrh and aloes, with all the chief ointments.

He shows how the temptations of the body are overcome by means of such plants. For they are *myrrh and aloes*, that is, they preserve the body from putrefaction. And this: *with all the chief ointments*, that is, with all the principal ointments that preserve it from putrefaction. Even myrrh preserves it from putrefaction, as the gloss says. Aloes too do the same, though not so well, as is said in the gloss. And the principal ointments can also do this. And because avoiding temptation particularly preserves us from corruption, we are therefore given to understand by this that on account of the above-mentioned overflowing of grace the temptations of the body are overcome.

A garden fountain, a spring of living water streaming down from Lebanon (Sg 4:15).

He concludes that all the temptations are overcome without exception. Therefore he says that such plants are a garden fountain, as they are capable of producing pomegranates, by resisting the temptations of the world. They are also *a spring of living water*, because the water they contain cannot be destroyed by the temptations of the devil. And they are the kind of water *that streams down from Lebanon*, that is, of a dazzling whiteness unstained by the impurity of the body.

Awake, north wind; and come, south wind! Let them blow through my garden, and its fragrance will spread abroad (Sg 4:16).

Christ concludes that he intends to allow his bride to be tempted, so that through that she may merit the goal and the glory. It may be interpreted as follows: You, my bride, can endure all temptations and can endure them easily, since the overflowing itself and the gifts of grace overflowing to others can do this. Therefore: *awake, north wind; and come, south wind!* — that is, I intend to allow various kinds of temptations to arise. And *let them blow through*, that is, *trouble my garden*, that is, my bride, *and its fragrance will spread abroad*, because such incitements will give you the chance to gain merit and be rightly fragrant. For the north wind is a cold wind; but the south wind is a warm one. They symbolize every kind of temptation, and everything that can incline one to evil. For whoever does wrong does so out of chilling fear or wrongly inflaming love.

Lecture 10

May my beloved come into his garden to eat the fruit of his pomegranates.

Since it seems that the bride cannot by herself be converted to God and abandon the world and endure temptations, she turns therefore to her bridegroom seeking his help and support. This part is divided into two: the bride's request is given first; next is added Christ's reply, where it says: *I have come into my garden.* And it may be interpreted as follows: My bridegroom exhorts me to turn to him by abandoning the world, and to endure temptations, and says that I can easily do this. But, as I see, relying on my own efforts I certainly cannot do so. And if he says that I can easily do it, I realize this is true with his help. Therefore I ask *my beloved to come into his garden,* that is, to come to me who am his garden, *to eat,* that is, be kind enough to accept *the fruit of his pomegranates.* For I admit and acknowledge with thanksgiving that the fruit that I create, the pomegranates that I produce, of good thoughts, emotions, prayers, and works, I do not create by myself, but with his help. Therefore I am not mine, but his.

I have come into my garden, my sister, my bride (Sg 5:1).

Christ's reply is given. In her request the bride made two points to be noted. First that she was asking for Christ's help. Next, that she was acknowledging that the good things she possessed came from him. In replying to his bride Christ makes three points. He shows first that he anticipated the request; secondly he agrees that the bride's good possessions are from him, where he says: *I have gathered my myrrh;* thirdly he leads her toward contemplation in tranquility, where he says: *Eat, friends.* It may be interpreted as follows: You, my bride, who are a locked garden, ask me to come to you and help you; I have already anticipated your request. This is what he says, *My sister, my bride, I have come into my garden. I have come,* with *veni* taken as past tense. Hence the meaning: I have already come into my garden, in anticipation of your request, prepared to help you. However, it might be read as *come!* with *veni* taken as the imperative mood. But since that would not combine well with what goes before, it is not our business to consider such a meaning at the moment.

I have gathered my myrrh with my spices. I have eaten my honeycomb with my honey, and I have drunk my wine with my milk.

Christ shows how he agrees that the bride's good possessions come from himself. Hence it may be interpreted as follows. You, my bride, are afraid of failing in the struggle: do not be afraid, because *I have gathered,* that is, cut or picked *my myrrh,* that is, you, who are my myrrh for the mortification of the body, according to what extent you can avoid temptation. And this *with my spices,* because, as was mentioned, through your endurance of temptations fragrance flowed from you according to the goal and the glory you will merit. For Christ is said to gather myrrh with spices, as the bride does this, by overcoming temptations with his help. In this Christ agrees that such a good thing as the overcoming of temptation the bride owes not to herself but to Christ. Afterward he adds: *I have eaten my honeycomb with my honey,* that is, because you are converted to me, and according to this conversion you taste the sweetness of contemplation.

I have drunk wine with my milk, that is, I made you drink wine with my milk, so that you should abandon the world, and by abandoning it drink wine for its spiritual joy and drink milk for its shining whiteness and purity. It is clear from this that Christ acknowledges that it is not only through him that his bride conquers temptation, but also through him that she is converted to him and abandons the world. And it should be noted that because the first cause has more influence on its effect than the second cause, if the bride gathers myrrh by conquering temptation, and eats the honeycomb with the honey by being converted to God, and drinks wine with milk by abandoning the world, if she does this calling on the help of Christ, who is the head and origin of the Church, then to a great and more perfect extent it is Christ who is to do this.

Eat, friends, and drink; lovers, drink your fill.

He exhorts the Church to contemplate in tranquility. Therefore he says: my *friends*, because I am always with you, you need not be anxious; *eat* the sweets of the spirit, *drink the wine* of spiritual joy, and *lovers, drink your fill* in the intoxication of the spirit, in the continuous sweetness of contemplation. But it should be noted that Christ first spoke to the Church in the singular, when he said *I have come into my garden, my sister, my bride;* but now he speaks to the Church in the plural, saying: *eat, friends.* The reason for this is that although the Church in relation to Christ, as his bride, is one, because a bridegroom must have one bride, nevertheless because the sweetness of Christ is not received in one way exclusively throughout the Church, for one is attracted to the sweetness of contemplation sometimes by its authority, another sometimes by devotion, and another by its profound wisdom; on this account the Church, in the plural, is said to eat and drink.

Lecture 11

I sleep, but my heart is awake (Sg 5:2).

After the state of the present-day Church has been described with regard to contemplation, here it is described with regard to action or the ministry of the children. And it should be noted that Christ thus exhorts the Church to contemplation and nevertheless invites her to minister to the children. And therefore he said: *eat, friends; and, lovers, drink your fill,* in exhorting the Church to contemplation. But here, like a good bridegroom caring for the children, he invites her to minister to her children. And this part is divided into two. For the contemplation of the Church is described first. Next Christ's exhortation is added, in which he invites the Church to awake from contemplation to action, where she says: *the voice of my beloved.* The contemplation of the Church is symbolized in the words: *I sleep, but my heart is awake.* For the contemplatives are said to sleep because they shut their eyes to the world. Nevertheless, their hearts are awake, for they are more prepared to perceive inward inspiration and divine influence. As was mentioned earlier, just as the blind, who have no contact with the visible world, have better memories, so the contemplatives, who have withdrawn their attention from the external world, have a better perception of inward inspirations.

The voice of my beloved knocking at the door; open to me, my sister, my love, my dove, my perfect one.

Christ's invitation is described. And this part is divided into two: first his invitation; next the bride's excuse, where she says: *I have taken off.* Two points are made about the first. First there is the description of the above-mentioned invitation; then the reason for the invitation is added, where he says: *my head.* It may be interpreted as follows: while in contemplation, I heard within me *the voice of my beloved,* that is, the voice of Christ knocking, and saying: *my sister,* for the likeness of nature, *my love,* for affection, *my dove,* for simplicity of heart, *arise* from the state of contemplation, *open to me,* by preaching to my children, by opening their hearts so that I can enter them. But it should be noted that the Church, through the active life, by exercising the office of preaching, opens to Christ in two ways in the faithful themselves, for: *what you did for one of the least of mine,* Christ says, *you did for me* (Mt 25:40). Again we also open to Christ himself, when through our preaching the heart of another is opened, through which opening Christ himself enters him.

For my head is wet with dew, and my locks with the dampness of the night.

He gives the reason for the said invitation. I ask you, my bride, to open to me by preaching the true faith and by good behavior. *For my head,* that is, my intellect, *is wet with the dew* of faithlessness, *and my locks,* that is, my hair, or my feelings, *with the dampness of the night,* that is, with the coldness and darkness of sin, which is understood as night by reason of privation, which is the essence of all wickedness, and because: *everyone who does evil hates the light* (Jn 3:20). But it should be noted that the intellect can be called the head, and the will can be called the head. For the will is called the head by reason of predominance, in the way that one who rules over others is said to be their head. So because the will seems to rule in the kingdom of the soul, because the rest of its powers come into action at the command of the will, therefore the will is called the head. But if we consider the head as the place where knowledge and perception flourish, and because the rest of our members are directed into action by the head, it is the function of the intellect and reason to direct, so reason and intellect deserve the name of head. Therefore it is not inappropriate that by the head the intellect should be understood, and that the hair rooted in the head should signify the emotions rooted in the will, since not only the intellect but also the will can be called the head.

I have taken off my garment, how shall I put it on? I have washed my feet, how shall I defile them? (Sg 5:3).

The bride's apology is described, and divided into three parts. First the nature of the apology is stated; secondly the attraction of

Christ is added, where she says: *when my beloved.* Thirdly by means of such an attraction the bride's readiness to serve is revealed, where she says: *I arose to open.* But it may be interpreted as follows: You, my beloved, invited me to take care of the children, to return from the contemplative state, for which I gave up worldly concerns, to the active state, according to which I had busied myself with worldly matters. But *I have taken off my garment,* that is, I have given up those temporal concerns, *how shall I put it on?* — that is, how shall I return to caring again for temporal affairs? as if she said, it is hard for me. *I have washed my feet,* that is, my feelings, which are called feet because they brought me to you. I have washed away such feelings, because not only have I given up temporal concerns, but I have also given up the desire to have any. *How shall I defile them?* — that is, how shall I defile my feet, that is, my feelings, by wanting to busy myself with temporal affairs again?

When my beloved put his hand through the latch-opening, my stomach trembles at his touch (Sg 5:4).

Christ's attraction is described. For though the bride apologized, yet such was Christ's power of attraction that he succeeded in persuading her to take care of the children. It may be interpreted as follows: I, the bride, apologized for not wanting to return to the active life, but *my beloved,* Christ, whose power is infinite, *put his hand through the latch-opening,* that is, through the intellect, or volition; for the intellect or even the emotions are like kinds of openings and cracks through which Christ enters us. And *at his touch,* that is, at his power to inspire me with which Christ touched me, *my stomach,* that is, the softest part in me, *trembled,* that is, was consumed with fear, since I did not dare to refuse the bridegroom's wish. As if she said: so great was Christ's power that not only the strongest parts of her soul were ready to obey Christ, but even the weakest.

I arose to open to my beloved. My hands dripped with myrrh, and my fingers full of the choicest myrrh (Sg 5:5).

For, as was said, Christ's power was so great that he converted the bride totally to his will. Therefore the bride's confession is described here, and her devout undertaking of the duty to which she was invited, that is, the care of the children. And because, as was mentioned above, in the ministry of the children the mind is distracted by external matters, therefore two points are made: first the bride's readiness to serve is described; secondly there is added the distraction of her mind, where she says: *the bolt of my door.* It may be interpreted as follows: My bridegroom so attracted me that, being unwilling or unable to resist, *I arose* from contemplation *to open to my beloved* through preaching. And I not only opened to him by preaching in word, but also by preaching in example. Therefore she adds: *my hands,* that is, my works, *dripped with myrrh,* that is, with the mortification of the body, which is understood by myrrh, as was said above, as people have sometimes been moved by the example of my works and done penance by mortifying their bodies. For we have the same duty to lead others to penance as we have to observe penance ourselves. So she adds: *and my fingers are full of the choicest myrrh,* as if saying: my hands dripped with myrrh, for others caught some of the drippings and droppings of my penance, carrying them in their own bodies. But *my fingers,* that is, various works of mine, which are called fingers, as the gloss suggests because of their separateness, have remained *full of the choicest myrrh,* because I carried in my own body a more excellent penance than I showed to others.

I unbolted my door for my beloved, but he had turned away and gone (Sg 5:6).

The bride tells of the distraction of her mind. And it should be noted that when we are distracted in mind and can no longer taste the same sweetness as we did before, we must return to the inmost depths of our hearts by seeking Christ, and by scrutinizing our thoughts and emotions. And since in such seeking and scrutinizing we are sometimes seized by vain and various thoughts, which are called the watchmen of the city, we must get rid of such idle thoughts and search carefully for Christ. And if we cannot find him by ourselves, we must implore the help of others. According to this sequence of events this part is divided into four: first the distraction of the mind is described; secondly there is added the double search for Christ, where she says: *my soul;* thirdly the being seized by vain thoughts is intimated, where she says: *they found.* Fourthly the search for help, where she says: *I adjure you.* It may be interpreted as follows: I, the bride, after I had opened the door to others by preaching and had been attending to the progress of others, wished to attend to my own progress by returning to the contemplative state. Therefore *I unbolted my door for my beloved,* that is, Christ. We call a bolt the bar with which a door is closed. This can symbolize the concern with temporal affairs which the church leader must lay aside for a time, so that he can return to contemplation by opening his door to Christ. But because on account of his concern with temporal matters the church leader is very much distracted in mind and fails to find Christ, she says: *but he,* that is, Christ, *had turned away and gone,* because being distracted in mind I did not find Christ, my bridegroom, as I wished.

My soul melted as my beloved spoke. I sought and did not find him; I called and he did not answer me.

The search for Christ is described. But it should be noted that when someone returns from the active state to contemplation, if he does not find Christ as he wishes, among other things that incite him to seek Christ is the memory of the lost sweetness. For when we feel we have sometimes tasted the divine sweetness in prayer, if when we return later to prayer and cannot experience a sweetness as great as before, the memory of such sweetness incites us to scrutinize such thoughts and feelings of ours, in case we might have displeased Christ with these, to be able to discover the reason why we can no longer experience the sweetness which we have felt before. Therefore she says: *my soul melted* for the sweetness of contemplation *as my beloved spoke,* that is, when the beloved spoke to me in prayer, and I to him. And because I no longer have such feelings, in returning to contemplation I have not found Christ. Hence remembering the said sweetness, *I sought* Christ, by scrutinizing the thoughts of my intellect: *and I did not find him; I called him* by the yearning of my affection, *and he did not answer me.*

The watchmen found me as they went their rounds of the city. They struck me and wounded me; the watchmen on the walls took away my cloak (Sg 5:7).

After she has told of the search for Christ and of not finding him, she tells of being seized by diverse thoughts. As proof of this it should be noted that the early Church had in a way more troubles, and in a way less, then the present-day Church. For in regard to persecution the former was more disturbed than the latter, which is no longer at the mercy of cruel tyrants. But with regard to dissension the latter is more troubled than the former, because nowadays the Church is endowed with immense wealth, and is therefore more divided within itself because of worldly concerns than the early Church was. Therefore, when the dissension of the early Church was described above, it was simply said that she sought Christ in her bed. But here it is said: *I unbolted my door for my beloved,* because worldly concerns literally create an obstacle and are a bolt in the door of the mind which has to be drawn back if we wish to discover Christ. Again, there it was said: *I sought him and did not find him.* But here it is said that the bridegroom turned away and was gone, and that she sought and did not find him, called him and he did not answer. In this the Church of the present day shows herself to be further away from Christ than the early Church was.

Thirdly, it was said on the former occasion that the watchmen guarding the city found the bride. Here it is said: *the watchmen found me, as they went their rounds of the city* — diverse thoughts found me. Such diverse thoughts *struck me, wounded me, and took away my cloak,* these thoughts are *the watchmen on the walls.* In this the present-day Church shows herself to be more overwhelmed by vain thoughts than the early Church was, because it is also indicated that the early Church found him on her own; hence she said: *A little while after parting from them, I found the one whom my soul loves.* But here the present-day Church, in order to be able to find Christ, entreats the children to help her, when she says: *I adjure you, daughters of Jerusalem.* It should be carefully noted, however, that the thoughts or watchmen of the city strike us when we give them the opportunity. They wound us when we are delighted by them, but they take our cloak from us by robbing us of virtues and gifts when we agree with them.

I adjure you, daughters of Jerusalem, if you find my beloved, to tell him I am faint with love (Sg 5:8).

The bride, in order to be able to find Christ, requires the help of the daughters; this request is to the advantage of the Church and to the advantage of the daughters. To the advantage of the Church insofar as, on account of the prayer of the daughters, the bridegroom bestows some blessings on the Church. It is to the advantage of the daughters because, on account of the earnest entreaty of the mother, the daughters are moved to seek Christ more eagerly. So two points are made: first such an entreaty is described; secondly there is added the more eager questioning of the daughters, where they say: *what kind of person is your beloved?* It may be interpreted as follows: daughters of Jerusalem, I took up your cause for you, and in my anxiety over it, with distracted conscience, I sought Christ, my bridegroom, but could not find him. Therefore *I adjure you,* I implore you, *if you find my beloved,* for perhaps he speaks to you in your prayers because you are not so intent on outward matters, but does not speak to me because I am more so than you are — so if this is the case, I beg you *to tell him that I am faint with love,* that is, I am weak with love. I wish to be caught up in his love, and feel the sweetness of his contemplation, and I am not strong but weak.

Lecture 12

What kind of person is your beloved of the beloved, most beautiful of women? (Sg 5:9).

In this part the eager questioning of the daughters is described. And this part is divided into two. First the daughters of Jerusalem ask their mother, that is, the Church, what is special about Christ, her bridegroom, so as to understand his goodness; secondly they ask where he is, so as to have his companionship, where they say: *Where has your beloved gone?* But these two questions follow each other in a natural order. The first is to discover the reason for something, so that in discovering its goodness we may desire it, moved by the desire for it. Secondly we ask where its goodness is, so as to be able to attain it. The first part is divided into three. First it asks what the nature of Christ's divinity is, where it says: *what kind of person is your beloved of the beloved?* Secondly it asks what the nature of Christ's humanity is, where it says: *what kind of person is your beloved?* Thirdly it gives the reason for the questions asked, where it says: *that you adjure us so.* It may be interpreted as follows: Bride of Christ, *most beautiful of women, what kind of person is your beloved of the beloved?* For the Father is not beloved of the beloved, because he comes from nothing; the Holy Spirit is beloved of all the beloved, because he comes from many, as coming from the Father and the Son; but only the Son is beloved of the beloved.

What kind of person is your beloved?

This verse asks what the nature of Christ's humanity is. Hence it does not add there: *of the beloved,* because just as by being born according to divine nature he is without a mother, so in a certain way by being born according to human nature he is without a father. For since the son must be like the father in nature, and since no human was the father of Christ, we can say that in a certain way Christ as a man did not have a father.

That you adjure us so?

This gives the reason for the said questions. It may be interpreted as follows: We want to know what the nature of your beloved's or bridegroom's divinity is, and what the nature of his humanity is, because you have roused our desire for this: for as you adjured us, so you implored us.

My beloved is fair and ruddy, he is one in a thousand (Sg 5:10).

The bride's answer is described, in which she makes four points. First she indicates the nature of Christ's divinity; secondly the nature of his humanity, where she says: *his head is golden;* thirdly the nature of his relationship to both, where she says: *his appearance is like Lebanon.* Fourthly she sums it all up, where she says: *such is my beloved.* So she first explains the nature of Christ's divinity. For the nature of Christ's divinity can be considered or explained in three ways: first in comparing him with the Father; secondly with the Holy Spirit; thirdly with ourselves. However according as he is compared with the Father, he was begotten by him, and proceeds by means of the intellect, and is called light and dazzling beauty; and with regard to this, she says: *my beloved is fair.* But according as he is compared with the Holy Spirit, so he breathes out the fire of love; and with regard to this she says: *and ruddy,* with the love of charity and of the love proceeding from him. But according as he is compared with ourselves, he is the son by nature, but we are adopted. Therefore she adds: *he is one in a thousand thousands.*

His head is pure gold.

She indicates the nature of Christ's humanity, and makes two points. First she declares what Christ is like in himself; secondly what he is like in his members, where she says: *his locks.* But according to his humanity Christ is our head, because the head must be of the same nature as the members. This is not appropriate for Christ according to his divinity but only according to his humanity. This head, however, is pure gold, because it has not been tarnished by the contagion of sin. For original sin passes by a common law into all at birth, except Christ, who was not conceived and born by the common law of concupiscence, but by the Virgin through the Holy Spirit.

His locks are like the leaves of palm trees and black as the raven.

She explains what Christ is like in relation to his members. But the members of Christ can be divided in two ways, that is, according to the matter of his teaching and of his life. Therefore she makes two points: first she explains the members of Christ by reason of doctrine, secondly by reason of diversity of life, where she says: *his hands.* But the diversity of teaching in the members of Christ is fourfold. First there are the apostles; secondly the prophets, who saw Christ from a greater distance than the apostles; thirdly there are the doctors of the Church, who interpret and teach the words of the apostles and the prophets; fourthly and lastly there are the preachers, who transmit to the people what they learn from the doctors. She therefore makes four points: first she explains the nature of the apostles, where she says: *his locks.* Secondly the nature of the prophets, where she says: *his eyes;* thirdly the nature of the doctors, where she says: *his cheeks;* fourthly the nature of the preachers, where she says: *his lips.*

First, then, she says: *his locks,* that is, the apostles, who are called locks, or hair, because they adhered closely to Christ's head, *are like the leaves of palm trees.* For such locks, that is, the apostles, were raised to a height like palm trees, and hence are like the leaves of palm trees. Or, *the leaves of palm trees* are certain trees like palms, and are aromatic, and symbolize the apostles for the fragrance of their good reputation. Hence another translation, as the gloss says, has: *his hair is like fir trees,* on condition that by fir trees we understand aromatic trees, not those used to build houses. And she adds that such locks are *black as the raven,* which could refer to the persecution that the Church suffered in the time of the apostles.

His eyes are like doves beside streams of water, washed with milk, as they sit beside the numerous streams (Sg 5:12).

She shows the nature of the prophets, who are called eyes because of their vision, according to 1 Samuel 9:11: *For he who is now called a prophet was formerly called a seer.* These, *his eyes,* are *like doves beside streams of water,* because of their knowledge of mysteries. Just as doves beside streams of water see the reflection of an approaching hawk in the water, so the prophets saw mysteriously, as if in the water, the snares of the devil, and warned the people in advance to beware of them. But she adds that these *doves were washed with milk,* for purity. For although the knowledge of the prophets was mysterious, it was nevertheless free from all thought of error. And she adds: *as they sit beside the numerous streams,* for revelation; for what the prophets saw they know through divine inspiration, by way of the numerous streams of the scriptures.

His cheeks are like beds of spices planted by the perfumers (Sg 5:13).

She shows the nature of the doctors, saying: *his cheeks,* that is, the doctors who are the cheeks masticating the food of doctrine. But these cheeks are *like beds,* that is, small plots *of spices,* because in the doctors, as in certain little plots of the scriptures, spices are threshed and broken up as on a great threshing-floor, to the extent that the doctors teach those things that are in the sacred canon to others, in a measure proportionate to them. And such small plots are constructed or *planted,* that is, established and organized, *by the perfumers,* that is, by the prophets and the apostles, from whom they receive the doctrine and then teach it to others. But the apostles and prophets are called perfumers for the fullness of their knowledge.

His lips are like lilies distilling choice myrrh.

She shows the nature of the preachers, saying: *his lips,* that is, the preachers, who are the lips transmitting what they have heard from the doctors. These *lips* are *distilling myrrh,* that is, preaching voluntary poverty or voluntary penance, which is called myrrh from its bitterness. And she says: *choice myrrh,* because, literally from a tree containing myrrh a drop or a liquid flows spontaneously, and such a liquid is called choice myrrh, and symbolizes voluntary penance. After such liquid stops flowing from the said tree, an incision is made, and because of the incision there flows from it another liquid, which is called second-rate myrrh, which is not so choice.

His hands are beautifully turned and golden, full of hyacinths (Sg 5:14).

She explains the members of Christ as they are differentiated according to their true life, that is, in the three ways, because some are active, some contemplative, but some, like the clergy, are both. So she makes three points: First she describes the active; second the contemplatives, where she says: *his belly;* thirdly the clergy, where she says: *his legs.* First, then, she says: *his hands,* that is, the active, who are called hands, which are the chief instrument for action or work: and they *are turned as on a lathe,* for easily performing good works, for something round is easily moveable. They are also golden, because it is not enough for anything to be classed as good unless it is founded on love, which is symbolized by gold, which is a glowing reddish color. Again these *hands are full of hyacinths,* for a right intention, which is required for all good works. For the hyacinth is a precious stone, the color of the heaven, and symbolizes right intention, because in all our good works we must lift our intention up to the heaven of the Trinity.

His belly is of ivory, set with sapphires.

She shows the nature of the contemplatives, saying: *his belly,* that is, the contemplatives, who are a belly filled with spiritual food, for it is especially filled with spiritual sweetness. For this *belly is of ivory* by reason of its purity, because the contemplatives most of all are cut off from the earthly defilements of humanity. And such a belly is *set,* that is, artistically inlaid, *with sapphires,* on account of its cleaving to God. For the sapphire is a precious stone, the color of the heavens like the hyacinth, which in the highest degree and especially fits the contemplatives. Therefore they most of all cleave to the supreme food.

His legs are marble pillar, set on golden bases (Sg 5:15).

She describes the nature of the clergy, saying: *his legs,* that is, the clergy, who are called legs because they carry others. These *legs* are *pillars* because of their straightness. They are *marble* because of their firmness. *They are set on golden bases* because of their love. Hence if the clergy are found lacking in these qualities they are rather the legs of the devil than the legs of Christ.

His appearance is like Lebanon, noble as the cedars. His speech is most sweet, and he is wholly desirable. Such is my beloved, and this is my friend, daughters of Jerusalem (Sg 5:16).

She shows the nature of Christ according to his humanity and divinity together. And she mentions three things which suit him according to both natures. First is his beauty, for insofar as he is human, he is beautiful, according to that verse in the psalms: *You are the fairest of men* (Ps 45:3). Insofar as he is God, he is beautiful, because he is the splendor of glory (Hebrews 1), and because he is true wisdom, of which it is said in Wisdom 7:29: She is more beautiful than the sun and surpasses every constellation of the stars. Secondly what suits him is incorruptibility, and this even as a man, according to that verse in the psalms (16:10): *You will not let your faithful one undergo corruption.* And insofar as he is God, even as true wisdom: *wisdom is radiant and unfading* (Wis 6:12). Thirdly, what suits him according to his humanity and divinity is sweetness and pleasantness, because we shall enter heaven by contemplating Christ's divinity, and leave it by contemplating Christ's humanity, and in both cases find pasture, that is, abundant refreshment of sweetness. But three points are touched on in this part. For beauty is mentioned, when it is said: *his appearance is like Lebanon,* that is, his beauty is bright and shining; incorruptibility, when there is added: *noble as cedars,* for the cedar is said to be a tree that cannot decay. Then sweetness is revealed, when there is added: *his speech is most sweet,* that is, his nature is sweetness itself. Therefore it is added that he is *wholly desirable* according to his humanity and divinity. And she concludes: *such is my beloved,* drawing my love to himself; *and this is my friend,* sharing his love with me.

Lecture 13

Where has your beloved gone, most beautiful of women? Which way did your beloved go, and shall we seek him with you? (Sg 6:1).

After the daughters of Jerusalem asked to have the nature of the Church's beloved explained to them, so as to understand him, they now ask where he is, so as to enjoy his company. But this part is divided into two: first there is the said question; next the bride's answer, where she says: *my beloved has gone down.* Concerning the first, it should be noted that in accordance with his divinity Christ goes away and is taken from us; but in accordance with his humanity he comes down and takes his way toward us. So in the first part three points are mentioned. First it is asked where Christ is according to his divinity. Secondly it is asked where he is according to his humanity, when it says: *Which way did your beloved go?* Thirdly the reason for both is given, when there is added at the end: *and shall we seek him with you?* as if to say, the reason we want to know where he is, is to enjoy his company.

My beloved has gone down to his garden to the bed of spices, to browse in the gardens and to pick the lilies.

The bride's answer is described. In proof of which it should be noted that the *where* of anything is understood in the appropriate way; there is nothing in nature that corresponds to it as such. For nature, as it is nature, has no *where*, nor what could be in a place; but taken in the wide sense, the *where* of anything in nature can be defined by the appropriate principles. For such things are said to be *where* they actually are in nature, because just as nothing is in fact without its own place, nothing is in fact without its own principles.

But taking Christ himself according to his divinity, he is not confined by any *where*, because his divine nature is infinite and unconfined by any limits. But according to his humanity some *where* is appropriate to him, since his humanity is finite and confined within the principles of its species. And so the bride does not answer the question: *Where has your beloved gone?* as it is asked of the divinity. But she answers the one where the words are: *Which way did your beloved go?*; or where did he go down to, as it is asked of his humanity. But in giving her reply she does three things: first she gives her reply; secondly she adds his reason in her reply, where she says: *to browse*, thirdly she shows her true love for Christ, where she says: *I am my beloved's*. It may be interpreted as follows: You, daughters of Jerusalem, have asked me where my beloved has gone. You also asked me where he went down to. To the first question I make no answer, because I am unable to. In reply to the second, I say that *my beloved has gone down to his garden to the bed of spices*, that is, he has gone down to the Church, which is his garden, to the bed, that is, to the blessed Virgin, who was a garden bed full of spices of virtues and gifts, by becoming incarnate in her, according to which incarnation he has associated with me, who am the garden in his Church. Next she adds his reason in her answer, when she says: *to browse in the gardens*, that is, to delight in our good works, as the gloss says, by helping us to do good, *and to pick the lilies*, that is, the elect, by gathering them together at his will.

I am my beloved's, and my beloved is mine, who browses among the lilies (Sg 6:3).

She shows her true love for Christ, saying: *I am my beloved's*, that is, I am preparing in myself a place of reception, as the gloss supplies. And *my beloved is mine*, is preparing in his home a place to receive me, so that he *who browses among the lilies*, that is, among pure desires, may be in me and I in him. In this she shows her true love for Christ, and Christ his true love for her: *For those who abide in love abide in God, and God in them* (1 Jn 4:16).

You are beautiful, my love, sweet and lovely as Jerusalem (Sg 6:4).

He defines the unity of the Church, or removes a certain doubt which might arise from previous statements. For it was said that in the Church there were different positions: some are beginners, some progressing, and some fully instructed. Again it was said that for the same position there were many requirements; for in relation to any position there must be some kind of beauty of substance, power, and effect. And in works particularly there must be multiple diversity. And because there is such great diversity in the Church, Christ wishes to show that his bride is one, whose unity is not destroyed because of such diversity. And he makes two points: first he repeats those things which appear to create diversity in the Church; secondly he shows that this is no hindrance to the unity of the Church, where he says: *my dove is one alone.*

The first part is divided into two, as two things seem to hinder the unity of the Church, namely, the diversity of the requirements for all the positions: secondly, the diversity of the positions themselves, where he says: *there are sixty queens.* The first part is divided into three, as there are three requirements for all the positions, that is: excellence of substance, power, and effect. And all these were touched on earlier in a sense. Therefore to reiterate them is in a sense to repeat what was referred to before. First, then, he mentions the excellence which the Church requires with regard to substance; secondly with regard to power, where he says: *terrible as . . .*; thirdly with regard to effect, where he says: *your hair.* So he says: *you are beautiful, my love,* with regard to outward substance; *sweet and lovely as Jerusalem,* that is, like the early Church, with regard to inward substance, for that Church was shapely and beautiful within, though it was very dark outwardly through persecution. But now persecution has ceased, and therefore the Church is outwardly beautiful.

Terrible as an army drawn up for battle. Turn your eyes away from me, for they have made me flee away (Sg 6:5).

He shows that she has beauty with regard to power. And because beauty comes through divine inspiration, therefore he says that the means must be removed, where he says: *Turn your eyes away.* He says, then, that because of its magnitude and its excellent beauty the Church is terrible as an army drawn up for battle, which fears no enemy because of the power it has from God's help and inspiration. Thus he says: *Turn your eyes away,* that is, lay aside the methods by which you want to question me. *For those eyes,* that is, your methods, *have made me flee away,* because those methods are insufficient to question me, which agrees with the words of the psalm: *Man will reach into the depths of his heart, and God will be exalted.* For the harder we try to discover God through common sense, the further he withdraws from us. And though there are good ways for defending the faith, they are no use for proving it. So the fact that we are terrible for teaching and defending the faith by divine wisdom and miracles, we are so through grace and especially through divine inspiration.

Your hair is like a flock of she-goats that have appeared from Gilead.

He first describes the beauty which she has through the operations of feeling; secondly that which she has through the operation of intellect, where he says: *like the bark.* Therefore he says: *your hair,* that is, your affections, is *like a flock of she-goats that have appeared,* or have come down *from Gilead,* which may be explained in the same way as before.

Your teeth are like flocks of ewes which have come up from the washing, all with twins, and not one of them is barren (Sg 6:6).

He describes her beauty in relation to intellectual activities, saying: *Your teeth* are *like flocks of ewes,* implying shorn ewes, *which have come up from the washing, all with twins, and not one of them is barren,* which was also explained earlier.

Your cheeks are like the bark of a pomegranate, apart from what is hidden within you (Sg 6:7).

He repeats the beauty of works, saying: *Your cheeks,* that is, external activities, *are like the bark of a pomegranate,* containing ruddy pomegranates, that is, fervent love, *apart from what is hidden within you,* that is, apart from what lies concealed inside, because she is not only beautiful in outward appearance but also inwardly.

There are sixty queens, eighty concubines, and young girls without number (Sg 6:8).

He describes the diversity of the Church regarding position. But such diversity can be understood in many ways. First by the diversity of the contemplative life, which is divided into beginners, those progressing, and those fully instructed. Or in relation to way of life, for some are active, some contemplative. Or in relation to fruit: for some, like virgins, bear fruit a hundredfold; some, like widows, sixtyfold, some, like married women, thirtyfold. And he describes this diversity: thus he says of *queens,* that is, the virgins, who have conducted themselves best, *there are sixty,* that is, their number is small and excellent. Sixty, as such, is a small number and yet a superabundant number: because its parts taken together amount to more than the whole, and symbolize the virginal state; for virgins are comparatively few and surpass others in fruitfulness. Next: *concubines*, that is, widows, who are called concubines because at some time they had a husband other than Christ. And there *are eighty concubines*, which is a number greater in quantity than sixty, and less in virtue; for it is not so superabundant a number if its parts are considered as aliquot. And it symbolizes the widowed state, in which there are more people than in the virginal state, but they are not so fruitful. Lastly, *there are young girls*, that is, the imperfect, or those living in the married state, *without number*, because these surpass the others in quantity but lag behind them in virtue. However, different reasons can be assigned for the diversity of the Church through what has been said; but nothing of this at the moment, because it would hold us up too much.

My dove, my perfect one, is one alone; she is the only one for her mother, the favorite of her who bore her (Sg 6:9).

He shows that such things are no hindrance to the unity of the Church. And he makes two points, as there are two sorts of diversity which seem to hinder such unity. First he shows that such unity is not hindered by the diversity of those things that are required for any state; secondly that the diversity of state does not hinder it, where he says: *they saw her.* For the first, it should be noted that the universal Church is united in four ways: first in faith, because there is one faith for all; secondly in love, because one chain of love links all who are in the Church together; thirdly in grace, which can be called our mother, because we owe our spiritual existence to it; fourthly the Church is united in its goal because we are all traveling toward the heavenly Jerusalem, which can be called she who bore us, because we should imitate her as daughters imitate their mother.

It may be interpreted as follows: Such diversity in the Church is inevitable, because in any position throughout the universal Church, there has to be beauty of substance, power, and effect, and there has to be such diversity in works. Nevertheless the unity of the Church is not destroyed by this because all these things are united by faith, united in love, in grace, and purpose. And if through these the concerns of different people became one, much more do substance, power, and effect become one, which can be the concern of a single person. And this is what he says: *my dove is one alone,* for the unity of faith, which is symbolized in the dove which is a simple animal thing. In the same way the faith of the Church is simple and without a shred of error; and also that we cleave simply to our beliefs, since we do not adhere to them through argument about faith. And he adds: *my per-*

fect one is one alone, for love; because love is the bond of perfection. And he adds: *she is the only one for her mother* by reason of grace; from which, as from a mother, we have our spiritual existence. *She is the favorite one of her who bore her,* for unity or purpose; because our substance, power, and effect, and all that is in us, is according to the measure of our faith; and all this, together with the order of love and the perfection of grace, we must direct toward that heavenly Jerusalem, which we should resemble, as a daughter her mother.

The daughters saw her and declared her most blessed: the queens and concubines praised her.

After showing that the unity of the Church is not hindered through the diversity of substance, power, and effect appropriate to any position and existing in any person and any member of the Church, he shows here that such unity is not hindered through the diversity of positions or even of people. His argument runs as follows. Outside the Church there is no salvation for anyone in any position, so that no one is saved except within the unity of the Church. Therefore queens, concubines, daughters or young girls, and all who are in the Church in any position and any circumstances are saved to the same extent as they praise and approve and declare most blessed the one Catholic Church united by faith and love. Therefore although these are different positions, still the Church is one, in which all these positions are saved. This, then, is what he says: the children or young girls *saw her,* that is, they saw the Church united by faith and love and *declared her most blessed* by approving such unity. So also *the queens and concubines praised her,* that is, her unity. By the daughters, concubines, and queens are understood the various positions in the Church, requiring a diversity of people, as was explained earlier.

Who is she appearing like the dawn, beautiful as the moon, bright as the sun, terrible as an army drawn up for battle? (Sg 6:10).

He ends the treatise on the Church of the present day in praise of her, saying: *Who is she appearing like the dawn?* For the early Church rose through the desert like a column of smoke, because of the persecution of tyrants. But the Church of today *appears like the dawn;* for persecution has ceased and day is approaching, and this Church is *beautiful as the moon* through faith. For what we know by faith, we see as it were in the light of the moon, because we do not apprehend it clearly. It is *bright as the sun* by reason of hope, according to which it is uplifted to the desire for the heavenly Jerusalem, which by reason of its brightness can be called the sun. It is *terrible as an army drawn up for battle*, for love; for by our possession of this we terrify the devil, because we keep unity and peace on earth and are humbly subject to God, which he refused to keep in heaven.

Lecture 14

I went down to my garden to look at the fruits in the valleys, and to see if the vines had blossomed and the pomegranates were in flower (Sg 6:11).

As was said earlier, this whole book is divided into three parts, according to the three stages of the Church. Two parts have been gone through, and it remains to examine the third stage, as the final stage of the Church. And because in the first stage the branches were broken, because the Jews in general deserted Christ, in the second stage, as in the present-day Church, the plenitude of the Gentiles has come in; but in the third stage, in the final centuries, all Israel will be saved, as was mentioned earlier. Therefore to determine the last stage of the Church is to determine the conversion of the Jews or the synagogue. And this part is divided into two: first the conversion of the synagogue is determined; secondly the Church is invited to take care of the synagogue now converted, in the words: *under the apple tree.* The first part is divided into two. For just as the state of the early Church was determined by first describing its state, and after that with the treatise ending in its praise, in the words: *who is she ascending through the desert?* so likewise in the treatment of the present-day Church, first there was a description of its state, and after that a conclusion in praise of it, saying: *who is she appearing like the dawn?* So now, first the conversion of the synagogue is described; secondly this treatise on its conversion ends in praise of it, saying: *who is she who comes down from the desert?* The first part is divided into three: first Christ encourages the synagogue to recognize his incarnation; secondly, encouraged by Christ, the synagogue apologizes for her ignorance, where she says: *I did not know,* thirdly, with the synagogue aware of her ignorance, Christ calls her back to mercy, saying: *Come back, come back.*

145

Concerning the first, it should be noted that when the Church came to the end of its early stage, it entered its present-day stage in peace, when it was said: *Look, Solomon's bed,* to give one to understand that now persecution had ceased. In the same way now when the conversion of the Jews has been settled, the treatise begins with a descent, when it is said: *I went down to my garden,* because Christ descended in a special way for the Jews, as shown in his words: *I was sent only to the sheep, etc.* (Mt 15:24). It may be interpreted as follows: synagogue, you so often asked me to come down and save you. Certainly *I went down to my garden,* that is, to my Church, or also to you, who were my garden by my assuming mortality. And this I did to view with a merciful eye *the fruit in the valley,* that is, the state of the active, who are called the fruit in the valley because they are in the lowest position. And to look with a devout eye to see *if the vines had blossomed,* that is, if the contemplatives had blossomed, who are called flowers of the vineyard for the fragrance of holy prayer. Also *to see if the pomegranates were in flower,* that is, the clergy, who are called pomegranates, because they have to lead two lives, the contemplative and the active. Therefore they are symbolized by pomegranates, which have reddish seeds inside, symbolizing the fervor of the contemplative life, but outside they have a rough rind symbolizing the turbulence of the active life. In this way, then, I came down to examine the state of all, and to help you in accordance with the state of all, and to unite you if you had no objection.

I did not know: my soul troubled me for the chariots of Aminadab.

The synagogue apologizes for her ignorance. It may be interpreted as follows: You say, my Lord, my savior, that you came down and assumed mortality in order to help me. *I did not know,* that is, I was unaware that you were the one who was to come; for I should never have crucified you if I had believed that you were the God of glory. But the reason for my blindness was that *my soul,* that is, my animal nature and sensuality, or my people, *troubled me,* by paying no attention to your warnings. And this *for the chariots of Aminadab,* that is, on account of the scribes and pharisees persuading the people, so that I did not believe in you but crucified you. For the scribes and pharisees are called the chariots because they carried and led the people. And these are chariots of Aminadab, which is translated as my voluntary people because they led the people according to their will.

Come back, come back, Shulammite maiden, come back, come back, so that we may gaze at you (Sg 7:1).

Christ calls the synagogue back to him; and he makes two points. First he explains the nature of the recalling; secondly he adds the reason for the recalling, where he says: *why should you look at the Shulammite maiden?* It may be interpreted as follows: since you, synagogue, or Shulammite maiden, acknowledge the captivity of your misery and blindness, and are aware of your animal nature, *Come back,* by abandoning your mental blindness. *Come back, Shulammite maiden,* by abandoning your animal nature and sensual wickedness. *Come back,* by cleaving to the truth and trying to be good. And this *so that we may gaze at you,* with a compassionate eye, taking pity on you.

Lecture 15

What will you see in the Shulammite maiden, but assembled armies?
(Sg 7:2).

He gives the reason for such a conversion, and argues as follows:
All must turn to him from whom they have all their good and all
their beauty; but the premise is that you, synagogue, must have all
your beauty from me, Christ; therefore you must turn to Christ. In
this argument he proceeds as follows: first it is said that the beauty
of the synagogue was intended by God; secondly it is shown that the
synagogue has to obtain such beauty through Christ, where he says:
I said: I shall climb the palm tree, thirdly the synagogue agrees to these
words, where she says: *worthy for my beloved;* fourthly she turns to
Christ, where she says: *I am my beloved's.* With regard to the beauty
of the synagogue he makes two points: first he describes the beauty
of the Church-synagogue intimately and diffusely; secondly he repeats its beauty in general and succinctly, where he says: *how beautiful.* But in describing the beauty of the synagogue in detail, he
shows that she is very beautiful in every respect. For just as beauty
of soul consists of the perfection of the virtues and the gifts which
adorn the lustful and the irascible person, as well as the practical
and speculative intellect and the will, so for the synagogue the
beauty which she had to achieve through Christ was intended. And
because some things perfected in this way concern powers which
are connected with instrumentality and some with those which are
not, so this part where such beauty is defined is divided into two.
First he defines the said beauty by comparison with the perfection
of powers connected with instrumentality; secondly by comparison
with powers not connected with instrumentality, where he says:

149

your two breasts. But the powers which are connected are two, anger and lust. First, then, he speaks of beauty as it concerns anger; secondly as it concerns lust, where he says: *your thighs.* But the perfection or beauty of the power of anger is courage, which drives us to resist and attack our enemies. For first he defines courage, or the perfection of anger, insofar as we resist our enemies; secondly insofar as we attack them and are victorious, where he says: *how beautiful are.* It may be interpreted as follows: The synagogue is now the Shulammite maiden, that is, a captive in miserable captivity. But if we look at her in the light of the beauty which God has foreseen for her, then she is wholly beautiful. For she is beautiful in relation to anger, to the extent that the perfection of anger has been foreseen for her, enabling her to resist her enemies. So he says: *what will you see in the Shulammite maiden,* for the reason mentioned, *but assembled armies,* that is, strong fortifications by means of which she can resist her enemies, as if to say: no giving in!

How beautiful are your feet in sandals, prince's daughter.

He shows that she is able to attack and defeat her enemies. It may be interpreted as follows: Not only was it foreseen, synagogue, that you could resist your enemies, but also that you could attack and defeat them. Therefore, *prince's daughter,* that is, synagogue, who were foreseen as my daughter, I who am the prince of earthly kings, *how beautiful are your feet,* that is, how beautiful are your actions and works, according to which you attack and invade the enemy. Your feet are not bare, but neatly shod, that is, molded by love. For love dresses and adorns our whole body and everything we have, insofar as it is the form and perfection of all our powers and all our works; and everything we do takes its perfection from life. And therefore according as our works are called feet, love gives them shoes, but according as they are works of the hands, love gives them gloves, metaphorically speaking.

Your rounded thighs are like jewels, the work of a craftsman's hand.

He defines her beauty as it relates to the lustful. Concerning lust, however, there are in fact three ways in which people commit this sin: for some are weak, some are incontinent and some are intemperate. The weak are those who are overcome by a little temptation. The incontinent are those who are not overcome by a little temptation, but fall when provoked by much temptation. Hence the weak know nothing of a struggle because of course they have had no struggle, as their name itself signifies. The incontinent, however, do put up a fight, and when they are beaten they cannot restrain themselves. For if they put up no fight they would not be incontinent; yet there would be nothing to struggle with. The intemperate, however, are those who have already acquired a tendency toward lust. So for such people wrongdoing is a pleasure, and they sin from choice. Hence they rejoice in wrongdoing and exult at the most evil things. And all this can be clearly seen from the book of *Ethics* 7, 1, 1. And because one of the opposites is multiplied so many times, the rest too are multiplied as many.

Just as there are three ways in which people sin with regard to lust, so there are three ways in which they act correctly. For some people are persevering, some are continent, and some temperate. But the persevering are those who are not tempted and do not fall and hence are the opposite of the weak, who fall without temptation. The continent are those who stand firm at every attack, and do not fall; they are the opposite of the incontinent. The temperate, however, are those to whom it is a pleasure to act correctly; for they have purified their desires, and achieved perfection through an inclination toward the good.

But in describing the beauty and perfection of the synagogue foreseen by God, he makes three points regarding lust. He first describes it with regard to temperance; secondly to continence, where he says: *your navel*; thirdly to perseverance, where he says: *your belly*. It may be interpreted as follows: synagogue, you not only possess beauty with respect to anger, but also with respect to lust. For according to divine foresight: *your rounded thighs are like jewels*, for your thighs are closed and by no means open. And this, *like jewels, the work of a craftsman's hand*, that is, my hand, I who am that craftsman and artist who made the dawn and the sun. Since, then, a woman's thighs are opened in sexual acts, it is shown that the perfect chastity of the synagogue was foreseen, when it is said that her thighs are *like jewels*, which are ornaments used to fasten things together; and that perfect chastity is symbolized by temperance in what has been said. But it should be noted that the word: *femur, femoris*, means a man's thigh, but the word: *femen, feminis*, means a woman's, for the synagogue assumes the character of a woman, in the person of the bride. And so he says: the thighs of a woman, and not of a man. Again it should be noted that he says: *like jewels*. But a jewel is a clasp, which women wear on the breast, to fasten their clothes on the breast. In this it is given to understand that chastity, for which the synagogue is commended, not only knows no opening of the body, but also knows no division in the heart; for perfect chastity requires the integrity of body and mind. Again it should be noted that such jewels are *the work of a craftsman's hand,* that is, the hand of God, because temperance, for which it is praised, is not acquired but imbued.

Your navel is a rounded goblet that never lacks mixed wine (Sg 7:3).

He commends her for continence. For the navel is the part where wantonness flourishes in women; as Gregory says: for men the loins are the home of wantonness, but for women it is the navel. This navel of the synagogue, according to divine foresight, is *a rounded goblet,* for a correct disposition, *that never lacks mixed wine,* that is, is never without drafts of sacred teaching on account of its clear-sighted intellect. The incontinent person contracts two evils through incontinence: He contracts malice in dispositions; hence he is not *a rounded goblet,* because he is not easily moved to do good work. He is no rounded goblet because he has no right intention, since he does nothing for eternal life, symbolized by a rounded goblet, in which because of its roundness there is neither beginning nor end. He also contracts blindness of intellect; for being blinded by passion, he observes neither good laws nor the lessons of sacred teaching.

Your belly is a heap of wheat surrounded with lilies.

He commends her for perseverance. The belly is a rather soft part of a woman. According to divine foresight, however, the belly of the synagogue will be without softness, and possess the strength of persistence and endurance. Hence according to such foresight the belly of the synagogue will be *a heap of wheat,* because others are invigorated and sustained by the wheat. By this it is given to be understood that, according to divine foresight, the synagogue is bound to attain such perseverance or such persistence that not only will it not fall itself but it will also keep others from falling. And this will be literally so at the end of time, when the whole of Israel will be converted to Christ, for by that time many will be stronger in faith and morals. And then *your belly will be surrounded with lilies,* for purity, because by opposing weakness with perseverance the defilement of the body is avoided.

Lecture 16

Your two breasts are like two fawns, twins of a gazelle (Sg 7:5).

After a description of the beauty which God foresaw for the synagogue with regard to the powers connected with a bodily organ, in this part there is a description of the beauty foreseen for it with regard to the powers not connected with a bodily organ. But these powers are two, namely, the intellect and the emotions. The intellect is divided into the speculative and the practical. So he makes three points: first he describes beauty in regard to the speculative intellect; secondly in regard to the practical intellect, where he says: *your eyes;* thirdly in regard to the intellective desire, where he says: *your head.* The first is divided into two, because in the speculative intellect there are knowledge and faith. So first he describes beauty in regard to knowledge and doctrine; secondly in regard to faith, where he says: *your neck.* The text: *your two breasts,* may be read according to the divine foresight, as symbolizing knowledge and doctrine. They are called two breasts for the two testaments, like breasts containing milk, that is, the sweetness of doctrine. These breasts, however, or her knowledge and doctrine, are *like two fawns, twins of a gazelle.* For fawns are nimble and gazelles sharp-sighted, symbolizing sacred doctrine, in which we easily discover what is true, and see truth itself sharply and judge it precisely. And these two fawns of a gazelle are called twins of a gazelle for their twofold meaning, the literal and the mystical, and are *twins* because these two meanings are always visible in each other and accompany each other, since in any part of sacred doctrine both these meanings can somehow be assigned.

Your neck is like a tower of ivory (Sg 7:5).

He describes the beauty foreseen for her in relation to faith, saying: *your neck*, that is, the faith foreseen for you, which is called the neck, because it is by this that you must be united with me, the head, just as it is by the neck that the head is united with the body. But this neck, or faith, is like a tower for defense. For although faith cannot be tested, yet it can be defended; and this *tower is of ivory*, that is, clear and firm, with no admixture of error.

Your eyes are like the pools in Heshbon, beside the gate of Bethrabbim.

He commends her with regard to practical intelligence. But two things seem to be applicable to the practical intelligence with regard to the present day. The first is judgment. For even prudence, which also seems to be decisive and perceptive for good morals, is as in subjection to the practical intelligence, as it is applicable to this practical intelligence to distinguish spirits, and particularly according as things that are contrary to good morals are suggested to us through such. For we should not believe every spirit, *but test the spirits, to see whether they are from God* (1 Jn 4:1). Therefore he makes two points. First he commends her with regard to the teaching of morals; secondly with regard to the discernment of spirits, where he says: *your nose*. So he says: *your eyes*, that is, your thoughts, by which you judge between good and bad morals, are *like the pools in Heshbon*. Heshbon is said to have been a city of King Sehon beyond the Jordan, which the children of Israel captured at the gates of which there were pools from which the multitude of people were given to drink.

Such is the teaching of morals in the Church, because the multitude of people, that is, all true Christians, drink it and all are invited to do so. John 7:37: *Let anyone who is thirsty come to me and drink*; and Isaiah 55:1: *All you who are thirsty, come to the waters.* Hence it is added that *these pools are beside the gate of Bethrabbim*, that is, beside the gate where there were always crowds of people. For son or daughter in holy scripture sometimes stands for abundance, as in the passage in Isaiah 5:1: *My beloved had a vineyard on a fertile hillside* (literally: on a horn, tongue of land, the *son* of oil) that is, on a long, low promontory, rich and full of oil. Another example of the same usage is: when someone is rich, he is called a son of money.

Your nose is like the tower of Lebanon, looking toward Damascus.

He commends her for distinguishing between spirits, saying: *your nose,* that is, your discrimination, the way you distinguish between good spirits and bad, *is like the tower of Lebanon,* that is, a shining tower, not disfigured by the devil's deception. This tower *looks toward Damascus,* that is, toward the devil. For Damascus is interpreted as a drink of blood, and symbolizes the devil who, thirsting for our blood, *like a roaring lion, prowls about looking for someone to devour* (1 Pt 5:8).

Your head crowns you like Mount Carmel (Sg 7:6).

He commends her with regard to intellective desire. In this we can consider two things, potentiality and actuality. So he commends her in two ways, first in relation to the will itself, secondly in relation to its actuality, where he says: *and the hair of your head.* So he says: *your head,* that is, the will which can be called the head, as was shown earlier, is like *Carmel,* a high mountain, because it is not directed toward earthly things but heavenly. Carmel is interpreted as the knowledge of circumcision, because we must accustom ourselves to an appetite cut off from earthly desires.

Your hair is like purple draperies; a king is held captive in its tresses.

He commends her for the acts of the will itself, saying: *the hair of your head,* that is, your acts and affections which are rooted in the will, which is suitably called the head, as has been said. These affections are *like purple draperies; a king is held captive in their tresses,* because they are always connected with Christ's passion. For purple is a dye made from the blood of a fish; seashells, as was said earlier and the gloss mentions, when cut round with a knife emit drops of purple color. And this purple can symbolize Christ's body, which was dyed red by his blood. And perhaps literally, when purple is dyed, it is placed in tresses through which that blood is drawn off to the purple itself, because as long as the purple is held fast in the tresses, it is unlikely to be able to lose its color, since it is through such a conjunction that it acquires that color. Our affections, then, must be like a king's purple, in memory of Christ's passion. They must also be held fast in the tresses, for they must never lose the blood-red dye and the beauty which they acquire from the memory of Christ's passion.

How beautiful you are and graceful, my dearest, my delight (Sg 7:7).

He repeats in general and concisely what he had mentioned in particular. For all the beauty specified can be reduced to three kinds, for it pertains to contemplation, action, or instruction. So he makes three points, because first he commends her in relation to the contemplative life; secondly in relation to the active, where he says: *your stature*; thirdly in relation to instruction and learning, where he says: *your breasts*. So he says: You, synagogue, according to my foresight, my dearest in delights, in the sweetness of contemplation, *how beautiful you are*, externally, *and graceful* within. Or: *how beautiful you are* in relation to the powers connected with a bodily organ; *and how graceful* in relation to those not connected.

Your stature is like that of a palm tree (Sg 7:8).

He commends her in relation to the active life, saying: *your stature*, that is, the active life, according to which you stand upright and do not bend toward forbidden things, *is like that of a palm tree*, that is, to a struggle, because in such a life people always seem to be at war, that is, in motion. Hence it is symbolized by Martha, who worried and fussed about so many things (Lk 10:41).

And your breasts are like clusters of grapes.

He commends her in relation to teaching or instruction, saying: *and your breasts*, that is, your teaching (understand: are like) *clusters of grapes*. For just as there is wine in readiness in clusters of grapes, so your teaching has cupfuls of scripture ready to offer.

I said: I shall climb the palm tree and take hold of its fruit. May your breasts be like clusters of the vine, and the scent of your breath the scent of apples, and your mouth like the best wine (Sg 7:9-10).

After describing the foreseen beauty of the synagogue, he now shows that she has to attain that beauty through Christ. But it should be noted that the beauty of the synagogue, as attributed to her and described, is not to be understood as referring to her actual existence, since these words concern a synagogue not yet fully converted. But they are to be understood as referring to the divine foresight, that is, that it was foreseen for her by God, that she must have such beauty through Christ, and therefore must be converted to him. It may be interpreted as follows: synagogue, the beauty already mentioned has been foreseen for you, but you must attain it through me. For *I said: I shall climb the palm tree,* that is, the cross, which is called a palm tree for victory. Or, literally (as the gloss seems to suggest), the cross is called a palm tree because part of it was made from a palm tree. *And I shall take hold of its fruit,* that is, the fruit of the cross. And he explains what this fruit is, saying: *may your breasts be like clusters of the vine,* that is, may one fruit be that your breasts, that is, your teaching, may be clusters of the vine; and this, for the beauty that God has foreseen for the synagogue through the instruction or teaching. And may the fruit of the cross, through my climbing the cross, be fragrant. Hence follows: *like the scent of apples,* for good reputation in regard to behavior and the active life. And also for climbing the cross, *may your mouth,* that is, the sweetness of your contemplation, be *like the best wine,* for the abundance of its spiritual joy. This makes it perfectly clear that, through Christ's climbing the cross, the synagogue must acquire beauty in relation to teaching, and the active and contemplative life. And because all the beauty foreseen for her bears some relation to those three, it justifies our previous conclusion that the synagogue has to achieve through Christ all the beauty that God has foreseen for her.

Worthy for my beloved to drink, and to savor with his lips and teeth.

This describes the synagogue's confession, in which it agrees that the aforesaid beauty has to be attained through Christ. It may be interpreted as follows: You, say, Lord Jesus Christ, that I can only reach such beauty through your passion and your climbing the cross. I acknowledge that the wine, that is, the passion through which I must obtain the things foretold, is *worthy,* that is, is right and proper for *my beloved to drink.* For the sufferings of no other would be sufficient to obtain such beauty for me, only your sufferings and the suffering of your members, insofar as their suffering proceeds from yours. He adds therefore that such a wine is worthy *to be savored by his lips and teeth,* that is, by the lips and teeth of Christ, because through the suffering of the members of Christ the Church has gained much beauty. And this beauty is extended as far as the synagogue, when at the end of time it is converted to Christ.

That the passion of Christ may be called a drink is clear from the words in Matthew 26:42: *My Father, if this cup cannot pass unless I drink it, your will be done.* But it should be noted that Christ is said to have drunk the passion, but the members of Christ, namely, the teeth and lips, such as the apostles and other saints, savored Christ's passion. Also for the above reason they did not receive suffering to the same extent as Christ, because in a way it was easier for Christ to suffer than for the other saints. And so Christ is said to have drunk his passion, but the other saints are said to have savored it, as the gloss appears to suggest.

I am my beloved's; and he is mine (Sg 7:11).

The conversion of the synagogue is described, and this part is divided into two: First, knowing the great beauty she is to obtain through Christ, the synagogue turns toward him; secondly, she seeks support and help to do this, where she says: *come, my beloved.* But it should be noted that, for the interpretation of the text, it is necessary to explain the part from the words: *What will you see in the Shulammite maiden,* to the words: *I said: shall climb,* as concerning the beauty which God foresaw for the synagogue, and the passage following this, as was said. But in explaining the words describing the beauty foreseen for the synagogue, whether that beauty ought to be explained in relation to anger and lust as was suggested, or in relation to all the members of the synagogue, making the eyes stand for preachers, the head for prelates, or in any other way, providing the interpretation is based on the literal text, no harm is done. And what has been said of the exposition of this part is to be understood for the many expositions made earlier. We, however, in accordance with the scanty measure of intelligence divinely bestowed on us, have made our commentary reasonably clear, and have tried to make some things suit the contexts of the text as a whole. But the text may be interpreted as follows: *I,* the synagogue, understand that I cannot achieve the beauty foreseen for me by God except through Christ, therefore *I am my beloved's,* that is, I turn toward my beloved, and ask him to be mine.

Lecture 17

Come, my beloved, let us go out into the fields (Sg 7:12).

After turning to Christ, the synagogue seeks his help and support. She does two things: first she seeks support, secondly she recognizes and acknowledges his incarnation, where she says: *If only you were my brother.* About the first she makes three points: first she seeks Christ's support; secondly she specifies the support, where she says: *let us see if the vine has budded;* thirdly she shows the disposition of the Jews to receive such support, where she says: *I shall give you my breasts.* But in seeking Christ's support, she does three things. First she asks Christ to help her in proportion to her need; secondly to help her constantly, where she says: *let us stay in the vineyards;* thirdly to help her carefully and eagerly, where she says: *let us go early.* It may be interpreted as follows: it is through you, my beloved, that I must achieve my beauty. Therefore, as she says: *come, my beloved,* to my help; and *let us go out into the field,* that is, to the Jews, who are an untilled field. And she says that the Jews, still small in faith, can neither gain access to you nor rise to your level, so you must go out to them and come down to them and thus she seeks help in proportion to her need.

Let us stay in the vineyards (Sg 7:13).

She asks for such help constantly. But it may be interpreted as follows: It is not enough, my beloved, that we go out into the field, that is, to the Jews themselves, helping them in proportion to their need, but we must stay in the vineyards, that is, the Jews who are the vineyards, and as it were rustic and thus uncultivated. Hence we must *stay in the vineyards,* helping them constantly.

Let us go early to the vineyards (Sg 7:13).

She asks for such help to be given to her carefully and eagerly. Hence she says: *let us go early,* that is, at the right time. Let us not be lazy, but eagerly and carefully *let us go early to the vineyards,* that is, to the Jews, helping those who were your vineyard before, and still want to return to being your vineyard.

And see if the vine has budded, or its blossom has opened, and if the pomegranates are in flower.

She specifies the help and support she needs. As proof of this it should be noted that our goodness, as it relates to the present, appears to consist of three things, namely, good thoughts which belong to the intellect, good feelings which belong to the emotions, and works which belong to achievement. Goodness of thought, understood by the blossom, depends on a good will; similarly goodness of external acts. For the thoughts that a man has, however intelligent and intellective, lacking a right will, cannot please, and are blossoms that fail to open. In the same way external acts without a good will cannot prevail, but are useless fruit, and rightly so, for nothing is meritorious except as it proceeds from the will. But external acts are symbolized by pomegranates which contain many seeds. For what is inwardly perceived by the intellect is indicated outwardly by a diversity of works; sometimes what is uncompounded in the heart is multiplied in numerous ways in action and is explained. Therefore in specifying the help she needs from Christ she mentions three things: First she asks Christ to come to her help by moving the hearts of the Jews to think the right thoughts. Therefore she says: *to see,* with the eye of mercy, that is, with you and I cooperating in many ways, *if the vine has budded,* that is, if the intellect produces good thoughts. Secondly, she asks him to move their hearts to a right will. Therefore she adds: and see if *its blossom has opened,* that is, if good feelings are produced through good works, which with your help must be so. Thirdly she asks Christ to move the Jews to good works outwardly. Therefore she says: and see *if the pomegranates are in flower,* that is, the good works done with your help. But there is good authority for using blossom and fruit as symbols for good thoughts and good works, for fruit is food, and we are fed by good feelings, as it is said in Sirach 15:3: *She has fed him with the bread of life and understanding;* and likewise by good works, according to the psalm: *Because you will eat the fruit of your labor, you will be blessed* (Ps 128:2).

Good thoughts are rightly the blossom which precedes the fruit of good feelings and works. Again these three can be compared to a reward: and so, since all the above-mentioned, that is, thoughts, feelings, and actions, come first, they can be called the blossom of the reward, which is called the fruit, as in the psalm: *Since he grants sleep to those he loved; this is the inheritance of the Lord: children, the reward of the fruit of the womb* (Ps 127:2-3).

It is clear, however, that works can individually be called blossoms; for as they, first appear on the tree with fragrance, they are blossoms. But the odor of a good reputation for the edification of others a man has from the goodness of his works, not of his thoughts or feelings, which make no outward appearance. Rightly, then, the flowers of the pomegranate stand for good works, which must show successive growth or increase, like the flowering pomegranates; for some will be at the preparatory stage or new-born, some in fullswing or in flower.

I shall give you my breasts.

After seeking Christ's help, and in describing the help the Jews need in particular, that is, for thinking, willing, and acting properly, she shows here that the Jews are disposed to receive such help. And she makes three points to correspond with the threefold help required. First she shows them well disposed with regard to the intellect; secondly with regard to the emotions, where she says: *the mandrakes*; thirdly with regard to external works, where she says: *all choice fruits.* It may be interpreted as follows: therefore I ask you, my beloved, to come into my vineyard, for *there I will give you my breasts*; that is, my Jews, meaning my dearest ones, because of a pastoral relationship, who are called breasts because of their disposition to receive the milk of your learning. For just as breasts are properly the receptacle of milk, so because of the disposition of the intellect, they will properly be the receptacle of your teaching, which is milk for its whiteness and nutritive value, when no error is mixed with it.

The mandrakes give out their fragrance at our door (Sg 7:14).

She shows them to be well disposed with regard to the emotions or will. Hence it is interpreted as follows: Not only, my beloved, are the Jews well disposed with regard to the intellect, but also with regard to the emotions. For *the mandrakes*, that is, the Jews, *give out their fragrance* because of the goodness of their desires and the disposition of their emotions. They give out, I say, their fragrance, and this *at our door*, that is, in their approach to us. For they wish to be converted and to enter us, you principally, and me, the Church, in consequence, insofar as the gifts of grace or the sacraments are to be derived from you, and passed on to them through me as through their mother.

It should be noted that the mandrake is a plant, whose root has members like those of a human being, but no head. Hence it symbolizes the Jews, because now they are without a head; but in the end they too will express a desire for the preaching and fragrance of the Church, so as to be joined to Christ the head.

All choice fruits, new and old, I have stored up for you, my beloved (Sg 7:14).

She shows that the Jews are well disposed with regard to the goodness of external works. Hence she says: *my beloved, I have stored up for you,* that is, have trusted to your providence, *all choice fruits, new,* that is, when they had to be gathered and how preserved. Hence she also adds: and *old,* as if to say, only the providence of your grace knows when the Jews must be gathered and how preserved, who by the gift of your grace will be gathered as choice fruits, new and old. For according to the examples and first witnesses of the New and Old Testament, they will be busy with good works.

Lecture 18

Who will give you to me as my brother, sucking the breasts of my mother? (Sg 8:1).

Here she recognizes and acknowledges Christ's incarnation. She makes four points. First, showing her confidence in Christ because of his incarnation, she asks him to allow her to receive his true teaching. Secondly she asks if she may taste his delightful sweetness, where she says: *so that I may find you.* Thirdly she seeks to avoid the disgrace she had endured in former times because of her blindness, where she says: *and now no one may despise me.* Fourthly she desires to keep hold of Christ for the benefit of her children, where she says: *I shall take hold of you.* It may be interpreted as follows: As you have become my brother through teaching me, therefore *who will give you to me as my brother, sucking the breasts of my mother?* — that is, explaining the law to me, and holy scripture, which is as it were my mother. For one who sucks milk concealed in the breast draws it out. Christ did this, by drawing out into the open the milk and sweetness concealed in the divine law, as we are told in the last chapter of Luke (24:27): *Beginning with Moses and all the prophets, he explained to them what was said about himself in all the scriptures.* Therefore to have Christ sucking the breasts of the law means to have him as teacher and master of the law. But it should be noted that although we can all call Christ our brother because he assumed humanity, yet the synagogue in particular can call him brother because he was born of a Jew.

So that I may find you alone outside and kiss you.

The synagogue asks to taste the delight of Christ. It may be interpreted as follows: Lord Jesus Christ, not only do I seek you as sucking the breasts of my mother, in other words, teaching me, but I seek *to find you outside*, that is, not enclosed in the law nor concealed in the bosom of the father, but outside in human nature, according to which you are my brother. And so through knowing and loving you, *I may kiss you*, through receiving delight and sweetness from you.

And now no one will despise me.

She seeks to avoid the disgrace she endured in the past for her blindness. Hence she says: *And now no one will despise me*, as if to say, up to now I have been despised as if I was blind, because I did not know you, my redeemer; but now that I recognize you, I ask no one to despise me, in reproach for my former blindness.

I shall take hold of you and bring you into my mother's house and into the bedchamber of her who bore me.

She shows that she wishes to keep hold of Christ for the benefit of her children. But this part is divided into four. First the synagogue announces the benefit as such. Secondly it reveals what kind of benefit it is, where she says: there you will teach me. Thirdly, because it seemed from this that the synagogue had undertaken the care of the children, she explains what kind of care is to be used, where she says: *his left arm under my head*. Fourthly and lastly Christ's words are quoted, in approval of such an explanation, where he says: *I adjure you, daughters.*

It may be interpreted as follows: Not only, my beloved, do I wish to have you outside to kiss you, receiving your sweetness: but I also want to have you for the benefit of my children. Hence I ask you to allow me to *take hold of you* and thus *bring you into my mother's house*, that is, into the hearts of those who know more about the law, the law that I regard as a mother, whose commands I must keep as those of a mother. And also *I shall bring you into the bedchamber of her who bore me*, that is, into the hearts of the children who know less about the law, which I regard as my mother, and her who bore me. For a house is larger than a bedroom. Hence the hearts of those who have a more abundant and more perfect knowledge of the law are the house of the law, or of the mother of the synagogue, while those who know less about the law are the bedchamber of the law, or of her who bore the synagogue. There is also another possible way of interpreting it: that those who know more about the law are the bedchamber, for they are experts in deciphering the law and its obscurities, while the house represents those who know less about the law, that is, who know only what is obvious and anyone can easily understand. However, this is quite irrelevant, as the basic interpretation remains the same.

There you will teach me; and I shall give you a cup of spiced wine and the juice of my pomegranates.

She shows what kind of benefit there would be for the children, if Christ was brought into their hearts. And she mentions three in particular: the illumination of the intellect, the kindling of the emotions, good works, or increased effect. The illumination of the intellect is suggested in the words: *there you will teach me*, if I bring you into the hearts of my children by illuminating their intellect, because otherwise they could not be taught. For what is done for her children, like a good mother the synagogue regards as done for herself, and therefore she says: *there you will teach me.* Then she suggests the kindling of emotion in the words: *And I shall give you a cup of spiced wine,* that is, after such enlightenment of the intellect, the not ungrateful children will give you a cup, that is kindled affection and desire, *of spiced wine,* that is full of abundant spiritual joy, or the sweetness of grace and the delight of contemplation. She suggests good works, in the words: *and the juice of my pomegranates,* that is, external works, which are called juice, because just as such juice is squeezed out of pomegranate seeds, so are external good works from a pure heart and perfect love. And the heart can be called a pomegranate because it contains the affections like small seeds reddened and adorned by love. This I shall give you, Christ, as a pleasing gift. These, therefore, are the benefits for which I desire you, Christ, to come into the hearts of my children, that is, to illuminate their intellect, kindle their emotions, and increase their effectiveness.

His left arm will be under my head, and his right arm will embrace me.

For because the synagogue had sought to hold Christ for the benefit of her children, she seemed to be caring for her children. Here she explains how this care is to be understood. Her explanation runs as follows: that the synagogue, or Church or church leader, who can be understood by the foregoing, must first attend to himself through the contemplative life and then to his subjects through the active life. Therefore the synagogue, the Church or the church leader says: his left arm, that is, Christ's left arm, by which is understood the active life, will be *under my head*, that is, a secondary concern, *and his right arm*, that is, the contemplative life, through which I attend to myself, *will embrace me*, that is, will be over me and cover me, because first I shall attend to myself, afterward to you.

I adjure you, daughters of Jerusalem, not to wake and not to disturb my love until she is ready.

Christ confirms what the synagogue had made clear, saying: *daughters of Jerusalem, I adjure you,* I beseech you, *not to wake* from rest, *and not to disturb my love,* that is, the synagogue our mother, who is my beloved, from the sleep of contemplation, because she has converted to me, *until she is ready,* since she must first attend to herself, afterward to you.

Who is she coming up from the desert, full of delight, leaning upon her beloved?

There follows the final part of the treatise on her conversion, and it ends in praise of her. She is commended in four ways, first for her ascent, because to ascend to God is praiseworthy and even wonderful. Therefore it says in admiration: who is she coming up? Secondly, she is commended for the place of her ascent, in the words: *from the desert,* that is, from the thorns of tribulation and the thistles of affliction. For in the early Church there was great tribulation and persecution, and there will be greater in the end. Therefore though it has praised the Church of the present day, it has not praised it as it coming up from the desert or through the desert, but as the rising dawn. Thirdly the Church is commended in her final stage for her adornment, in the words: *full of delights,* that is adorned with good desires and good works, as the gloss seems to explain. Fourthly and finally she is commended for the manner of her ascent, in the words: *leaning on her beloved,* that is on Christ, by whose power she ascends. For that very reason the Church herself is worthy of commendation, for it is a great honor to follow one's Lord (Sir 24:27) but a greater one to lean on him, because it is a sign of greater love, as it is said of Saint John, the evangelist, that he reclined on the breast of the Lord (Jn 13:25).

Lecture 19

Under the apple tree I raised you up. There your mother was corrupted, there she who bore you was violated (Sg 8:15).

Earlier a description was given of the conversion of the synagogue. In this part the Church is invited to take care of and help the synagogue now converted. This part is divided into three: first Christ reminds the Church of the kindness and help he has given her; secondly in repayment for this he asks for her perpetual love, where he says: place me like a seal; thirdly, for the very love which the Church is bound to have for Christ, he invites her to help the synagogue, where it is said: *we have a little sister.*

Christ therefore reminds the Church of the Gentiles of the gift he has bestowed on her, saying *under the apple tree,* that is, under the cross, which is called *arbor malus* (apple tree or evil tree), either because it was there literally for evil, or because the tree of the cross was fruitful, like an apple tree. Under the cross, then, or under such a tree, *I raised you up.* For the Church of the Gentiles was dead, but by accepting the gift of the cross, it came to life again. But he tells how he raised the Church of the Gentiles up, saying *there,* that is, *under the apple tree,* or under the cross, *your mother was corrupted,* that is, by idolatry, which you followed like a mother, and which made you blind; *there she who bore you was violated,* that is, you accepted your wickedness, which you copied as if you got it from your mother, and so your affections became perverted.

Place me like a seal on your heart, like a seal on your arm (Sg 8:6).

He asks for perpetual love, and makes two points: first he begs for the aforementioned love; secondly he produces various reasons for doing so, where he says: *For love is strong.* It may be interpreted as follows: You, Church of the Gentiles, have been raised up by me through the passion of the cross: for by such suffering I have removed the error of idolatry from your intellect, and wickedness from your affections. Therefore since I have bestowed such great good on you, *place me like a seal on your heart,* by loving me forever, doing nothing against my wishes, and you must do nothing to displease me. So what we must understand by the seal on the heart is the love stamped on it, by which the soul becomes one with God, cleaving inseparably to him, and, by the seal on the arm, external good works, because the arm is outside.

For love is as strong as death; jealousy as cruel as hell.

He gives various reasons for what he had said. As proof of this it should be noted that one reason for which we owe God perpetual love is inferred from the benefits bestowed on us. And he touched on this earlier, in saying: *Under the apple tree I raised you up.* Another reason is inferred from love itself. For since God loves us, it is right that we should love him. But Christ's love for us has four conditions, which four reasons can be inferred for which we owe him perpetual love. The first reason is inferred from the immensity of his love. The second from the advantage of his love, where he says: *its lamps.* The third from the strength or stability of his love, where he says: *many waters cannot quench love.* The fourth from the value of his love, where he says: *if a man gave.* The first reason runs as follows: Everyone owes perpetual love to one who loves him immeasurably and to the last degree; but, Church, I, Christ, love you beyond measure, so to show your gratitude, you owe me perpetual love. For this reason only one condition is assumed, that is, Christ's immense love for the Church. Hence the text is interpreted as follows: Church, it is right that you should place me like a seal on your heart and your arm, so as to love me perpetually, and not work against me; for the love that I have for you is and has been surpassing and boundless. It is *as strong as death,* and was literally so great that death separated soul from body when I chose to die for love of you, so that you should live. Also *jealousy,* that is, the violation of love, which I felt for you, was as *cruel as hell,* because the pains that I endured for love of you were like the pains of hell. For no pain on earth could compare with mine, as in the words of Lamentations 1:12: *all you who pass by, come and see if there is any sorrow like mine.*

Its lamps are lamps of fire and flames.

It induces a second reason, which runs as follows: everyone owes perpetual love to him from which love he gains great benefit. You, Church, have gained great benefit from the love which I have had and have for you; therefore, etc. For this reason only one condition is assumed. It may be interpreted as follows: I am right to say that you must love me perpetually, for its lamps, that is, the lamps of love, which I have and have had, are understand lamps of great advantage; for they are lamps of the fire that purified your intellect and kindled your affections toward all good. They are lamps *of flames* insofar as they have illuminated your intellect toward all essential truth, for from Christ's love for us we gain the perfection of intellect and emotion, than which nothing is more useful to us in this life.

Many waters cannot quench love, nor rivers sweep it away (Sg 8:7).

For this he addresses a third reason, which runs as follows: Everyone owes perpetual love to one who loves him perpetually and constantly. I, Church, have loved you perpetually and constantly; therefore, etc. For this reason only one condition is assumed. The text may be interpreted as follows: Church, by rights you ought to love me perpetually, because I have loved you perpetually and constantly. This is clear because *many waters*, that is, many troubles, numerous in quantity and disastrous in magnitude, *cannot quench love, nor rivers*, swiftly flowing, *sweep it away*, that is, the love with which I have loved and love you.

If a man gives away the whole wealth of his house for love, he will despise it as nothing.

For this he assumes a fourth reason, which runs as follows: Everyone owes perpetual love to one who loves him with a dear and previous love. Such is the love, Church, with which I have loved you; therefore, etc. For this reason only one condition is assumed. The text may be interpreted as follows: Church, by rights you ought to love me perpetually for I have loved you with a love very dear and precious. For my love is so precious that *if a man gives away the whole wealth of his house for the love* which I had and have for you, it cannot be made to equal the price of that love by its weight on the scales. On the contrary, if he thinks it over, *he will despise it as nothing*, and assess his wealth in respect of my love, to which nothing earthly can be compared since it surpasses it beyond comparison.

We have a little sister who has no breasts. What shall we do for our sister on the day when she has to be spoken to? (Sg 8:8).

For the love that the Church must have for Christ, Christ invites her to help the synagogue now converted. But it should be noted that, not without cause, Christ gave so many reasons to show that the Church must love him greatly. For if out of such love Christ means to persuade the Church for love of himself to come to the aid of the converted synagogue at the end of time, because at that time there will be a great persecution, it was not superfluous to give the aforesaid reasons. But this part is divided into three: first, there is Christ's invitation; secondly is added the specific nature of the said invitation, where he says: *if she is a wall;* thirdly the Church's answer, where she says: *I am a wall.* His invitation, then, implies the following argument: Whoever loves someone very much must, for love of him, come to the aid of all who have an affinity and connection with him; but you, Church, owe me great love, as has been shown; therefore you must support the synagogue which matters to me and is connected to me, for she is my sister. And the greater her need the more energetic must be your support. And so it will be for the synagogue at the end of time, for he says: *we have a sister,* by my carnal affinity, by your spiritual affinity, for she is to be gathered into the fold for the same grace.

And so you must be moved by affection, because she is connected to me and is to be connected to you. You must also be moved to this by her need, because she is *little,* recently converted, and so needs confirmation. And *breasts,* that is, teachers, *she has not* of her own, nor can have except her own, and therefore she needs your instruction for you to nourish her with the milk of doctrine. Accepting this invitation to help the synagogue, the Church asked to be taught by her bridegroom and master, saying: *What shall we do for our sister on the day when she has to be spoken to,* to censure her error? — as if asking what help she needed.

If she is a wall, let us build bulwarks of silver on it. But if she is a door, let us frame it with panels of cedar (Sg 8:9).

Christ replies to the question, and specifies what help ought to be given to the synagogue. As proof of this it should be noted that, as in a natural being a thing first receives that by which it can subsist in its acquired form, this being the first thing it is capable of doing from its begetting, and later receives the power to produce a being like itself in form which it is unable to do before reaching maturity, since each single thing reaches maturity when it is to beget its likeness (*Physics* 7, 18), so in a spiritual being, man first receives the power to stand up as a gift imbued in him from heaven, and then he is called a wall, because he has the power to stand up, not to move others; and later when he has reached maturity in that gift, he receives the power to lead others to Christ, and then he is called a door because he is able to introduce others to Christ.

In view of this, the text may be interpreted as follows. You, Church, ask me and want me to teach you what help ought to be given to the synagogue. This I say specifically, that *if she is a wall*, that is, not yet mature in spiritual being, because she has no power to introduce others to me, but only to stand, then so that she may persevere more firmly and more constantly, *let us build*, I principally, with you as my subordinate cooperating with me, *on it*, that is, on the said wall, *bulwarks of silver*. These stand for the firm and shining sayings of scripture, as silver is firm and shining, by which hearts are strengthened in faith and love, as is said in that passage of the psalms: *Strengthen me with your words*. Through these we avoid the temptations of heretics and demons. *But if*, that is, if *she is* not a wall *but a door*, that is, if the synagogue has already reached such perfection that others can be introduced to me through here, *let us frame it with panels of cedar*, that is, let us so adorn her with texts and examples of the saints that, by the loveliness of her company and the good odor of her reputation, others may more easily be induced to come to me through such a door.

I am a wall, and my breasts are like towers (Sg 8:10).

The Church's response is given, and this part is divided into two. First in her reply the Church indicates that she is ready and willing to help the synagogue; secondly, as a result of this, the synagogue becomes eager for the Church's love and acknowledges her to be derived from Christ, and that the Church is her guardian and protector, where she says: *then I became*. It may be interpreted as follows: I, the Church, have been invited by you, Lord Jesus Christ, to help the synagogue, whether it is a wall or a door. And I say that for love of you I am prepared to help the synagogue, not only insofar as she is a door, that is, insofar as she has reached maturity of being, because this would be no great but a trifling matter; or rather, as she is a wall, that is, has not yet reached maturity of being, I am prepared not only to build *bulwarks of silver* of divine gifts, but also to make myself a wall for her confirmation, as it is written in 2 Corinthians 12:15: *I myself shall spend and spend myself to the limit for your sakes.* This, then, is what the Church says: *I* want to be a wall to strengthen the synagogue, that is, to give myself; *and therefore my breasts,* that is, my teaching, will be *like towers,* because through all the devotion I give to it the teaching will be manifestly clearer, more exalted and more efficacious as a defense.

Then I became in his presence like one finding peace. There was a vineyard belonging to the peacemaker, in that which holds the peoples (Sg 8:10).

The synagogue, seeing the Church's love for her, because for love of God she was prepared to give herself for her confirmation, becomes eager to love the Church. She who before used to call the Church adulterous, degraded and alienated from God, acknowledges now that she is the true bride of Christ, derived from him and preserved by him. So this part is divided into two: for first there is the synagogue's confession concerning the Church; secondly, in case the synagogue's confession seems inadequate, there is Christ's supplement, where he says: *my vineyard.* The first is divided into two: first the synagogue acknowledges the Church's derivation from Christ; secondly she acknowledges that the Church is protected and preserved by Christ, where she says: *he has let it out.*

The first part may be interpreted as follows: I, the synagogue, out of my hatred for you, formerly neither recognized nor considered him to be the true God, in the blindness of my understanding. Therefore I hated the Church too, and did not believe her to be the true vineyard of Christ. But then *I became in his presence,* that is, Christ's, *like one,* expressive words, spoken with certainty, *finding peace* through the illumination of faith and the remission of sins. I am correcting my error and my sin and acknowledging the Church to be the true spouse of Christ, for love of whom she is ready to do everything she can to enable me to obtain the salvation that is to be forever in Christ. Hence with mouth and heart I truly acknowledge her to be the true bride of Christ. *And there was a vineyard belonging to the peacemaker,* that is, to Christ, who brought peace to the world, *in that which* (understand: faith) *holds the peoples,* that is, in the Catholic faith, which is the same because universal, that is, of many peoples. It should also be noted that she does not say in that faith, that is, which the peoples hold, but which holds the peoples, for any divine gift possesses us more than we possess it, insofar as gifts of such kind of respect of good works are (far above) our own free will.

He has let it out to guardians; a man brings for its fruit a thousand silver coins (Sg 8:11).

She shows that the Church is protected and maintained by Christ, saying: I was right to say that the Church was a vineyard belonging to Christ himself. For Christ *has let it out to guardians,* that is, to the angels, apostles, and clergy, one of whom *a man (vir),* that is of vigor *(vires),* working in that vineyard, with a heart full of faith brings to Christ himself *a thousand silver coins,* that is, he gives Christ all the income from its fruit, whether temporal or spiritual.

My vineyard is in my own hands. You have a thousand peacemakers; and there are two hundred for the guardians of its fruit (Sg 8:12).

Because the foregoing confession might be wrongly understood by some, in this part Christ supplements the synagogue's confession. And concerning this, he makes two points: first he supplements the said confession; secondly, because of the synagogue's love for the Church, he invites the Church to support the synagogue, where he says: *you who dwell in the gardens.* In two ways however, someone might think that desertion was implied in the synagogue's aforementioned confession. First, in the assignment to tenure; because she had said that Christ has let it out to guardians, someone might think that Christ had deserted it. To prevent this, Christ supplies: *My vineyard is in my own hands,* as if to say, I let out my Church to be guarded by others in this way, because I myself was also in direct charge of it, since I am the true God who maintains all things without intermediary. Secondly, in the assignment of the fruit, because she had said: *a man brings for its fruit a thousand silver coins.* Since, in the Church, by the name "men" the active members may be understood, anyone might think from this that only those active in the Church bore fruit. Therefore the Lord supplements this confession, showing that the contemplatives in the Church also bear fruit. And so he adds: Church, *your peacemakers,* that is, contemplatives, who are called pacific because they are secluded from the disturbance of worldly affairs, there are (I say) *a thousand* such as these, that is, yielding perfect fruit.

It was said above that *a man brings for its fruit a thousand silver coins, and the peacemakers are a thousand,* that is, the contemplatives, perfect in number and fruitfulness. Since for the perfect life it is essential to have not only the contemplative but also the active life for the care of others, nevertheless there is greater merit in contemplation than in action. And so after it says: *you have a thousand peacemakers*, it adds: *and two hundred who guard the fruit*, that is, the merits of the Church. Here a large number is doubled, namely, a hundred, which even doubled fails to reach the ultimate limit of the numbers, which is a thousand. For even though the contemplative life is of greater merit, nevertheless the active combined with the contemplative is meritorious in a greater number of ways. Hence above the words: *two hundred*, etc. the interlinear gloss says: "He merits a double reward who both looks after himself and converts others."

You who dwell in the gardens, my friends are listening; let me hear your voice (Sg 8:13).

Christ invites the Church to come to the aid of the synagogue, because the synagogue loves her. In this there are two stages: first there is his invitation; secondly the Church's response, where she says: *Come away, my beloved.* It may be interpreted as follows: Up to now I have been persuading you, Church, to come to the aid of the synagogue for love of me. Therefore since the synagogue herself clearly loves you, for she has confessed that you, the Church, are my true bride and my vineyard, such a friendship, which has been formed with you through me, by a single confession, love and faith, ought to move you to come to her aid. And this is what he says: You, Church, *who dwell in the gardens* in spiritual delight, *my friends*, that is, the Jews, who have now become your friends for being my faithful one, are listening, that is, are ready and *waiting for you*, to hear and be taught by you. They show their desire, their heart's wish, saying: Church, *let me*, the synagogue, united to you by faith and love, *hear your voice*, that is, through preaching. This can also be taken as the words of Christ, inviting the Church to teach the synagogue. And he says: let me hear your voice, because he considers that what is done for others for his sake is done for himself.

Flee, my beloved, and be like the roe or a young stag on the spice-bearing mountains (Sg 8:14).

This is the Church's reply, which is that, like a good bride, she wishes for a time to be separate from Christ, not from his faith or love, but from his sweetness, that is, to cease from the sweetness of contemplation for a time, so that, now that the Jews have been converted and thus have become brothers, she can apply herself to instructing them in morals and doctrine. So she says: *You, my beloved*, that is, you, Christ, who dwell on the spice-bearing mountains, for the height of devotion and the repute of good behavior and holy works, *flee*, that is, take away the sweetness of contemplation from me, to give me more time for teaching and training the Jews. All the same I do not wish this to be forever, but only for a time. So she says: *and be like the roe*, observing my defects; and since you are essential to me for contemplation, *be also like a young stag*, so as to return to me swiftly through contemplation, and imbue me with delightful contemplation. And may Christ think us worthy to have such an experience in this present life through our status as wayfarers, and in the future life through the clear vision of understanding, Christ, who with the Father and the Holy Spirit lives and reigns forever. Amen.

Treatises

The Ark of Noah

Noah's ark signifies redemption in Christ

On the creedal formula that Christ is "one person in two natures," which we firmly believe in the Catholic faith, the gloss says: "This was prefigured in the ark of Noah, where the redemption of the saints was accomplished through two natures, according to opinion and truth." But since this gloss is obscure, I have sought how to understand it, and have concluded that the words should be construed in this way: This (that is, how there is a double nature in Christ) was prefigured in the ark of Noah, where (that is, in which ark or by which ark) the redemption of the saints was accomplished through two natures, according to opinion and truth (that is, as far as figure and reality; the former is figurative rather than an expression of literal truth, and thus can be called an opinion, something inferred and related to the truth). Three things, then, shall be discussed: first, how there is a double nature in Christ and how this was prefigured in the ark of Noah; second, how the redemption of the saints was accomplished through two natures in the ark according to truth; and third, how this was accomplished according to opinion or figuratively.

Multiplicity of natures

In the first place it must be known that Christ's nature can be understood in two ways, either simply or with qualification. Simply speaking, there was a double nature in Christ because both divinity and humanity were in him. But in a qualified sense, or speaking from the perspective of his humanity, there were various natures within him, or each nature was assumed differently in him. In

179

Christ were reason and emotion: superior and inferior reason, and irascible and concupiscible appetites.

We also observe that in Noah's ark existed a variety and diversity of four natures. First was the nature of birds and animals. The nature of animals was also multiple, namely rational and sensible, since there were humans and beasts in the ark. The rational nature was further divided into male and female. The sensible nature was also distinguished into wild and tame, since there were wild and tame animals in the ark.

We may apply and fit these four natures to the natures of Christ and say that avian nature, which is heavenly, signifies his divinity, while animal nature, which is earthly, signifies his humanity. The rational nature signifies his reason and the sensible nature his emotion. Masculine nature signifies his superior reason, feminine nature his inferior reason, for between superior and inferior reason there is a certain joining, as between male and female, according to Augustine in his book *The Trinity*. Wild nature signifies his irascible appetite and tame nature his concupiscible appetite. Thus all the differences of animal nature residing in the ark may be linked with the variety of Christ's nature according to this correspondence. It is well said, then, that this (that is, how there is a double nature in Christ) was prefigured in the ark of Noah.

Literal correspondence

With this first matter discussed, namely how the double nature in Christ was prefigured in the ark of Noah, we now wish to address the second matter, namely how the redemption of the saints was accomplished through two natures in the ark according to truth. This can be approached in four ways: first in terms of the persons dwelling within Noah's ark; second in terms of those who descended from them; third in terms of Christ, who assumed flesh from their stock; and fourth in terms of the other creatures dwelling in the ark.

As to the first it must be said that in terms of the persons dwelling within Noah's ark, the redemption of the saints in the ark was truly through two natures, that is, through male and female. And this was a liberation of saints in truth because both natures were truly liberated by the ark. Thus it is written in Genesis 6:9 that *Noah was a just and perfect man in his generation.* Concerning Noah himself there is no doubt that he was just when he entered the ark. But the others as well, both male and female, during their time in the ark, truly held themselves pure and holy. When it records that *Noah entered and his sons, his wife and his sons' wives* (Gn 7:7), the gloss says it was rightly commemorated that the males entered, followed by the females, because the time of marital embracing had not yet come. It should be understood, then, that they were obligated to hold themselves clean and holy within the ark. Thus the four men and four women in the ark were redeemed and liberated through the ark according to truth. And because they conducted themselves in this way, it is well said that the redemption of the saints, the liberation through the ark according to truth, was accomplished through two natures.

This is understood secondly in terms of those who descended from them. Since the whole human race, in which are many saints and elect, was multiplied from the few of Noah's family, the statement that redemption was accomplished in two natures is not at all figurative, but literal. In other words, salvation was accomplished through the ark in truth, because truly many of both natures, male and female, have been saved who descended from those in Noah's ark.

This can be confirmed thirdly concerning Christ, who assumed flesh from the stock of those within the ark. Since the entire human race was multiplied from those individuals, in literal truth the Son of God, who entered the Virgin after the flood, assumed his flesh from the stock of those in the ark. Through the two natures sheltered in the ark, the redemption of the saints was accomplished, for the human race was multiplied from the male and female nature kept in the ark, and from it the Son of God was incarnate, through whom was accomplished the redemption of the saints.

This is shown fourthly by considering the animals that were in the ark. Scripture records no eating of animal flesh before the flood, but only afterward. Thus many bodies of the saints were formed from food taken from the flesh of animals that were in the ark, or of other animals descending from them. Materially at least those animals served in forming the bodies of the elect who were saved and redeemed.

Figurative correspondence

Having seen, in the foregoing exposition, how redemption was accomplished through the two natures existing in the ark according to truth, it remains to show how this was so according to opinion, that is figuratively. Since the salvation of the just was accomplished in the ark, because Noah and many other just people were saved, and since the salvation of the just was also prefigured by the ark, the gloss makes a comparison in truth and in opinion or figure. The salvation of many was accomplished in Noah's ark, the redemption of the saints who took their being through the double nature within the ark.

We may take up again the four natures that we related to Christ, showing how the diversity of natures dwelling in the ark signified the diversity of natures in Christ, through whom the redemption of the saints was accomplished. Furthermore, if we wish, we can describe the four things by which the redemption of the saints is designated: first from the size of the ark, second from its form, third from its structure, and fourth from its material.

The first is evident since the size or length of the ark was 300 cubits, its width 50 cubits, and its height 30 cubits. Concerning these dimensions, Augustine says in Book XV of his *City of God* that it corresponds to the measurements of the human body, for the ark was six times as long as wide and ten times as long as thick, which is the proper proportion of the human body. That the ark's size followed the proportion of the human body signifies that the Son of God would come in humanity, by which the redemption of the saints was accomplished, as Augustine indicates in the same place.

This is clear secondly from the ark's form, for the ark was large at the bottom and narrow at the top; it was finished with one cubit at the top according to Genesis 6:16: *You shall finish its height in a cubit.* This well designates the present Church in which is salvation and the redemption of the saints. The Church is surely the large part below while the upper part is finished in a narrow space of one cubit, that is, in the one man, Christ. Hence the gloss says in the same place that the ark was wide below where the beasts were, but narrow above where the people resided, because the Church opens out into a wider hold where it sustains bestial men, while the space that holds rational men comes down to a point. For the holier in the Church are fewer, and this holds true until reaching the one who is at its height, who alone is without corruption: the holy Son, Christ.

This is evident in the third place from the ark's structure: there were upper rooms in the ark and third stories, that is, chambers with two and three compartments, as other passages suggest. And the gloss says there was also a door in the side. Augustine treats this subject in Book XV of *The City of God*, chapter 26, and teaches that all these things must be understood in such a way that the ark signifies the Church: It was two-chambered because the Church contains converted Jews and Greeks, or Jews and Gentiles. It was three-chambered because all of humankind was multiplied from the three sons of

Noah; and out of this human race many were converted to the faith, from whom the Church is made. The door in its side signifies the opening in Christ's side (as Augustine affirms there), out of which flowed the sacraments of the Church, whence is the entrance into the Church. Since the redemption of the saints must be through Christ and the Church, that structure of the ark signifies the redemption of the saints.

This is shown in the fourth place from its material, which was from smoothed, that is, squared, planks, and glued together with pitch. In the squared planks of wood the gloss understands the constancy of the saints, because a squared plank stands firm on every side. By glue is understood the bond of love that perfectly unites and glues together the saints. Through constancy and love we become partakers of redemption. Thus the material of the ark, smoothed and glued together in this way, signifies the redemption of the saints.

The ark having two natures, then, is understood as the redemption of the saints according to literal truth, as was argued, and also according to opinion, that is, figuratively, as is now manifest. And this suffices for the proposed question.

The Divine Influence in the Blessed

In which it is shown in five ways that God, not through another but immediately through himself, grants the influence by which all angels, both higher and lower, and also human beings, are beatified.

Our venerable father, lord of legions, has deigned in person to move our soul to consider a certain pregnant question that pertains to the Church triumphant, namely whether the lower angels, and each of them in particular, receive some special influence from God beyond the influence they receive through the mediation of higher angels. Now we call this question pregnant because by it we come to a question concerning the Church militant, namely whether it is useful to the saints that our father and lord, the highest pontiff, practice exemptions in the Church of God, so that divine influence flows immediately to some and rules them immediately within God's Church without the mediation of superiors. Although God rules physical substances through spiritual mediation, and lower bodies by the mediation of higher ones, nevertheless he sometimes acts beyond this order, for he heals many of the sick, who were incurable according to the order of superior bodies. Thus he raised Lazarus from the tomb where he had lain for four days, returning his body to the same identity it had before, which is against the order of planetary influences, as the philosopher says in *On Generation*: When their substance is lost they do not return to the same identity.

Concerning the first question, whether the lower angels, and each of them in particular, receive some special influence from God beyond the influence they receive through the mediation of higher angels, it must be said that this is not a question about bea-

tific influence since that influence is general and does not pertain
to the proposed question. Speaking about the influence according
to which the beatitude of the blessed exists, which is God himself,
it comes immediately from God to all angels and blessed souls, for
God himself, through himself, and without any mediation, is our
beatitude according to Genesis 15:1: *Fear not, Abraham. I am your
protector and your very great reward.* Thus God is our reward, and we
do not serve God in order to obtain any other reward besides God.
We must first seek the kingdom of God, which is God; afterward, all
else will be added to us. It follows, then, that when we seek additional things from God, we should seek them for God as our beatitude and our principal reward, as Augustine says in the first book
of his *Confessions*: "You have made us for yourself, O Lord, and our
heart is restless until it rests in you." Our proper beatitude, then,
in which our heart and our mind rest, is God.

We may enumerate five ways by which it is established irrefuta-
bly that our beatitude is God through himself, and that nothing
less than God and nothing other than God can beatify us, and not
only us but all angels as well. Our principal question is addressed
in these ways: the first is taken from the divine immensity; the second from his interiority; the third from his reality; the fourth from
his universality; the fifth from his rest and contentment.

The first way is clear because it is self-evident, for if some vessel
is able to hold so much wine, less wine than that cannot fill the
vessel. If some vessel is able to hold a fifth or full measure or whatever amount of wine, less than that cannot fill the vessel. Therefore
since a soul or an angel is able to contain such a good as God, a
lesser good than God cannot fill either soul or angel. According to
Augustine in book ten of his *Confessions*, "we cannot be blessed until we say it is enough," that is, until we are satisfied with the joy and
goodness of God. Being thus able to hold as much as God is, a
lesser good than God cannot beatify or satisfy us. That we can contain such a good as God follows from our being made according to
God's image and likeness.

According to Augustine in many places in his *Confessions*, God is
more intimate to anything than the thing itself to itself. God is
more intimate than our innermost being. Therefore since an angel
or an intellect is not quantitative, has no dimensions, and is not
divisible, according to the Master in discussing causes, an intellect
is an indivisible substance. And nothing can penetrate angel or
soul or any spiritual being except what can penetrate its very substance. We may assert, then, that if an angel or soul or any spiritual
substance desires to be beatified or satisfied by any good other than

the divine good, this is to desire to be satisfied by a good that does not penetrate itself nor enter into itself. It is clear that if the whole ocean encircled the shell of one egg or one nut, none of the water would enter the shell, and the entire ocean would not fill the shell. Therefore it is great foolishness for someone to desire to fill his soul with money and other external goods when they cannot enter into the soul. Such goods can fill a bag into which they can enter, but they cannot enter into an angel or soul, they cannot satisfy it. Only God, who is able to penetrate us and come under the essence of angel or soul, can satisfy and beatify angel or soul.

The third way for establishing this is seen from divine reality. There is a vast difference between having a thing itself principally and having its likeness or having it in intention. A person experiences this in himself, as James says about someone looking at his natural face in a mirror: *For he regarded himself and went his way, and presently forgot what kind of person he was* (Jas 1:24). Everyone experiences this in himself, for even if he has regarded the image of his face in a mirror a hundred times or more, he does not remember it as well as he remembers the face of another he has seen only once. From this it is evident how great a difference there is between a thing and the likeness or image of a thing. According to the philosopher in book three of *The Soul*, "Things are not in the soul, but likenesses or similitudes of things." Thus no matter how much these likenesses or similitudes are multiplied, they will not fill or satisfy a soul. God alone, who is able to be in the soul through himself in reality, can satisfy and beatify the soul. Augustine confirms this in book four of his *Confessions* where he speaks to the Lord within and above himself: "Where shall I find you teaching me unless in you and above me?" The soul, then, finds God in itself and above itself, for the soul is not in God unless God is in the soul: *Whoever abides in love, abides in God, and God in him* (1 Jn 4:16). We do not seek God in reality far off from us, God is in reality within us. Indeed according to Augustine in book three of his *Confessions*, "When we are far off from God by turning ourselves away through sin, he is still near to us in compassion and mercy, supporting and conserving us in our being."

The fourth way to show that God is our beatitude is from divine universality. Every creature is some particular good, but God alone is universal good. Augustine discusses this subject throughout book eight of *The Trinity*, chapter three, where he says: "What are all these many things, this good and that good? Remove this and that and behold good itself if you can, and you will see God, not a good beside another good, but the good of all good." Every creature, then, is a particular good because this is good and that is good, but God alone is universal good. He is not this or that particular good, but is all good universally, the good of every good, as is clear from the above passage.

We may argue thus: the soul or angel, possessing reason and understanding, is naturally suited to be brought into the universal good because, as the commentator says in *The Soul*, intellect is what makes universality in things. No particular good can satisfy or beatify an angel or soul since the universal good is far more than any particular good. God is universal good, unlike every creature which is some particular good, and thus God alone is able to satisfy and beatify the soul.

The fifth way is from divine rest and contentment. As long as something is in motion, it is not at rest. Therefore when we tend to the end itself through things that are directed toward the end, as long as we remain in the things toward the end we are in motion and do not rest. Since all creatures are ordered to God as to an end, strictly speaking there can be no rest in any creature, since no creature is the end simply or the end of all things. Only God is the end of all things because God alone, as the commentator maintains in book one of the *Metaphysics*, is a triple cause with respect to all things: God is the efficient cause of all, the formal and exemplary cause of all, and God alone is the final cause or end of all things. Thus our rest and beatitude can exist only in God. Since every creature is perishable and moveable, rest cannot exist simply in any creature, for whoever depends on something perishable must himself perish when it does.

God, without any mediating creature, beatifies both angels and souls. Returning, then, to the proposed question, when it is asked whether lower angels, and each of them in particular, receive any special influence from God beyond the influence they receive through mediation of higher angels, if this question concerns the divine influence whereby we are beatified by God, then because such influence cannot exist without the bestowal of consummate grace or without the bestowal of glory by which God beatifies and glorifies us, it is clear that the question is null, for God glorifies and beatifies every angel and every soul. Therefore with regard to such influence and beatification, God does not beatify lower angels through higher angels, but God beatifies every angel, both higher and lower, and also every soul.

Chapter Two

While angels were blessed by seeing and loving the one and triune God,
humans before the coming of Christ were never actually blessed by seeing the
deity and humanity of Christ, although they were blessed in hope.

After declaring what must be held concerning the influence
God gives to angels to make them blessed, namely that God beatifies all angels, both higher and lower, and also all souls immediately through God, we now wish to determine what should be held
concerning the influence or force that God brings to bear on angels, by which God reveals to them what pertains to the governing
of the universe. But we must first address a different point, because
some are mistaken about beatitude, saying that it is not necessary
that those who are blessed see the trinity of persons, but it is sufficient that they see the unity of essence. But this cannot stand, for
vision follows faith, according to the psalms: *As we have heard, so*
have we seen in the city of our God (Ps 48:8). Thus those things we now
hear of through faith (since *faith comes by hearing*— Rom 10:17) we
shall see in the city of our God, that is, in our heavenly homeland.
And we will proclaim the words of this psalm: As we have heard in
our wayfaring, so have we seen and will see in heaven. Keep in mind
that it is common for holy Scripture to use the past for the present
or even for the future in order to denote the stability and certainty
of the things spoken of in Scripture. For what has happened cannot be held not to have happened, inasmuch as a past or accomplished deed is so immutable that even God cannot make what has
happened not to have happened or what is past not to be past, as is
said in the *Ethics* of Agatho: "For God is deprived of this alone: to
undo what has already been done." To indicate this stability and
immutability, it may be stated in the present tense, that when we
are in heaven we will say: As we have heard in this life concerning
the unity of essence and the trinity of persons, so shall we see in
heaven. But holy Scripture expressed in the past what was able to
be stated in the present: As we have heard, so have we seen, though
it can be faithfully rendered: so shall we see.

Now let us return to the question and say that vision in heaven
follows faith in this life, which vision will be the full reward, as is
shown by Augustine in book one of *The Trinity*, chapters 8 and 9.
The truth that this vision is the full reward should not be understood in such a way that vision is separated from love and delight,
for to see what is not loved or what is not enjoyed would be more
conducive to pain than joy, it would be more misery than beatitude.

We accept the belief, which always gladdens us, that our beatitude consists more principally in love or delight, which is an act of the human will, than in knowledge or vision, which is an act of the intellect. Our beatitude consists in both an act of the will and an act of the intellect, but it consists more principally in love, an act of the will, than in vision, an act of the intellect. It is often said in our vernacular, when a person sees something he does not love, and perhaps it is hateful or displeasing to him, that he should have eyes when he sees it. It is impossible that someone should see such a surpassing good as God and not love God or delight in God, in whom there is nothing unlovable and nothing that does not delight. Therefore Augustine says in the aforementioned chapters that vision is the whole reward, taking vision in such a way that it includes love and delight.

Having examined these matters in light of the fact that vision succeeds faith, since these are articles of faith — not only that God is one in essence, but also that God is three in persons — our blessed vision in heaven which replaces faith in this life will not only be of God, one in essence, but also of God, three in persons. Thus we will see clearly and openly both one God essentially and the three persons. Yet even this vision will not suffice for our beatitude, just as it is not enough for faith to believe that God is one and three, unless we also believe that he was incarnate in the person of the Son, since only the person of the Son was incarnate.

The whole Trinity clothed the Son in flesh, since the Father and the Holy Spirit covered the Son in flesh, and the Son clothed himself in flesh. But although the three were engaged in covering, only one person was clothed in flesh according to the Athanasian Creed: "Whoever would be saved must acknowledge the Trinity, but for eternal salvation it is also necessary to believe in the incarnation of our Lord Jesus Christ." It is not enough, then, to believe that God is one and three if we do not believe that God the Son was incarnate, suffered, died, was buried, and rose again. The Lord himself, wishing to explain eternal life, which is our beatitude, touched upon all of these when he said: *This is eternal life: that they know you, the only true God, and him whom you have sent, Jesus Christ* (Jn 17:3). As Augustine establishes in his commentary on John, and as is maintained by the common tradition, these words should be understood as also referring to the Holy Spirit, who is love, the substance of both Father and Son. Thus the entire Trinity, Father, Son and Holy Spirit, is the one and only God, as Augustine explains in this place.

But it may be claimed to the contrary that vision of only one divine person seems to suffice for beatitude since it says: *Show us the*

Father and that is enough for us (Jn 14:8). But this is easily resolved by
the words of Christ himself when he answered Philip: *Philip, he who
sees me sees the Father also* (Jn 14:9). With regard to divinity, one person cannot be seen without another being seen, for all three persons have one and the same essence, one and the same power, and
one and the same operation. Because of their unity of essence, one
person cannot be seen without the other. They are joined by nature, that is, in natural intelligence. One person, then, is always
seen with the others not only on account of their essential unity
(since essence is the object of the intellect), but one person is not
seen or understood without another because of their relation to
each other, since they are joined to each other by nature.

It may also be objected that since deity is the principal object of
beatitude, humanity has no part in this object. To this it can be said
that while humanity is not the principal object of our beatitude, it
is nevertheless a connected object without which our beatitude
could not exist. For until the passion of Christ, however many holy
fathers passed away, they were not blessed in fact, since they did not
see God, but were only blessed in hope, having a firm hope of seeing God. All those dying before Christ's passion, even if they were
purged, still went to purgatory. After they had been purged they
went to the bosom of Abraham, that is, to the limbo of the holy
fathers.

As is often said, the order in Adam and in us is reversed, for with
Adam the infected person infected nature while with us the infected nature infected the person. For this reason we cannot see
God unless satisfaction be made for both infections, namely of nature and of person. Every generative and corruptible nature, including human nature, is of itself unlimited, at least in potential,
because it can multiply itself without end, although its essence cannot be multiplied forever. Only God is infinite essence and thus
only God was able make satisfaction for all human nature. According to Augustine in the first book of *The Trinity*, chapter 10: "If any
other way were possible to heal our misery, none was more fitting."

Therefore until the day of the passion of Christ, who died for
our salvation, there was no satisfaction sufficient for our nature;
but with his death the gate of heaven was opened and all that were
in the limbo of the holy fathers saw God. Thus the thief was told:
Today you will be with me in paradise (Lk 23:43), because on that day
the thief and Christ both died, and the thief's soul saw God. Our
beatitude, then, will consist in both the vision of divinity and the
vision of Christ's humanity, although more principally in the vision
of divinity.

Even though our beatitude will not be simply in the vision of Christ's humanity, it will nevertheless consist in his humanity insofar as without it our beatitude would not have happened, since before the incarnation of Christ, and before his passion and death, no pure person was beatified. The words of John can be interpreted with regard to this truth: *I am the door; if anyone enters through me he will be saved. He will go in* (by seeing divinity) *and go out* (by seeing the humanity of Christ) *and shall find pastures* (Jn 10:9) because both will be our joy and delight. It should be noticed, however, that before the resurrection of Christ the holy fathers in limbo saw the humanity of Christ, at least his soul that descended there, but that after his resurrection they saw his humanity in itself and his whole humanity. Therefore we conclude and declare that some things all the blessed see, namely the unity of God's essence, the trinity of persons, and the humanity of Christ. While the beatitude of angels existed without the vision of Christ's humanity, the beatitude of people did not.

With regard to the unity of essence and trinity of persons, then, every angel and person is beatified by God through God and in God through God. But with regard to the governance of the universe for the salvation of the elect, not only does the higher order of angels illumine the lower order, but also higher angels illumine the lower within the same order. For when it is declared in Isaiah 6:3 that the seraphim were crying out one to another, their cry may be understood as coming from angels seeking to be instructed, one from another. Our question, then, whether the lower angels, and each of them in particular, receive any special influence, etc., can be adapted to address this mediation of knowledge, which will be discussed in the following chapter.

Chapter Three

While God beatifies all angels and people immediately, as far as concerns the governance of the universe, God illumines and teaches intermediate angels through higher ones and lower angels through intermediate ones.

We were asked about the influence or illumination of lower angels by higher angels, and in order to answer the question we must discuss the verse: *Then comes the end, when he will have handed over the kingdom to his God and Father and abolished all rule and power and might,* etc. (1 Cor 15:24). The gloss maintains that as long as the world endures, angels rule angels, demons rule demons, and people rule people, to the benefit or to the deception of the living; but when all things are united, all rulership shall cease because it will no longer be necessary. At the consummation of the world, when the number of the elect is complete, all illuminations will cease, whereby lower angels are taught by the higher concerning the governance of the world so that the elect may receive their inheritance. Hence it is said *they are all ministering spirits, sent to serve those who receive the inheritance of salvation* (Heb 1:14), that is, to serve the elect.

Let us observe that angels have a twofold mission: to external and internal affairs. This is clearly shown in Isaiah: *And one of the seraphim flew to me, and in his hand was a coal he had taken with tongs from the altar,* etc. (Is 6:6). But it is certain that an angel from the order of seraphim was not sent to Isaiah, for the entire first hierarchy, containing the three orders whose highest is the seraphim, is in the inner court of God according to Dionysius, and no angel from these orders is sent to external things. According to Dionysius, *The Angelic Hierarchy*, book eight, this angel was from the lower orders since only the lower orders, not the higher, are sent, or at least no angel from the highest order is ever sent to external things. This angel, then, is called one of the seraphim, not by reason of his order, since he was of a lower order, but by reason of his mission, that is, by reason of his office. For "seraphim" means burning, that is, flaming, because they are completely aflame in love. The angel sent to Isaiah took a coal or stone from the altar with tongs. This coal or stone was burning or aflame with the fire in the censer of the altar. And he touched Isaiah's lips with the burning coal, which burned and scorched them, and thus purged his lips. Because of this burning and scorching he was called one of the seraphim, that is, a burning angel.

According to Dionysius, not all angels are sent, but only the lower ones. Yet the apostle says in Hebrews that all angels are ministering spirits, sent to serve those who will receive the inheritance of salvation, that is, for the salvation of the elect. Therefore it is necessary to distinguish their missions, as we have said. Let us say, then, that all angels are sent either to interior things, and the highest angels are sent in this way, or to external things, and only the lower are sent in this way. Even divine persons are said to be sent. The Father alone is not said to be sent, according to Augustine, because he is not from another. But the Son and the Holy Spirit are said to be sent visibly and invisibly. The Son was sent visibly in the flesh when he became human, and the Holy Spirit was sent visibly in the form of breath, when Christ blew upon his disciples, saying, *Receive the Holy Spirit.* The Spirit was also sent in the form of a dove when Christ was baptized by John, and again in the form of fire on the day of Pentecost. Just as both the Holy Spirit and the Son were sent visibly, so they are both sent daily invisibly. For the Son is sent invisibly to illumine the mind and the Holy Spirit to inflame the heart. But when divine persons are sent, they are not sent where they had never been, but where they had not been in a certain way, not by changing their location, but by repairing a defect in our nature, as Bede argues.

In the same way we can understand how the higher angels are sent. For when higher angels illumine lower angels, they are said to be sent to those whom they illumine concerning the governance of the world and the ruling of the universe. When it is asked, then, whether the lower angels, and each of them in particular, receive any special influence from God beyond the influence they receive through the mediation of higher angels, it can be said that if we are speaking about the influence by which an angel or person is made blessed, God alone produces this in us immediately through himself; but if we are speaking about the influence of illumination for the ruling of the universe, God produces this in lower angels by the mediation of higher angels. Dionysius affirms this in book four of *The Angelic Hierarchy*, saying: "By divine ordination promulgated through primary beings, secondary beings are brought back to God." And in chapter eight of the same book he says: "In the divine ordination from above, this is wholly promulgated by primary beings, that secondary beings may participate in divine illuminations." Thus it is the order and law of divinity that lower angels are brought back through the mediation of higher ones.

Every angel is beatified immediately by God by seeing God and loving God, but while each angel sees God as a kind of mirror, he does not yet see in that mirror all things shining in it. Continually, as long as the world endures, God reveals to higher angels those things which he ordains to accomplish in the universe for the salvation of the elect. And there is such order and harmony in the heavenly realm that the illuminations concerning the governance of the universe come to intermediate angels through their superiors, and these illuminations reach to the lower angels through the intermediate. And the higher order not only illumines the lower order with such illuminations, but also a higher angel within one and the same order illumines a lower angel, for it is held that the seraphim cry out one to another, which cry is nothing else than one angel seeking to be taught and illumined by another.

The question is not completely answered, when it asks whether lower angels receive any influence immediately from God beyond what they receive through the mediation of higher angels. Even if it is said that they receive the influence by which all angels are made blessed immediately by God, since God beatifies all without mediation, the question still remains concerning illumination for the governance of the universe, whether with regard to the ruling of people God immediately illumines lower angels through himself. It can be responded that just as there is one teacher in his chair, who speaks and moves the ears of all his students, so God is one teacher in heaven, who propels and moves the minds of all his angels. And while there are some things in a master's teaching so easy and light that all grasp them, there are other things that only the more astute grasp; and concerning these things the more astute teach and illumine the less astute. So God, remaining motionless in himself, makes all else to move, and he propels and moves them in regard to the universal government, how he wills the universe to be ruled and governed; and by such motion and force, there are some things that all angels perceive, but others that only the more astute perceive; and concerning these things the more astute and higher illumine the lower and less astute. Hence Dionysius, in book four of his *Divine Names*, says that God is like the sun because the sun illumines all things and yet creatures with clearer eyes perceive more of the sun's light, and by means of the light they see many things that others do not see.

With regard to our question, in this way the matter is resolved as far as it pertains to the Church triumphant. Yet it may be remembered that the question was called pregnant, and through it we can come down to the Church militant as to the exemption by which what was not so immediate might be made more immediate. For always the highest pontiff is understood to be the ordinary in all places and to be able to reserve to himself the oversight and immediate jurisdiction over any Church. Yet this does not prevent any bishop of a diocese from judging the cases of his diocese, and he is the ordinary in the whole of his diocese. This is the case because bishops are raised to part of the responsibility, but the highest pontiff is raised to the full plenitude of power. And because the whole remains together with the part, so the immediate jurisdiction of the highest pontiff also remains together with the ordinary jurisdiction of every bishop. And because this exemption removes and deprives the middle jurisdiction of bishops, it may be called a certain irregularity, because it circumvents the authority of bishops. But since we have discussed this matter more fully in a book, where we argued against exemptions, in this treatise we can pass over this matter in silence.

The Body of Christ

Purpose of the treatise

I have been asked by my lords and by friends who have been unable, due to the demands of their office, to read my *Propositions* on the body of Christ, to abridge it, and to expound clearly the beliefs which according to holy scripture we are obliged to hold concerning the body of Christ and what must be our disposition toward the reception of it. I have decided, therefore, to write a treatise in which I shall point out what the Catholic faith imposes concerning the body of Christ in accordance with holy scripture, and what our disposition toward it should be so as to receive the sacrament of the eucharist in a manner that will lead not to our judgment but to our salvation. By way of proof, attention must be directed to the statements of scriptural authorities on the sacrament of the eucharist under five headings, namely: 1) content; 2) prefigurations; 3) meaning of the sacrament; 4) effect of the sacrament; 5) its use or purpose. However, with regard to those who receive the sacrament itself, holy scripture lays down the proper disposition necessary for the worthy and salutary reception of it.

Plan

Under those six headings that I have listed I wish to make six points in this treatise on the sacrament: of these, five will concern the sacrament, the sixth however will concern those who receive it. First I shall discuss the content of this sacrament so that the truth of the sacrament may be clearly seen. Secondly, I shall demonstrate how this sacrament was prefigured in the Old Testament. Thirdly, I shall make clear the meaning of the sacrament. Fourthly, I shall see what are its effects. Fifthly, I shall speak of its use. And under these five headings will be defined the sum total of what we are bound to believe concerning the sacrament of the eucharist in accordance with the judgment of holy scripture. Sixthly and finally will be discussed the preparation required on our part for worthy reception of communion. And on that point this treatise will conclude.

Content of the sacrament

As regards the first point, that is, the investigation of the content of the sacrament itself, it is the real body of Christ, which was formed from a virgin mother, which he drew from the Virgin, which hung on the cross, which was sacrificed for the redemption of the whole human race. The holy scriptures make this clear in many passages; for instance it is said in Matthew 26:26-27: *When they were at supper, Jesus took bread and blessed it and broke it and gave it to his disciples and said: "Take and eat. This is my body."* Likewise in Mark 14:22: *When they were eating, Jesus took bread and blessing it he broke it and gave it to them and said: "Take it, this is my body."* The same is read in Luke 22:19, where it is said: *And having taken the bread, he gave thanks and broke it and gave it to them, saying: "This is my body which will be given up for you: do this in memory of me."* And in 1 Corinthians 11:23-24 it is said: *For I have received from the Lord that which I have also passed on to you, that the Lord Jesus, on the night on which he was betrayed, took bread and giving thanks he blessed it and said: "Take and eat: this is my body which will be given up for you: do this in memory of me."* And in John 6:51 we read: *My flesh is life for the world.* This should be understood not only as concerning spiritual eating and the death which the son of God suffered according to the body he had taken on, but as concerning also the sacramental eating whereby there is given to us the real flesh of Jesus Christ. Finally there is in 1 Corinthians 10:16: *The cup of blessing which we bless, is it not the communion of the blood of Christ? And the bread which we break, is it not the communion of the body of Christ?*

From these passages it is obvious without resorting to any metaphor or simile or parable that the true body of Christ is contained in this sacrament, as I have said before. However, arising from its content, this sacrament is designated by a variety of names. For it is called, in the first place, eucharist, that is "good thanks," insofar as it contains him, of whom it is said in Ephesians 5:2: *He offered himself up as a sacrifice for us, a victim to God for an odor of sweetness.* In the second place it is called "synaxis," is said in Ephesians 2:14: *For he is our peace, who has made both one.* And in John 11:51: *Christ had to die not only for the people but to gather into one the children of God who had been scattered.* Thirdly and lastly it is called "viaticum" (food for a journey) insofar as it contains him who said of himself: *I am the way, the truth and the life* (Jn 14:6). And he instituted this sacrament also when he was about *to pass over from this world to the Father,* as is said in John 13:1. Hence also those who pass from this world will be strengthened by this food as if by food for a journey, according as it is symbolically read in Elijah (1 Kgs 19:5-8): He walked in the strength of that food as far as the mountain of God, Horeb. And this clarifies the first point.

Prefiguration in the Old Testament

I have explained what is contained in this sacrament and that by reason of the content it is designated by various names, the first point, as I said, which was to be clarified. I intend now to show how in the Old Testament it was prefigured by various models. As proof of this, attention must be drawn to the fact that different forms of this sacrament came before it in accordance with the different ways in which it can be considered. In the first place it can be regarded as a type of sacrifice: and as such it is prefigured in the sacrificial offering of Melchizedek, of whom it is said in Genesis 14:18: *He offered bread and wine; for he was a priest of the most high God.* And because of this it is said of Christ in Psalm 110:4: *You are a priest forever according to the order of Melchizedek.* And it is also prefigured as some kind of sacrificial offering by all the sacrifices of the Old Testament, all of which were directed toward what is said in Hebrews 10:14: *By one oblation he perfected those that are made holy.* Secondly it is considered as the sacrifice of a victim and thus it was foreshadowed in the paschal lamb, of which it is said in Exodus 12:3.5.47: *There shall be a lamb, a male one year old . . .* etc. And afterward there is added: *And the entire multitude of the children of Israel will sacrifice it . . .* etc. And in general all the sacrifices of the Old Testament were prefigurations of this one sacrifice, just as it is said in Colossians 2:17: *Those are foreshadowing what was to come,* and in Hebrews 10:1: *The law having a shadow of the good things to come.*

Thirdly, it may be considered to what extent it is spiritual and heavenly food: and it is thus prefigured by the manna given by the Lord to the children of Israel in the desert, as described in Exodus 16:4 and in Numbers 11:9. But this seems a definite foreshadowing of the sacrament. In the first place in relation to the species, because it is said to be bread, in accordance with that passage in

Psalm 78:24-25: *God has given them bread from heaven; human beings have eaten the bread of angels.* And the Lord called his own flesh bread, according to John 6:51: *The bread that I shall give you is my flesh for the life of the world.* In the second place, as to its source: this prefiguration is indeed mentioned in Wisdom 16:20: God *gave them bread from heaven without toil, having in it all delight.* Indeed of this prefiguration it is said in John 6:51: *I am the living bread which has come down from heaven.* In the third place, as to those to whom it is given: just as manna was given to the children of Israel after the crossing of the Red Sea, so also that spiritual food is given only after baptism, for which the Red Sea provided a prefiguration according to that passage in Paul, 1 Corinthians 10:1-4: *Our fathers were all under the cloud and all crossed the sea and all in Moses were baptized in the cloud and in the sea.* And after these words there is added, in regard to the prefiguration of this sacrament: *And all have eaten the same spiritual food and all have drunk the same spiritual drink.* In the fourth place, as to the murmuring: for it is said in Numbers 11:6 that the children of Israel murmured about the manna that was supplied to them, saying: *Our soul is dry: our eyes look on nothing else but manna.* Likewise we find in John 6:42: *The Jews therefore argued among themselves saying: How can he give us his own flesh to eat?*

On this fourth point consideration may be given as to the administration of the sacrament being the responsibility of priests, who are by rite ordained according to the power of the keys of the Church which Christ entrusted to the apostles and to their successors. And in this manner it was prefigured by the loaves of proposition of which it is said in Exodus 25:30: *And you shall place upon the table loaves of proposition in my sight always.* Of those loaves it is said in Mark 2:26 that it was lawful for the priests alone to eat them. In the fifth place this sacrament is considered as spiritual viaticum: and so it was prefigured in the bread in the strength of which Elijah walked as far as the mountain of God, Horeb (1 Kgs 19:8). And so the second point is clarified.

Meaning of the sacrament

I have shown how by various models this sacrament was prefigured in the Old Testament, which came under the second heading. I wish now to examine the third, namely the meaning of this sacrament. To understand this it is necessary to discover the various things represented for us by means of this sacrament.

In the first place, it is said that it is a kind of memorial representing the passion of Christ and is truly his body in that it contains him. Hence it is said in Luke 22:20: *Do this in memory of me.* And in 1 Corinthians 11:26: *As often as you shall eat this bread and drink this cup, you shall show the death of the Lord until he comes.* In the second place, the mystical body of Christ also represents the assembly of the faithful, inasmuch as it has some resemblance to it. Because just as many grape seeds come together to make wine flow and for many grains of corn one loaf of bread is made, so from many different members of the faithful the Church is constituted and the mystical body of Christ is brought about. This is the assembly of Christians in accordance with that passage in Paul, 1 Corinthians 10:17: *One bread and one body, we are many, all of whom share in the one bread.* In the third place it represents the spiritual restorative by which the pure mind is refreshed. This refreshment, however, primarily resides in the contemplation of wisdom. Hence it is said in Proverbs 9:2: *Wisdom has mixed the wine and set forth her table.* And Sirach 15:3: *She will feed him with the bread of life and understanding and give him the water of healthful wisdom to drink.* Secondly it consists in the enjoyment of divine love of which it is said in Song of Songs 5:1: *Eat, friends; drink freely of love.*

In the fourth place it represents future happiness. Hence it is said in Luke 22:29-30: *I bestow on you as my Father has bestowed on me a kingdom, that you may eat and drink at my table in my kingdom and sit upon twelve thrones judging the twelve tribes of Israel.* And Luke 14:15: *Happy is the one who eats bread in the kingdom of God.* And Isaiah 65:13: *Behold my servants will eat and you shall be hungry.* And Psalm 36:9: *They shall grow drunk from the abundance of your house.* And Revelation 2:17: *To him who overcomes I shall give hidden manna.* And so we are clear on what we said came under the third heading.

Effects of the sacrament

Since we have seen the significance of this sacrament under the third heading, it now remains for us to see what, according to holy scripture, are the effects of this sacrament. This is proposed for clarification under the fourth heading: under this heading we must ascertain the manifold effects attributed to the sacrament of the eucharist. The first effect is that through this sacrament the soul is made alive. Hence it is said in John 6:58: *For it is the bread of God which has come down from heaven and gives life to the world. And whoever eats this bread will live forever.* The second effect is that by means of this sacrament we are given an increase of grace and of the virtues and a multiplication of them, as can be read figuratively in Isaiah 30:23: *The bread of the harvest of the land shall be most abundant and rich.*

The third effect is that through this sacrament we obtain spiritual delight. Hence of it is said figuratively in Genesis 49:20: *Aser, his bread shall be rich and he shall provide delights for kings* — those delights, I may mention, of which it is said in Job 22:26: *Then you will abound in delights over the Almighty and will lift up your face to God.* The fourth effect is that our heart is strengthened against all temptations. Hence Psalm 104:15: *Bread strengthens the heart of man.* And Psalm 23:5: *You have prepared a table in front of my eyes, against those who afflict me.* The fifth effect is that through this sacrament sins are remitted and especially the venial ones, and those of which we have no recollection. Hence the Lord says in Matthew 26:28: *This is my blood which will be poured out for you for the remission of sins.* And Hebrews 9:14: . . . *the blood of Christ, who through the Holy Spirit offered himself unspotted to God, has cleansed our conscience from dead works, to serve the living God.* About this it is said in Psalm 60:5: *You have given us to drink of the wine of remorse . . .* etc. And so it is quite clear what are the effects of this sacrament which we undertook to examine under the fourth heading.

Purpose of the sacrament

Having shown what are the effects of the sacrament, which was the fourth point for discussion, we must now make clear and demonstrate in accordance with the opinion of holy scripture the use or purpose of the blessed eucharist, as was proposed at the start as the fifth and final point for clarification. In this regard it must noted that the use of the sacrament consists in the eating and drinking. Hence it is said in John 6:55: *My flesh is truly food and my blood is truly drink.* And in Matthew 26:26: *Receive and eat.* And in Mark 14:22: *Take up,* that is "eat." And in 1 Corinthians 11: *Take and eat.* And so the supper, or dinner, is described as a banquet, as it were, in the scriptures: in Matthew 22:4: *Behold I have prepared my dinner . . .* etc; in Luke 14:16: *A certain man made a great supper . . .* etc. And in Isaiah 25:6: *And the Lord of hosts will make for all the people on this mountain a rich feast, a feast of vintage, a feast of fat marrows, a feast of wine purged of dregs.* But if I may say so, as I think it right to do, two doubts occur to me. First, that since it has to be said that the use of this sacrament consists in the eating and drinking, someone might find in that a source of error, inferring that Christ should not be worshiped in the host because it was not instituted for that purpose but for eating.

The second doubt is something like this: that if the purpose and end of the holy eucharist is that it be eaten and drunk, there is a fear that someone could say that outside of that purpose the body of Christ does not reside in it: that would be a very serious error. But those doubts are easily resolved. And because the solution of the first doubt draws its origin from the solution of the second doubt, so I shall speak first of the second question, and secondly of the first.

It must therefore be noted that by two ways we can pursue the question that the body of Christ is in the sacrament but outside of its purpose, with the result that the first way is demonstrative yet leads from the true to the impossible. Therefore it must first be made known that the end is twofold, inasmuch as it regards the bread, the purpose of the one who engenders, and the purpose of the thing generated. The purpose of the generator is said to be the form of the thing by which the thing itself receives being according to the requirement of its own nature, and without which it cannot be. The purpose of the thing generated is, however, the action itself of the thing, or its purpose, without which the thing itself could continue in its own being, and especially if it were among the number of permanent things of which neither their being nor their first actuality depends on action, or on their second actuality, but they can exist without it, as the philosopher says in the second book on the *Soul.* Therefore since the form of this sacrament and its internal purpose, which is its first actuality, is the word of God, namely *This is my body,* and since the sacrament of the eucharist is among the number of sacred things which possess permanent matter, but the purpose is its second actuality, the purpose of the thing already engendered and external, it is clear that its being and its perfection do not depend on its action and its purpose, and without any purpose at all it remains a sacrament as long as the accidents of bread and wine can be maintained, and as a consequence, apart from any purpose, there remains present there, by the power of the sacrament, the body of Christ, which was formed from the flesh of the Virgin and which was sacrificed for the redemption of the human race.

Hitherto it has been possible to prove this, but only by way of showing that in being eaten the body of Christ remains in the sacrament aside from its purpose, but also, as was said, by the way that leads to impossibility; and this is twofold. First, if the body of Christ were not in the sacrament apart from this purpose, the sacrament would not be determined by virtue of the passion of Christ, from the total contemplation of the word and of the form of the sacrament, and from the intention of the minister of the sacrament on reaching the word at the elevation, that is, saying the words of consecration over the bread, which is its proper matter, but depended on the in-

tention and will of those receiving it, to the point that because they
intended such a purpose for the sacrament and wished to receive the
sacrament, the sacrament would be duly performed, even if the
priest were to say the words of consecration over the bread. But this
is impossible and altogether contrary to the Catholic faith which lays
down that by virtue of the words which Christ handed down, since
the words said with the intention of fulfilling the sacrament are said
by the priest ordained in the rite, the substance of the bread is
changed into the real body of Christ, into that body, I say, which was
formed out of the flesh of the Virgin, which hung on the cross, which
was sacrificed for the redemption of the whole human race, as can
be seen clearly from what has been said earlier.

Secondly, it is proved also by the way which leads to the impossible and this second proof is based on the first proof. But if the
body of Christ were not in the sacrament apart from the purpose
in eating it, the word of God would not be the form of the sacrament but the will and agreement of the recipients. Also the priest
would not know when the sacrament was carried out but those
about to receive it would: but these are all impossibilities. Therefore we must acknowledge that the body of Christ is in the sacrament by virtue of the word, even if in the meantime no one makes
use of the sacrament by eating it. It does not therefore follow, as
those who disregard reason would argue, that this sacrament is
given to us to eat and drink, therefore it is not a sacrament outside
of this purpose: here one argues from the refutation of the second
impulse to the refutation of the first impulse, from the refutation
and negation of the action to the refutation and negation of being.
And later it becomes clear from those words that the end is twofold,
internal and external. The purpose of the sacrament is its external
end, the removal of which is not followed by the removal of the
sacrament, even if that did follow from the removal of the internal
end, that is, that should the word be removed from the sacrament,
the sacrament would be nothing other, as Augustine says, than the
element.

The second doubt being resolved, we want to solve the first; this
we shall easily do if we pay attention to what was said above. I have,
in fact, shown that in this sacrament while it contains the true body
of Christ formed from the most pure flesh of the Virgin, at the
same time there can be preserved the accidents of bread and wine,
even if there is no one to use it by partaking of it. Since this is so, it
follows that this sacrament must always be venerated and that they
would be damned who were unwilling to venerate the sacrament of
the eucharist, since in it there is manifest the same of which it was

written: *The Lord your God you shall adore.* And of the Son, who is not other than the Father but is the same God with the Father, it is said: *Let all honor the Son, just as they honor the Father.* And again: *And all the angels of God shall worship him.* And so it is clear that Christ is to be worshiped in the sacrament. And this is the opinion of Augustine when he says: "I find that without profanity the earth may be worshiped, without profanity his footstool may be worshiped. For he took up earth from earth, since flesh is from earth and he took flesh from the flesh of Mary. And because in the flesh he walked here and gave us flesh itself to eat for our salvation, no one eats that flesh without first having worshiped" (*Expositions of the Psalms* 98). Therefore it is found that the Lord's footstool may be worshiped and not only do we not sin in worshiping it but we do commit sin in not worshiping it. Therefore it is invalid to say: "Christ has been given to us in the sacrament in order that he be eaten by us, therefore he must not be worshiped in it," just as it is invalid also to say "Christ came into this world to seek out and to save that which was lost, therefore he must not be worshiped in this world." But just as in this world he is worshiped by many, since in assuming flesh he did not cease to be God, according to those words: *He remained that which he was and took upon himself that which he was not*, notwithstanding the fact that he came to seek and to save that which was lost; so he must be worshiped by us in the sacrament although he be given to us to eat, because he has not ceased to be God, and we can say to him: "But you yourself are the same . . ." etc.

Dispositions for communion

We have dealt with all the matters which we proposed to clarify in accordance with holy scripture, that is, those relating to the sacrament considered for itself, and have resolved the doubts which arise regarding the fifth point. It remains now to examine the sixth point we undertook to clarify as to the disposition required on our part for the worthy reception of this sacrament. As proof of this it is to be noted that we cannot adequately dispose ourselves for the reception of this sacrament without the grace of God who makes us worthy, according to the words of Paul, in 2 Corinthians 3:4-6: *We have such confidence through Christ in God; not that we are sufficient to consider anything of ourselves, as if by our own ability; but our sufficency is from God, that is, by the grace of God, who has made us fitting ministers of the New Testament.* And in Colossians 1:12: *Giving thanks to God the Father who made us worthy to participate in the destiny of the saints in light.* Therefore we shall rightly begin to dispose ourselves for reception of this sacrament if we confess our wretchedness and unworthiness from our whole heart, continually saying the words of the centurion: *Lord, I am not worthy that you should enter under my roof but only say the word and my soul will be healed.* For if we do this, God will bestow grace on us and will make us worthy.

In the second place it may be noted that we cannot adequately and perfectly dispose ourselves to receive the sacrament worthily, because such preparation and disposition comes when God moves us through grace and fills us with grace. This, however, in the case of adults, of which I mean to speak, only takes place if they are willing, according to the words of Augustine: "He who made you without your help did not justify you without your help." Therefore not only must we recognize and confess our wretchedness and unworthiness and ask God to make us worthy of so great a sacrament, but we also must consent to this with a free will and, through the grace we are given, have a conscience cleansed and purified. Hence it is said in 1 Corinthians 5:8: *Therefore let us feast not on the old leaven nor on the leaven of malice and wickedness but on the unleavened bread of sincerity and truth.* This accords with the directions given in Exodus 12 concerning the paschal lamb, that it should be eaten with unleavened bread. But one needs proof for oneself of a conscience so perfectly purified, according to the words of the apostle in 1 Corinthians 11:28: *But let a man prove himself and so let him eat of that bread and drink of that cup.* Man's own proof for himself consists in three things: contrition of heart, oral confession, and acts of amendment, so that through contrition of heart we may prove our thoughts, and through oral confession we may prove our words, and through acts of amendment we may prove our opinions. But if in this proof we discover such sorrow for our sins, then we are able to say these words of the Prophet: *I shall reflect on you all my years in the bitterness of my soul* (Is 38:15).

And so let us confess our sins to the priest, according to the words in James 5:16: *Confess your sins to one another,* so that we do not reiterate the words of Christ to the adulterous woman: *Go and sin no more* (Jn 8:11); and so we shall make amends that instead of evil deeds we may abound in good works and worthily be able to approach the reception of this sacrament. But anyone who approaches with an impure conscience not only is not enlivened but is taking on a burden, as in these words of 1 Corinthians 11:27: *Whoever eats and drinks unworthily eats and drinks judgment upon himself.* And according to the words in Jeremiah 11:15 it is said figuratively of the sacrament: *Shall holy flesh remove from you your wickedness of which you have boasted?* Hence also it is read of Judas that after receiving the morsel, that is, the body of Christ, Satan entered into him. And this took place not because he received something bad but because he received a good thing badly and unworthily.

And so an explanation has been provided for the problems I set out to clarify.

The Praises of Divine Wisdom

Chapter One

In which are shown the matters to be treated in this work, and what will be the order of treatment.

In the midst of our many and various occupations you have asked us certain questions, and we have decided to comply with your pious request according to our modest knowledge. You asked us seven questions: How should we believe? How should we hope? How should we confess and do penance for sins? How should we love God? How should we fear and obey God? How should we thank God for blessings received? And lastly, how should we serve God? After these questions you asked specifically about the interpretation of the verse, *My heart has thrown up a good word; I myself speak my works to the king; my tongue is the pen of a scribe who writes quickly* (Ps 45:1). You wished to know how to understand it and the gifts of the Holy Spirit. In order to understand and discuss all these questions, as Dionysius at the beginning of his *Ecclesiastical Hierarchy,* let us invoke Jesus, the beginning and end of all hierarchies, beseeching and begging his help.

We say there are two contrary movers within us, namely sense and reason, as those well-versed in philosophy maintain, arguing from the third book of *On the Soul.* And Paul asserts this quite clearly when he says: *I see another law in my members fighting against the law of my mind* (Rom 7:23). Reason, then, which is the law of the mind, intercedes for the best like a good mover or instigator, while sensuality and the law of our members attempts to incline us to the opposite, as is affirmed in Genesis: *The sense of person is prone to evil from his youth* (Gn 8:21). Leaving aside sensuality or the law of our members, which inclines us to evil, we must discuss reason, which inclines us to good. However, since we intend to discuss our salvation here, which is above what reason can attain, reason is not enough. It is necessary to go beyond a moving reason to a divine mover, so that we may attain our salvation and eternal inheritance as those moved by God and as children of God: *For those led by God's Spirit are children of God, and if children, then heirs* (Rom 8:14,17).

We need to speak about both good movers, namely reason serving God and God himself initiating. Traditional language and opinion propose two kinds of habits, namely virtues, when the soul's powers obey moving reason, and gifts, when all the soul's powers respond to God who moves and impels. In the questions to be discussed, then, we will treat the divine impulse that comes through his gift more than the impulse of reason. This is clearly the case because even the philosopher says in *On Good Fortune*, addressing people who are moved by divine impulse, that it is not expedient to counsel them, for they have a principle that is better than intellect and counsel.

Relying, then, on the impulse of the Holy Spirit, we will proceed in this treatise as follows: first we will interpret the verse, whose exposition was requested last, because in it are displayed the seven praiseworthy qualities or the seven praises of divine wisdom; then we will adapt these to the seven gifts and thus answer the seven proposed questions.

Chapter Two

In which it is shown that there are seven praises of divine wisdom and how they are adapted to the interpretation of Psalm 45:1.

With the order of treatment presented, we now wish to discuss the seven praises of divine wisdom and to adapt them to the exposition of the verse, and by this to distinguish the seven gifts and answer the seven proposed questions. Therefore it must be known first that divine wisdom is full and bountiful; second that it is high and deep; third that it is upright and true; fourth that it is good and holy; fifth that it is near to all; sixth that it is fruitful; seventh that it is efficacious and prompt. If we wish to answer the proposed questions we must taste and experience something of the divine wisdom, and we ought to recognize all the good qualities in that high wisdom in order to understand the divine gifts and answer all the questions.

We will discuss the seven gifts that are enumerated in order in the first verse of Psalm 45: plenitude or abundance of divine wisdom is noted when it says, *has thrown up*; height and depth when it says, *my heart*; rectitude and truth when it says, *word*; goodness and holiness when it adds, *good*; nearness to all when it continues, *I myself speak*; fruitfulness when it says, *my works to the king*; and finally efficacy when it says, *my tongue is the pen of a scribe who writes quickly*. The seven steps of wisdom are taken from these seven gifts, as will be clear when we deal with them.

The abundance and bounty of divine wisdom is described first, then, when it says, *has thrown up*. The prophet's heart was so full of divine wisdom that it was as though it were forced to eject it, like a bottle filled too full must reject what overflows. And this is how the gloss interprets it, saying, *has thrown up* — surely from fullness, because the prophet's mind (as expressed in the same place) was so full inside that it had to throw up. It is no marvel if the prophet's mind was so filled that it was forced, as it were, to throw up, for the treasures of divine wisdom and knowledge cannot be comprehended by anyone, but they fill all things.

The height and depth of divine wisdom is described second when it says, *my heart*. What is uttered by the mouth seems to come from the surface, but what proceeds from the heart seems to come from the lowest depth. This depth is so deep that no one can declare it in words.

The rectitude and truth of divine wisdom is described third when it says, *word*. A word speaks and cries out what is true, for "word" means something true and perfect. Augustine, wishing to exclude every imperfection from God, said in *The Trinity* XV, 16, that in God is not thinking, but the word. Divine wisdom cannot fail, nor has it any imperfection, and therefore it is expressed by the label "word." And God's very Son, to whom divine wisdom belongs, is properly called the Word. So too, because of its perfection and truth, the holy Scripture is called divine wisdom, since it is filled with divine wisdom. By reason of its content of truth, Scripture has such authority that Augustine says in his second work on Genesis that the authority of Scripture is greater than the capacity of every human mind.

The goodness and holiness of divine wisdom is described fourth when it says, *good*. The word that the prophet longed to throw up concerning divine wisdom was not just any word, but a good and holy word, as is confirmed by the verse: *The word of the Lord in your mouth is true* (1 Kgs 17:24). In this word a person lives as far as his soul, which could not happen were the word not good and holy: *A person does not live on bread alone but on every word that comes from the mouth of God* (Dt 8:3; Mt 4:4).

The nearness of divine wisdom to all things is described when it says, *I myself speak.* A person usually addresses distant people through messengers, but to those nearby he speaks for himself. And since anyone may speak for himself to those nearby, the prophet says, *I myself speak my works to the king,* to whom the divine wisdom is near. And no wonder, because *it reaches mightily from end to end, and orders all things sweetly* (Wis 8:1).

The fruitfulness of divine wisdom is noted sixth when it adds, *my works to the king.* Just as something is called fruitful as far as it produces offspring, so an action is called fruitful when it issues in works. Thus the philosopher, in book three of his *Ethics,* determines that we are related to our works as a father is related to his children. When the divine wisdom so fills those whom it would cause to advance in works that a person speaks good works to the king, it is evidence of tremendous fruitfulness.

The power and efficacy of divine wisdom is described seventh and last when it adds, *my tongue is the pen of a scribe who writes quickly.* To cause a person to declare quickly and to utter a word without impediment pertains to efficacy.

Chapter Three

In which it is shown how from these seven praises of divine wisdom we may draw the seven steps by which we ascend to divine wisdom, and from thence the seven gifts of the Holy Spirit.

From these seven praises can be derived the seven steps by which we advance to divine wisdom, and from the steps are taken the seven gifts of the Holy Spirit, as is found in the second book of Augustine's *On Christian Teaching.* For if we consider the abundance and plenitude of divine wisdom, which is its first praiseworthy quality or first praise, we are bound to depart from all carnal pleasures, which pertain to the gift of fear, that we might say with the psalmist (and as Augustine repeats in the same place): *Pierce my flesh with your fear* (Ps 119:120). Our flesh, that is, our carnal desires, is pierced with fear of the Lord when sensible pleasures seem detestable to us and only the Lord's pleasures delight us.

The abundance and plenitude of divine wisdom should bring about that we delight only in them, since it is said that *wisdom excels foolishness as much as light differs from darkness* (Eccl 2:13). Wisdom is like light; therefore if physical light is pleasant and it delights the eyes to see the sun (as is said in Ecclesiastes 9), how much more delightful is the light of wisdom, which cannot be extinguished: *Love wisdom because its light cannot go out* (Wis 7:10). And if it is delightful to consider the light of created wisdom, how much more and incomparably delightful it is to consider the light of uncreated wisdom. The delight should be so great when we contemplate the plenitude of divine wisdom that day and night we can never have enough of, but ought to scorn all sensible pleasures on account of its delight. The plenitude of divine wisdom should compel us to forsake sensible pleasures, which pertain to the gift of fear.

The second praiseworthy quality, or second praise, of divine wisdom, namely its depth, should induce us to be humble, which pertains to the gift of piety. For a person humbles himself and becomes meek when he considers his own weakness and the excellence of another. Therefore if we consider the vast depth and height of divine wisdom and the feebleness and weakness of our own intellect, we will regard ourselves as nothing, for our mind in the category of intelligible things is like prime matter in the category of being. And we will regard ourselves as beasts that lack understanding, and say to the Lord: *I have become like a beast before you and have been brought to nothing* (Ps 73:22-23).

The depth of divine wisdom is such that it should make us especially humble and meek, which pertains to the gift of piety. According to Augustine, *Teaching Christianity*, II, 7, just as fleeting pleasures pertain to fear, so becoming humble pertains to piety; for the gift of fear in us makes us behave well by detesting and fleeing sensible delights, while the gift of piety in us (taking piety in the broader sense) makes us behave well toward others by displaying proper honor to them. This happens especially if we are meek and humble.

The third praiseworthy quality of divine wisdom is rectitude or truth, which ought to make us studious. A person should be diligent and studious in regard to things he knows are upright and true, and through them he possesses the gift of knowledge. Knowledge is of human things, wisdom of divine things; to understand and judge human things correctly pertains to knowledge while to understand and judge divine things pertains to wisdom. And since no one can make good judgments about anything unless he is attentive, diligent, and studious, we may say with Augustine, in his second book of *Teaching Christianity*, that just as fleeing pleasures pertains to fear, and being meek to piety, so being studious pertains to knowledge. Without studiousness we are unable to judge human things well, which belongs to the gift of knowledge.

The fourth praise, or fourth praiseworthy quality, of divine wisdom is its goodness, which should keep us from being broken by adversities. This pertains to the gift of fortitude because, as the apostle teaches, *Our present tribulation that is momentary and light is working within us an eternal weight of glory beyond all reckoning, as we look not on what is seen, but on what is not seen* (2 Cor 4:17-18). What are seen are temporal things; what are not seen are eternal things. The divine goodness and that excellence of glory reveal to us what is good, what we ought to do, and how to surmount tribulations.

The fifth praiseworthy quality of divine wisdom is its nearness to us. Just as divine wisdom, like divine power, is within everything but not encompassed, and outside of everything but not excluded, so it is highest and yet not separated, and nearest and yet not contracted. This nearness should induce love within us, and delight in divine and eternal things, which pertains to the gift of counsel, according to Augustine, *Teaching Christianity*, II, 7.

The sixth praise or praiseworthy quality of divine wisdom is its fruitfulness, for *wisdom moves more than all moving things* (Wis 7:24). Divine wisdom is both immobile and mobile: immobile in itself, mobile in its effects, which extend to everything. Thus it is said to move more and be more fruitful in regard to its effects. By such fruitfulness we ought to be brought to purity of mind, which pertains to the gift of understanding. The purer the mind's eye, the more fruit is borne in the contemplation of wisdom.

The seventh praise of divine wisdom, and the last to be considered, is its efficacy or power, which ought to bring us to peace of mind. We should remain peaceful and restful in him who is the maker of all and possesses all power, which pertains to the gift of wisdom. Hence Augustine says, in the second book of *Teaching Christianity:* Such a son ascends to wisdom, the seventh and final gift, which he enjoys in peace and tranquility.

Chapter Four

In which the sufficiency of gifts is clearly presented, and it is more clearly shown how the seven gifts are received according to the seven steps.

To understand more fully what has been said, and that we might perceive all these things more clearly, we will speak about how the seven gifts of the Holy Spirit should be received. Some gifts pertain to the perfection of our reason, others to the perfection of our desires. Four things (as far as concerns us at present) belong to the perfection of reason, namely to apprehend the truth, then, according to this apprehension, to make good judgments about human and created things and to make good judgments about divine things, and, according to this apprehension and these judgments, to be directed rightly into actions and works. To apprehend correctly pertains to the gift of understanding; to judge human things well pertains to the gift of knowledge; to judge divine things well pertains to the gift of wisdom; to be thus directed rightly into actions pertains to the gift of counsel. Now three things (as far as concerns us at present) pertain to desires, namely to flee carnal pleasures, which is done by the gift of fear; to hold fast in adversity, which is done by the gift of fortitude; and to treat others properly, which is done by the gift of piety. Elaborated in this way we have a sufficiency of gifts.

Augustine arranges these in the following order: first we should flee carnal delights; second we should be humble, not looking out for ourselves, but growing meek; third we should be attentive and studious; fourth we should not be broken in adversities; fifth we should be turned to delight in eternal things; sixth we should have eyes wholly cleansed — for we are not fully purified as soon as we have fled carnal pleasures since some remnant of sin may still remain in us. When wine is taken out of a bottle the odor of wine still remains in the bottle; and when a fever leaves a sick person the remnant of sickness still remains. Thus when someone departs from sin, the incentives to sin still remain, and we must be cleansed of these by love of eternal things, for the more we love eternal things, the less we are incited to sin; seventh and lastly we are tranquil in mind from doing all the previous things.

The seven gifts are gathered from these seven, so that the gift of fear is possessed by fleeing carnal pleasures; the gift of piety by being meek; the gift of knowledge by being diligent; the gift of fortitude by standing firm in adversity; the gift of counsel by loving eternal things; the gift of understanding by having the eye of our mind cleansed; the gift of wisdom by being peaceful in mind. Therefore a person cannot come to the gift of wisdom and have peace of mind until he first flees carnal things, which is the beginning of all other gifts and pertains to fear. From this start, by fleeing carnal things, a person begins to know himself, becomes humble and shows due respect to others, which pertains to piety. Having fled carnal delights and become humble and respectful, he no longer thinks vain thoughts but is more attentive and diligent and begins to judge created things, which pertains to the gift of knowledge. By judging created things well, a person regards temporal things as nothing and is not broken by adverse circumstances; and this pertains to the gift of fortitude. Now possessing all these gifts he despises all low, temporal things and is brought to the love of eternal things, which pertains to the gift of counsel. For the gift of counsel is when someone is directed to good works, which happens especially through love of eternal things. Whatever a person loves, such will seem an end to him and he will do and speak accordingly. Thus if we have love of carnal things we will do carnal acts and speak carnal words, since carnal people are involved with carnal things. But if we shall have love of spiritual things, we will be involved in spiritual works, speaking and doing them, and we will be directed to good works. Out of love of eternal things the eye of our mind is purified, because *the commandment of the Lord is a light illuminating the eyes* (Ps 19:9). And the greatest commandment is of love or charity, by which the eye of our mind is cleansed. For just as by loving carnal things we are turned toward them and stained by them, so by loving spiritual things we are turned to them and cleansed by them. And to have cleansed eyes of the mind pertains to the gift of understanding. Through this gift we are able to apprehend truths well, just as through knowledge and wisdom we are able to make good judgments about them. Therefore as an impure eye of flesh cannot see well, so the eye of the mind that is not cleansed cannot apprehend well. On account of all these gifts a person becomes tranquil in mind, which pertains to the gift of wisdom. Whoever wants to judge rightly about such high and difficult things, as are divine matters, needs to have a tranquil and peaceful mind. Hence it is well said that *the beginning of wisdom is the fear of the Lord* (Prv 1:7), because from fear we begin to flee carnal pleasures so that we may finally come to wisdom and peace of mind.

Chapter Five

In which the discussion continues and it is shown how from the first praise of divine wisdom, namely from its plenitude, we can know how we should believe, and what things are to be believed.

With all these things discussed, the interpretation of the verse, *My heart has thrown up a good word,* etc. is clear. This interpretation was approached spiritually in the sense that the gifts of the Holy Spirit, about which you desired to know some things, were adapted to it. Now we wish to answer all seven of your questions according to the same verse and its seven praises of divine wisdom. From the plenitude of divine wisdom we will show how we ought to believe; from its rectitude and truth how we ought to do penance for our sins; from its goodness how we ought to love God; from its nearness to us how we ought to fear and obey God; from its fruitfulness how we ought to give him thanks; and seventh and lastly from the power of divine wisdom we will show how we ought to serve him. Thus shall we answer all seven questions from the seven praises of divine wisdom, which we have drawn from the first verse of Psalm 45.

Above all we must understand what should be believed by someone if he would fully know the truth of the question. And because Deity and Trinity are known only to God himself, we must find what is to be believed through divine revelation and the teaching of Christ. The plenitude of divine wisdom in which divine things are fully known informs us sufficiently how we ought to believe, because we should believe in them the way they have been revealed by divine wisdom. Therefore Dionysius, in the first book of *On Divine Names*, says: Of this supersubstantial and hidden deity we dare not say or think anything beyond what has been declared to us from above in the holy Scriptures. Therefore when it is asked how we should believe, or what must be believed, we can give a short response: What has been declared to us from heaven should be believed entirely, and everything must be believed, whether expressed *at various times and in many ways, as God once spoke to the fathers in the prophets, or spoken clearly and openly to us in the Son, whom God appointed heir of all things, through whom he also made the world* (Heb 1:1-2). Thus whatever is contained in the Old and New Testaments should be believed. Scripture does not contain one thing here and another there, but according to Ezekiel's vision it is *a wheel within a wheel,* (Ez 1:16). Things that are expressed hiddenly and in figures in the Old Testament are revealed clearly and in reality in the New Testament.

A twofold distinction is made concerning belief, one on the manner of believing, the other on the articles believed. And the manner of believing is further distinguished into believing in God, believing God, and believing unto God. For faith is in God as efficient cause; it has God as its object; and it tends to God as a final cause. As far as faith tends to God as to an object and end, we believe what should be believed about God; but as far as faith is efficiently from God as an exemplary cause, all that is proposed for us to believe we believe through God himself. All things shine forth clearly in the divine wisdom, from which they derive and which they reflect. Therefore what we now hear by faith we will see face to face in heaven. Then we shall say: *As we have heard, so have we seen in the city of the Lord* (Ps 48:8). When we are in the city of the Lord, that is, our heavenly homeland, the things proposed for us to believe and follow here will be offered to us as things to be beheld and seen there. This, then, is what it means to believe in God and to believe God: to believe the divine things in the manner in which they have been inspired by God. But as far as faith tends to God as final cause, we believe in God in such a way that by believing we tend to him as our end.

We may adapt these three aspects of belief to three kinds of people, namely to heathens, to faithful sinners, and to the just. Heathens, although they believe in God, do not believe God or unto God. Heathens are able believe in God by having some notion of divine things, because *what is known of God is manifest in them* (Rom 1:19). Yet they do not thereby properly believe God, because they receive their understanding of divine things not from the holy Scriptures God has inspired, but from the senses alone through the things God has created. They do not believe by receiving the testimonies of the saints through whom God has spoken. Thus heathens did not believe God, for while they believed in God by having some notion of divine things, they did not believe God, for they did not receive the testimonies of the holy Scriptures. Now faithful sinners, although they believe in God more fully than the heathen, because they have a fuller understanding than they, and although they believe God by receiving the testimonies of holy Scripture, yet they do not believe unto God since by believing they do not tend to God as an end, nor do they make the divine good their end. The faithful just, however, have all three aspects of belief.

While we may distinguish these three in terms of faith, as saints have distinguished them, to believe in God is a more formal cause, for if by faith we believe unto God and tend to him as an object, we ought to do it in the manner God has revealed to us and as he himself has taught us. Therefore by faith we believe in God as we believe God, for he has spoken to us about himself. Likewise as we believe unto God, we ought to do so as we believe God in terms of what he has spoken to us about himself. We should believe unto God and tend to him as a final cause in the manner he has taught us. And because to believe in this way is believing by formal cause, whereby we should be taught by God, it is well said that the manner of belief should be received from the plenitude of divine wisdom, for God alone knows himself fully and has a full understanding of himself. Therefore we ought to believe him concerning himself.

This covers what should be said about the manner of believing. But as to the matters believed, and what and how many things must be believed, we say that we should believe all the articles of faith, which are reduced to fourteen in number, according to tradition. Of these, seven pertain to divinity and seven to humanity. As to divinity, we should consider the unity of essence, the Trinity of persons, Father, Son, and Holy Spirit, and the three kinds of work that are proper to God alone, namely to create by giving nature, to recreate by infusing grace, and to glorify by granting glory. These will be the seven articles pertaining to divinity: first concerning the unity of essence: *I believe in one God*; second concerning the person of the Father: *the Father almighty*; third concerning the person of the Son: *and in Jesus Christ his Son*; fourth concerning the person of the Holy Spirit: *I believe in the Holy Spirit*; fifth concerning the work of creation: *creator of heaven and earth*; sixth concerning the work of re-creation: *the holy catholic Church, the communion of saints, the forgiveness of sins*; seventh concerning the work of glorification: *the resurrection of the body and eternal life*.

There are also seven articles pertaining to the humanity of Christ which must be believed: first that *he was conceived by the Holy Spirit*; second that *he was born of the Virgin Mary*; third that *he suffered, died and was buried*; fourth that *he descended into hell*; fifth that *on the third day he rose again*; sixth that *he ascended into heaven*; seventh that *he will come again to judge the living and the dead*. Because all these were revealed to us from the plenitude of divine wisdom, it is well said that from this plenitude we ought to be induced how and what to believe.

Chapter Six

In which it is shown from the second praise of divine wisdom, namely from its depth, how the second question is answered, how we can know what to hope for.

Having answered the first question, namely how and what we should believe, from the first praise of divine wisdom, that it is so full and abundant, we now wish to show how to answer the second question, namely what we should hope for, from the second praise, that divine wisdom is so high and sublime. We should keep in mind that hope always concerns something lofty and high, for properly speaking there is no hope concerning something small, but only concerning something great and lofty. Therefore, although we are in some way induced to hope in God from the abundance of divine wisdom, we are induced to such hope especially and properly from its height and loftiness.

We should hope for two things, namely that we will come to see that loftiness of divine wisdom through open vision, and that we will enjoy the excellence of divine goodness through perfect love. But the question about in which of these two our happiness more principally consists, whether in the vision of the loftiness of divine wisdom or in the love of its excelling goodness, we have discussed elsewhere, nor is it relevant to our present matter. Let it suffice here to know that our happiness exists in both and we should hope for both.

We can attribute five specific reasons for why the loftiness of divine wisdom leads us into what we should hope for and how. If we consider that loftiness we will see clearly that all things are ordered to it; that all things can be and are restored by it; that all things are seen by it; that all things are contained in it; and that all things are penetrated by it and it is itself penetrated by all things. Our hope ought to be in God alone so that we do not incur that prophetic judgment: *Cursed is the person who trusts in people and makes flesh his arm, and whose heart departs from the Lord* (Jer 17:5); but, on the contrary, incur the blessing: *Blessed is the person who trusts in the Lord and whose confidence will be in God* (Jer 17:7). All five things we have mentioned about the loftiness of divine wisdom should induce us more fully to trust in God and place our chief hope in him alone.

Divine wisdom, because of its loftiness, is that to which all things are ordered. Lower things are always ordered to higher things, and since that wisdom dwells in the highest place, all other things are ordered to it, as is held in Sirach 24. Therefore just as our mind never rests until it arrives at the final truth from which there is nothing further to seek (as wise philosophers have asserted), so our heart never rests in anything that depends on another and is ordered to another, but it only rests in that which is not ordered to anything else. Since we can claim with certainty from the loftiness of divine wisdom that God is above all things and is himself unable to be ordered to anything else, then we ought to place our hope only in that which can satisfy our heart, in that which is not ordered to anything else. Thus we should place our hope in God alone, and say with Augustine, in chapter one of his *Confessions:* You have made us for yourself, O Lord, and our heart is restless until it rests in you.

Secondly, the loftiness of divine wisdom is that from which all things can be restored or are restored. Besides the fact that God is not the effect of another, nor ordered to another, nor caused by another, so that our heart can rest in him since by having him we do not desire anything besides him, God is also the cause of all things so that he can reestablish and restore all things. Even if all things were to be brought to nothing, our heart could be at rest, for it rests in the fact that God can restore all things, which only God can do. Hence if we were annihilated, he could still restore us to being the same individuals. We ought to place our hope in such a one, who, if we are brought to nothing, if we are killed, can still restore, raise up to life, and beatify us. As Job has said: *Though he slay me, yet will I hope in him* (Job 13:15).

Thirdly, from the loftiness of divine wisdom we may declare that all things are seen by it. An eye down low can see very little, but the eye that is up high sees many things. And divine wisdom is so high that all things are apparent and clear to it. Hence it is said in Hebrews: *He is the searcher of thoughts and of the intentions of the heart, and no creature is hidden in his sight, but all things are naked and open to his eyes* (Heb 4:12-13). We ought to place our hope in him, who can see all our defects, knows all our thoughts, to whom nothing is invisible and nothing hidden. Just as a sick person should trust in a physician, who knows best how to diagnose diseases, so we ought to place our hope in God, to whom no defect of ours can be hidden.

Fourthly, from the loftiness of divine wisdom we can conclude that all things, that is, the perfections of all things, are contained in God. Since divine wisdom is the cause of all things, according to the verse: *I have made all things in wisdom* (Ps 104:24), and since what is in caused things is more fully in their causes, as Dionysius says in the second book of *Divine Names*, then from the loftiness of divine wisdom, by which we have shown that God is the cause of all, we can conclude that the perfections of all caused things are more fully and more perfectly in God. Therefore we ought to hope in God, in whom are all perfections and who can fill all in all, because he is the desire of all things and in him every heart finds rest. In the second book of his *Confessions* Augustine shows that even in all those who fall into sin is found a certain shadowy hope, but the perfect good without defect, which consists in its purity, is in God. Hence he says that there is a defective and shadowy hope in those who fall and are overcome by sin. Pride pursues loftiness, but you are the one lofty God above all things. And what does ambition seek besides honors and glory? But you are the one who is glorious forever and is to be honored above all things. Whatever good we can desire we find with fullness in God. Thus we should hope in the one who can fulfill all our desires. The defective things we wrongly seek in creatures are found pure and excellent in God.

In the fifth place, from the loftiness of divine wisdom we can show that it fills all things. We observe in the physical elements that the higher and loftier an element is, the more it may be penetrated, for water is more penetrable than earth, air more than water, and fire more than air. Divine wisdom, then, because it is highest and necessarily pure and most simple, by reason of its simplicity, is penetrated by all things and penetrates all things. The divine word or divine wisdom, because of its penetrability, is likened to a two-edged sword in Hebrews: *For the word of God is living and active and more penetrating than any two-edged sword* (Heb 4:12).

Therefore we ought to place our hope in one who can fill our heart, our mind, and our soul. And only he can do this who is able to penetrate our soul and enter into it. As in the physical world, where something cannot fill another unless it can enter into it, so nothing can satisfy and fill our soul except what can enter and be in our soul, which belongs to God alone.

If it is asked, then, in what and how we should hope, we say that our hope must be placed in God, so that through him we may come to him. For he alone can satisfy our desires, according to the things discussed above, all of which were established and concluded from the loftiness of divine wisdom.

Chapter Seven

In which it is discussed how, from the third praise of divine wisdom, namely its rectitude, the third question is answered, namely how we ought to do full penance for sins, which will happen especially if we know what good penance accomplishes.

Having shown how, from the fullness of divine wisdom, we can explain in what and how we should believe, and how, from its loftiness, in what and how we should hope, we now wish to lay down how, from the truth or rectitude of this wisdom, we can determine how we should do penance for our wrongs, defects, and sins. In temporal affairs we use a straightedge to see immediately what is crooked and what is straight, so that many things that seem straight to the eyes are revealed to be crooked when measured with a ruler. Likewise builders do not trust their own eyes concerning the rectitude of a building, but they drop a plumb line and apply a ruler to it so that what is crooked may come to light. Thus it is well said in the psalms: *When I take time I will judge justices* (Ps 75:2), for many things appear to be justices which will be revealed to be sins at the final judgment. And because the rectitude of this wisdom is so straight that whatever is out of line with it is crooked, we should be very intent upon how we do penance for our sins and how we correct our crookedness: *For if we judge ourselves well, we will not be judged by him* (1 Cor 11:31).

Penance is the second Tablet after baptism through which we can escape from the sea of this world, return to divine grace, virtues, and gifts, and rectify our crookedness. Thus, lest we be out of line from the rectitude of divine wisdom, we should do full penance for our sins. This occurs especially if we consider the many good effects that penance accomplishes. In his book *On True and False Penance*, chapter one, Augustine says that all Scripture cries out, and all the lives of saints try to show, how much the grace of penance should be sought. For penance, according to him, heals the weak, cures the leprous, raises the dead, and produces, increases, and preserves health. It restores walking to the lame, fertility to the barren, and sight to the blind. It chases away vices, adorns with virtues, and defends and strengthens the soul. It heals all things, it brings joy to all things. It tempers our thoughts, constrains passion, and controls excess. By it the ignorant come to know themselves, those who seek come to find themselves. It leads people to the angels and returns creatures to their creator. It shows the lost sheep to the one seeking it and presents the tenth coin to the one worrying over it. It brings the prodigal son back to his father, it delivers over the one wounded by thieves to be kept and cured. On it every good relies, by it every good is preserved, darkness flees, light comes, and everything is purified. It is a consuming fire.

Chapter Eight

In which it is shown how Augustine's words should be understood about the good effects penance accomplishes, as regards the powers, the perfections of the powers, the actions, and the ways of acting.

In order to understand the words of Augustine, we may say that, concerning our government and rule, we should consider five things, namely the powers by which we act; the dispositions and perfections of the powers by which we are enabled to act; the actions themselves; the manner of acting; and the end to which we tend by such actions. Sin corrupts all of these: it takes away the good dispositions and perfections of our powers; it impedes actions, it perverts the powers, it destroys the manner of acting, it makes us tend to the end wrongly.

With regard to the perfections and dispositions of the powers, sin does three evil things: it makes us weak, leprous, and dead. It makes us weak by debilitating us; leprous by infecting us; dead by taking away grace, love, and other good dispositions and perfections by which we live. Penance, which is opposed to sin, heals the weak, cures the leprous, revives the dead. Against these three, namely against weakness, leprosy, and death, penance provides, increases, and preserves health. It gives health and thereby removes weakness; it increases health because it not only protects us from the infection of leprosy, but also conserves health and preserves us from death.

Thus are sin and penance related to each other, with regard to the dispositions and perfections of our powers. But with regard to the actions themselves, sin does five evil things: it makes us lame, barren, blind, and above all it corrupts us and deforms our virtues. It makes us lame so that we are not inclined to good actions; barren so that we do not yield fruit in good works; blind so that we do not perceive and see the good actions that we ought to do. And sin not only impedes us from performing good works, it also corrupts us by inclining us to evil actions; and by so doing, it deforms any virtues that remain. Thus if faith and hope, which are numbered among the virtues, remain in us after sin, they remain not in a formed but in an unformed state. Penance, then, opposing itself to all five evils that result from sin, restores walking to the lame, abundance of good fruit to the barren, sight to the blind, it drives away vices, and puts on virtues.

Above all, this very same sin that corrupts us, with regard to the dispositions of our powers, and with regard to the actions themselves, in addition wounds us with regard to the powers themselves. In this area sin causes four evils: first by taking away the defenses and stability of our powers; second by bringing illness into them; third by dissipating them; and fourth by causing sorrow and sadness within them.

Through sin a person loses first his fortitude and strength so that he is unable to resist sin. For as long as we are in sin and apart from grace, we cannot avoid sinning. To say that we could avoid sin would be to fall into the error of Pelagius and claim that with mere natural powers a person is able to keep himself from sinning. Thus sin first takes away the defenses and stability of our powers.

Secondly it weakens them and makes them ill. For just as it is one thing to lose heat and another to become cold, so it is one thing to lose defenses and stability and another to contract the opposite vices and become weak and sick. These two are so related that one always occurs with the other, yet for the sake of understanding, we take up one, then the other.

Sin causes these two evils in us, and then causes yet a third evil, because it diffuses and dissipates our powers. In a sinner the powers are not united, but dispersed and diffused, for his reason commands him to do one thing while his sensuality another.

In the fourth place sin causes sorrow and sadness in our powers and in our mind. Just as the testimony of our conscience is our glory, so it brings sorrow and sadness to our mind to find things contrary to our conscience within us.

Opposed to these four evils which sin causes, Augustine discusses four things that penance accomplishes: Against the first it fortifies and strengthens the mind; against the second it heals all; against the third it reintegrates all; against the fourth it brings complete joy. It may be said that these were discussed above, when it was said that sin causes weakness which the removal of strength removes, and that sin makes a person leprous, which induces infirmity and disease, while penance causes the goods opposed to them. But we say that, although sin takes away good dispositions, impedes good actions, and wounds the powers, and that it does all these evils at a single blow, nonetheless these are many separate evils and the things penance does to oppose them are many separate goods. Therefore if Augustine, or other saints, in detesting sin and commending penance, seem to repeat the same thing in many places, the repetition can be attributed to their treatment of different evils, such as the removal of perfections, the wounding of powers, the impeding of actions, or some other evil.

It is clear how we should talk about sin and penance with regard to powers, good dispositions, perfections of powers, and actions; but as to the manner of acting we say that sin causes three evils: it distracts the mind, it disperses passions, and it leads to loose behavior. When we fall into sin, we first begin to think vain thoughts, and thus are said not to moderate our mind, as though thought followed thought without control. And thoughts are vain when not ordained to a proper end. Secondly someone who has begun to think vain thoughts and not to moderate his mind begins to delight in vain things, and is thus said not to restrain his passions. And thirdly he consents to vain actions, and then he is said not to control his behavior. Here, then, is the manner of sin, the way of acting by sin. But penance, being completely opposed to sin, moderates the mind so that we do not think vain thoughts, restrains the passions so that we do not delight in them, and controls behavior so that we do not consent to them.

Chapter Nine

In which it is shown how the words of Augustine should be understood concerning what penance accomplishes, insofar as we tend to our end through it.

It has been shown how we should speak about sin and penance with regard to our powers and actions, but with regard to the end to which we tend by them we are able to say that sin causes us to deviate from our end while penance causes us to tend toward our end. Concerning the deviation from our end, we can speak about it in two ways, either generally, or specifically insofar as we are related to Christ. And approaching it generally, sin makes us deviate from our end in four ways: first by impeding our understanding so that a person does not know himself. For if a sinner knew himself and looked carefully into himself in terms of the awful effects of sin, he would depart from sin at once. Secondly sin corrupts the affections so that a person refuses to seek himself and find himself. For if he sought and found himself he would see that he was a rational being who should act according to reason. Thirdly by sin we are separated from the fellowship of angels, into whose company we ought to be led in order to enjoy our end and our creator together with them. Fourthly by sin we are turned away from God our creator.

Since penance is opposed to sin in every way, penance causes four things contrary to the four ways we deviate from our end through sin: through penance an ignorant person comes to know himself; and seeking he finds himself. Penance leads people to the angels and brings the creature to the creator. This is how we ought to speak about sin and penance generally in terms of the deviation from our end or the following after of our end.

Approaching it specifically, as far as we are united to Christ, who is the mediator between us and God, we can say that sin causes seven things in us. It separates us from Christ while penance restores us to him. Sin makes us into lost sheep because it causes us to wander away from our shepherd. It makes us the lost coin because by sin our image is deformed. Just as an image of a ruler is on a denarius or drachma, so is the image of God in our soul. A denarius is not said to be a denarius if the image is removed. Likewise, when the image is deformed in our soul, or even somehow removed, which happens through sin according to the verse, *You will reduce their image to nothing* (Ps 73:20), then the soul ceases to be a coin or is called a lost coin. The way sin takes away the image, and how not, is clear: it does not take it away as far as the soul's powers. But even though sin does not strictly remove these powers, it does wound and debilitate them.

Thirdly sin makes us into prodigal children by taking from us our eternal inheritance. Fourthly it causes us to be robbed and wounded by thieves, that is, by demons or by carnal desires: robbed of graces, wounded in natural virtues. Fifthly through sin our will loses every good and is the captive of evil. Sixthly through sin our mind puts on darkness and is stripped of light. Seventhly through sin all our works become raw, cold, and without merit.

But penance, since it is wholly opposed to sin, causes seven things contrary to those just enumerated. Penance shows the lost sheep to the seeking Christ; it presents the lost coin to the searching Christ; it brings the prodigal son back to his father; it hands over to be guarded and healed the man wounded and robbed by thieves. In penance every good is found and preserved in the affections; it drives away darkness and brings light to the mind; as far as actions, it purifies all our works. But let us remember that we are able to assert all these things as we are united to Christ. Because in the Gospel he specifically speaks about the lost sheep, the lost coin, the prodigal son, the man wounded by thieves, we attain every good through him. He is our master that drives away darkness, brings light, and purifies all our works in the fire of love, for without him we can do nothing.

If some matters treated above are repeated here, it is because they can be discussed under one aspect or another. For penance causes the four things generally by not extending to our union with Christ, while it causes the seven things specifically by extending to this consideration, whereby through penance we are joined to Christ and attain all seven of them.

We should consider that while Christ's death was sufficient for the redemption of all, it does not accomplish the redemption of all because our iniquities separate us from him, and the influence of his holiness does not reach us. But when we are brought back to him and united to him through penance, then we are found by him as the lost coin, etc., as described above. We should consider as well that the losing of the coin pertains to the image, which consists in the soul's powers. We are wounded there by sin as far as they are natural powers; and we are robbed of graces as far as they are perfected by virtues and gifts. Therefore the losing of this coin seems to be identified with this wounding and robbing. But we will say that our coin, the image of God, consists in the higher powers. According to Augustine, in book fourteen, chapter three, of his *On the Trinity*, the image of God must be sought in the highest part of the soul. But the wounding and robbing takes place in the lower virtues, because the concupiscible and irascible appetites, or the sensitive appetite itself, is robbed of its perfections by sin, and it is wounded and debilitated in performing good. Therefore we can refer each to one or the other.

Chapter 10

In which it is shown that, if we want to be fully conformed to the rectitude
of divine wisdom, we should be fully contrite, confess, and make satisfaction
for our sins; and in which it is shown what contrition is, and for what
reasons we ought to repent of our sins.

We have spoken at length about all the good effects penance
brings about. Now, so that we might be encouraged to do penance,
and lest we deviate from the rectitude of divine wisdom, we wish to
speak about the parts of penance. Sin causes all the aforementioned
evils by which we deviate from the rectitude of divine wisdom as from
a straight and true measure by which all such deviations are known.
On the other hand, penance causes the good things opposed to
these evils and by which we are conformed to that rectitude and that
measure. But penance is made up of many parts, and nothing is complete without all of its parts. Therefore, that we might be fully conformed to that rectitude, we have decided to discuss all the parts of
penance.

There are commonly said to be three parts of penance: contrition in the heart, confession in the mouth, and satisfaction in
works. A sinner should first be contrite of heart. Metaphorically it
is said that a sinner's heart is like a bottle filled with foul liquid,
because it is filled with the filthiness of sin. Since making contrite
literally means to crush or break something into little pieces, the
heart of a sinner ought to be contrite, that is broken into little
pieces, so that all the foul liquid runs out. If it were only broken
into large pieces, then some of that liquid might be left. But when
it is completely shattered, nothing of the foul liquid will remain in
it. This contrition is remorse over sins, and through remorse over
them the heart is emptied of the stench and filth of sins.

Concerning this remorse that is required in penance, Augustine,
in his book *On True and False Penance*, says that a sinner should always
have remorse, and should rejoice in his remorse, and should grieve
that he has not always been remorseful. This remorse, then, ought to
be like contrition, that is, a shattering into small pieces. For we ought
to search our conscience in particular concerning all the things we
have committed against God, and we ought to have remorse over
each of them so that no sin, or complacency about any sin, lies hidden in any part of our heart. Indeed we should so repent of each sin
singly and particularly that our entire heart, in order to restrain sins,
is broken in every part and holds no sin in itself. As is said in the
fourth book of *Sentences*, distinction 14, where the authority of Gregory is cited, whoever deplores some sins while committing others
either does not yet know how to repent or is pretending. And it con-

tinues: What is the benefit if someone weeps over sins of lust but still follows the impulses of greed. And in *On True and False Penance*, chapter nine, Augustine says: It is a certain impiety of unfaithfulness to hope for halfway mercy from him who is just and justice itself. Our heart should be contrite and shattered in every part so that we repent of every single sin.

We can enumerate five causes why we should be contrite and remorseful over our sins: first that we might be turned away from the world, according to the verse: *Love not the world nor the things that are in the world* (1 Jn 2:15). Second that we might be turned toward God, as God himself urges us through the prophet Joel: *Be converted to me in your whole heart and rend your hearts* (Jl 2:12-13). Third that we might have God as our help. For just as someone who turns himself away from light does not have its assistance, so too someone who turns himself away from God has spurned God's help as much as he can; against whom it is said in the psalms: *Behold the person who has not made God his help* (Ps 62:7). Fourthly we should have displeasure over sin because we cannot begin a new life unless our former life displeases us. Fifthly we ought to be so contrite and remorseful that we avoid sinning in the future, for this is genuine repentance according to Ambrose: to weep for past evils and not to commit again what was wept for. And according to Gregory it is to mourn over sins committed and not to commit what was mourned over.

Chapter 11

In which it is shown that confession, which is the second part of penance, adorns the soul, and that we should confess to a priest for five reasons.

The second part of penance is confession, to which we are urged by the testimony of James, who says: *Confess your sins to one another* (Jas 5:16). The confession of sins adorns the soul and makes it beautiful. Confession is interchangeable with beauty and sweetness, and they entail each other according to the psalms: *You have put on confession and beauty* (Ps 104:1); *Confession and sweetness are in his sight* (Ps 96:6).

There were some who said that sins are forgiven in contrition alone, so that a person need not confess. And they argued from the account of the lepers, of whom it is said that *when they went they were cleansed* (Lk 17:14), although they had been commanded to show themselves to priests. This, they argued, signifies that sinners should confess their sins and show themselves to priests, but before they show themselves they seem to have already been cleansed. Therefore before a person confesses he is clean in his contrition and intention of confessing, which accords with the psalms: *I said I will confess,* that is, I was intending to confess, *against myself my injustices to the Lord, and you have forgiven the wickedness of my sin,* etc. (Ps 32:5). Thus if remission occurs from the intention itself, we need no longer confess.

But we say that the will is empty and vain if the disposition is present and yet it does not lead to action. A person's sin is not forgiven unless confession is present in his will and he intends to confess; otherwise there is no forgiveness for him. If such an intention and disposition to confess is in him, and yet he does not fulfill what he had in his intention and will, then his intention is deemed empty and insufficient for salvation. Therefore a person may be saved without confession, when he is contrite and intends to confess, but time for confession fails him. If, however, he has the disposition to confess, and either he was feigning when he proposed to confess or he departed from a good intention, he is thereby ungrateful to God, and he will be unable to attain salvation as long as he continues in this ingratitude.

We can assign five reasons why a person should confess: first that he might place himself in a state of assurance. When someone confesses he puts himself under the keys of the Church. Great is the power of the keys and often by virtue of the keys a person moves from attrition to contrition. A person does not know how to judge whether he has true contrition, and therefore he should place himself under the keys, hoping and trusting that, by virtue of the keys, any defect in his contrition will be made up. In this way he establishes himself on a firmer basis, saying with the wise: Hold to the certain and leave behind the uncertain.

Secondly a person should confess because he avoids transgressing a commandment, since we are commanded to confess. This was prefigured in Leviticus 14, where the rite for a leper is recorded: when he is cleansed he is brought to a priest. This reveals that the sinner cleansed from the leprosy of sin ought to show himself to a priest through confession.

Thirdly a person should confess to gain an increase of grace. Even if he attains grace by contrition, through devout confession he merits an increase of grace. Thus it is said in Proverbs: *He that hides his sins will not prosper, but he that confesses and forsakes them will find mercy* (Prv 28:13). Mercy here means either that he moved to a state of grace, if he was not in grace before confession, or that he obtained more grace, if already in grace he devoutly put himself under the keys of the Church.

Fourthly a person should confess to gain knowledge of sin. One confesses so that the priest might know how to discern between leprosies and to give an understanding of sins, for he knows how to bind and to loose. In *True and False Penance*, Augustine says that someone who wishes to confesses his sins in order to find grace should seek a priest, who knows how to bind and loose, who admonishes him mercifully and prays that both may not fall into a pit; otherwise, if he is neglectful of himself, he may be neglected by his confessor.

Fifthly a person should confess his sins to lessen the penalty owed for sin. The shame that comes in confession is part of satisfaction, and it lessens the penalty owed for sins.

Chapter 12

In which it is shown that satisfaction, which is the third part of penance, is necessary for the penitent because of five reasons.

The third part of penance is satisfaction, which can be related to five things. There are three evils in sin, namely pride, insofar as the sinner does not wish to be subject to God; avarice insofar as he wishes to follow his own will and desire; and obligation to receive punishment for transgression. Satisfaction, then, can be related to five things: either to the pride within sin, insofar as a sinner does not wish to be subject to another's will; or to avarice insofar as he wishes to follow his own will and desire; or to the obligation for punishment; or to the other parts of penance, which are contrition and confession; or to the one making satisfaction and doing penance. When the penitent makes satisfaction in this way, he puts himself under the will of another, namely of a priest, and forsakes his own will to do what the priest commands him, which is not easy or pleasurable.

Thus five things are required for good satisfaction: first, against the pride in sin, a sinner must subject himself to another's will; second, against avarice, which is also in every sin, he must forsake his own will; third he must undergo punishment in himself for the obligation in every sin. According to Augustine in chapter 19 of *True and False Penitence*, etymologically the word penitent means one who holds punishment. Fourth he must make up for any defect in his contrition and confession. The sorrow of contrition and the shame of confession are part of satisfaction. But perhaps a person was not so sorrowful nor so ashamed that he made sufficient satisfaction for sin. Then some other satisfaction beyond contrition and confession must be enjoined. Fifth it is good satisfaction when a penitent offers himself wholly to God. In satisfaction are imposed prayers, abstinence, almsgiving, pilgrimages, fasts, and other such things. When contrition is in the heart and confession in the mouth, so that the soul of the sinner is ordered to God, then satisfaction must be imposed that he might offer himself wholly to God, both his body and his possessions, if he has any.

Penances include fasts by which the body is afflicted; prayers by which the entire soul is ordered to God; genuflections by which the body is bent and the soul humbled; pilgrimages by which the body becomes tired; or almsgiving by which external goods are shared. In this way a person can be ordered to God according to himself and all that he owns. Hence a priest ought to consider with maturity and discretion what he should impose on someone, for the more a penitent repents and grieves, and the more he is ashamed of sin, the more satisfaction he makes and the less punishments should be placed on him. In the same way abstinence should be imposed more on youth, that they may be weakened in the flesh and, thus weakened, may keep themselves from sins.

Chapter 13

In which the fourth question is answered, namely how God should be loved, from the fourth praise of divine wisdom, that it radiates infinite goodness in which all creatures participate.

Now that we have discussed the three praises of divine wisdom, answering the three corresponding questions, we wish to discuss the fourth praise, which concerns the goodness of divine wisdom, which enables us to answer the fourth question: How should we love God? To understand this well we will have to know what should be loved and how many good effects love causes in us.

It should be known that to love and to will the good are the same thing. Hence the philosopher, in the second chapter of his *Rhetoric*, says about love: To those defining love we should say it is wishing for another what we consider good. We must take up our account of love from this understanding of it as goodness we wish for another, or for ourselves. Thus from God's goodness we will be able to know how God should be loved.

We say that the fourth praise of divine goodness is its love, for that wisdom is not only full, high, and upright, as the first three praises assert, but also good and the utmost good, as this fourth praise asserts. It is said that good is equivalent to being. Therefore just as something is good insofar as it exists, that which is infinite being is also infinite good; and because that divine wisdom is infinite being, it must also be infinite good. Thus if the account of love is taken up from the understanding of goodness, it follows that

God should be loved infinitely. And because we are not able to attain to this, since our love, either as an act or as a habit, is finite, inasmuch as it is created, it follows that we cannot love God so much that he should not be loved more. Hence, according to Gregory, the measure of love is to have no measure. And thus it is commanded in the Mosaic law and in the evangelical law that we should love God as much as we can with all our mind, that is, with our entire memory, with all our heart, that is, with our entire understanding, and with all our soul, that is, with our entire will, which are the three parts of the image of God.

And further we should love him with all our strength, which can be interpreted in two ways: first that "all our strength" refers to the powers of our soul. For we should order toward God not only the parts of the image, which are the higher powers of the soul, namely memory, understanding, and will, but all the other powers of the soul as well. We should be brought to God and love him not only with all our memory, understanding, and will, but also with all the other powers of the soul, and they should all be ordered to him through love.

Or "all our strength" may mean that we should have no measure in loving God, neither extensively nor intensively, but we should be completely ordered to God. We should love God with all our mind, with all our heart, and with all our soul, that is, by ordering everything, our whole being, to him. Thus our totality is in him extensively so that nothing is in us that we do not order to him. We should do this further with all our strength, that our totality might be in him intensively, so that we must order all of ourselves to him with all fervor, as much as we are able, and according to all our powers. The first totality, when it says with all our mind, etc., is understood extensively, so that our entire being might be comprehended in him. The second totality, when it says with all our strength, etc., is understood intensively, because we ought to order all our powers to God, not just in any way, but in the highest way.

Therefore from that goodness which shines in divine wisdom we can know how God should be loved. But this very divine goodness, which shines in God and in his wisdom, may be considered from three sides: first what it is in itself; second what it is in the production of its future effects; and third what it is in the conservation of its effects. From the divine goodness in itself we are shown how to love God, because he should be loved according to all that is in us, according to all our powers, according to every way, according to all our strength. This holds true not only if we consider the divine goodness in itself shining in the divine wisdom, but also if we consider it in the production of its effects, because, as the apostle teaches, *we have nothing that we have not received* (1 Cor 4:7). From him we have mind, heart, and soul; memory, understanding, and will, and all the powers of the soul; from him we also have every impulse for good that can exist through our powers; from him, therefore, we have everything extensively and intensively, as far as the powers possessed and the manner of possession, as far as their natures and as far as their impulses. And since it is terrible ingratitude not to order all things that we have to him from whom we have them, that we might not be ungrateful to God, we ought to order all our powers according to every impulse to God himself. Nor is this enough, because we cannot render equally to him. For if we consider the measure, we give nothing above and do nothing more than what we were obliged to do. Therefore the Lord said: When we have done all good works, we ought to say, *We are useless servants and have done only what we ought to do* (Lk 17:10).

The same is clear thirdly if we consider the divine wisdom shining in divine wisdom as far as the conservation of its effects. For God is not the cause of things as a builder is the cause of a house, but if at any moment God should desert his creation, it would immediately cease to exist. Hence Augustine, in book four of his *The Literal Meaning of Genesis*, chapter 12, says: "The world is not like a structure of rooms, which remains standing even when its builder departs and is gone; but the world would vanish in the blink of an eye if God removed his governance from it." And because God is above all things, conserving them, and because they are nothing without him, therefore we should be turned toward him through all things, and, with all our strength, we should direct all our powers to him through love. Speaking to God in book six of his *Confessions*, Augustine says: Leaving all things behind let us turn to you, who are above all and without whom all would fall into nothingness.

Considering the manner of divine love, that we should love him above all intensively, with all our strength, and above all things extensively, according to all our powers, let us appropriate this manner of loving to the praise of divine wisdom, insofar as infinite goodness shines forth in it. For inasmuch as God through his own wisdom knows himself as infinite good, he has communicated his goodness to things through his wisdom, so that all things may be said to be made in his divine wisdom. He has communicated his goodness to us through his wisdom and has made us his debtors, so that we are bound to love him without measure; and therefore we wish to adapt all things to the praise of divine wisdom, insofar as it is infinite good and infinite goodness shines forth in it.

Chapter 14

In which it is shown from the manner of love of divine wisdom how we can know what things should be loved, how many, and in what order.

We said above that if we know how God should be loved, then we can know what should be loved, how many things should be loved, and how many good effects love causes within us. In *Teaching Christianity*, chapter 23, Augustine relates four things that should be loved: One which is above us, namely God; another which is ourself; third what is near to us, namely our neighbor; and fourth what is below us, namely our body. But in the way he lays down these four, he really relates five things that should be loved, for we are divided into two parts, into the interior and exterior person, or, using Augustine's words in *Teaching Christianity* I, 26, 27, into soul and body. Thus we may divide the good of our neighbor and say that five things should be loved: God who is above us; the interior person within ourselves; the interior person of our neighbor who is near to us; our exterior person or our body, which is below us; and the external person of our neighbor or his body, which is near to our body.

But saying this we seem not to have enumerated all the things that should be loved, for love itself should be loved. This is why Augustine says in *The Trinity* VIII, 8: Let no one say, I know not what to love; he should love his brother, and love the love whereby he loves his brother. Therefore we say that there are two kinds of things to be loved: some we love as things for which we desire good; and some we love, not as things for which we desire good, but as good things that we desire for ourselves or for others. In the first category are three things to be loved in one account, four things in another, and five things in yet another. In *The Trinity* XIX, 14 and *Teaching Christianity* I, 26, 27, Augustine says there are three things to be loved: God, our neighbor, and ourself. These three things to be loved are declared when the Lord says: *You shall love the Lord your God, and your neighbor as yourself* (Mt 22:37.39). But in *Teaching Christianity* I, 23, 22 he says that there are four things to be loved, because he divides us into soul and body, or into ourself and our body. (For when something is composed of two elements, the higher receives the name of the whole, as the pope's actions are said to be the Church's actions because the pope is the head of the Church; and just as the pope is called highest in the Church, likewise our soul, or spirit, or interior person, is identified with our-self.) But just as we are divided in two, so we can also divide our neighbors in two, into corporeal and spiritual nature, at least our neighbors that are human. (We make this qualification on account of the angels, who are also our neighbors and are able to show us mercy; for that chasm between us and the angels is not so firm that we cannot go to them and they cannot be called our neighbors.) Therefore these five things we have discussed should be loved: the spiritual nature that is above us, namely God; the spiritual nature that we are, namely our soul, the spiritual nature of our neighbor who is near us, namely his soul, whether angelic or human; our corporeal nature which is below us, namely our body; and the corporeal nature of other people, namely their bodies that are near to our own.

We love all these as things for which we desire good, and they should be loved in this order: first God is to be loved, even more than we love ourselves, since that on account of which something is done is the greater cause (*Posterior Analytic* 1). God should be loved on account of himself, but a person ought to love himself, not on account of himself, since he is not his own end, but on account of God. It follows from this that a person ought to love God more than himself. And we cannot doubt the truth of this, for if love is a certain union, God is united more and is nearer to us than we are to ourselves, as Augustine argues in book three of his *Confessions*, chapter six. He should be loved more indeed, because our good cannot even subsist without God. Our good is found in God more than in ourselves because our good cannot subsist without God. Our good, then, would be unable to subsist in itself were it not joined to God. If we were annihilated, and if nothing existed in itself, all could be restored by God. Therefore every person should love himself more in God than in himself, and he should love God more than himself, since his good is more God's than it is his own.

Likewise we ought to love God more than our neighbors. Children are more united to their father than they are to each other, for they are united to each other only because they are united to a father from whom they derive. Thus the love of children for their father is greater than their love for each other. So too we bear the image of one God, and thus our union with others is from the union we have with God; therefore we should love God more than all others.

We should love God more than all others, but we should also love ourselves more than our neighbors. We are not commanded to love our neighbors more than ourselves, but as ourselves, that is, to the extent we love ourselves. Just as we love ourselves unto eternal life, so we should love our neighbors unto eternal life. It is right that the full account of love be taken from its end, for an end acts in lovable things as first principles in speculative things. We believe first principles in themselves but conclusions on the basis of first principles, and thus we believe first principles more than we believe conclusions. Likewise we love the end on account of itself but love other things on account of the end. God, then, should be loved because he is our final end and beatitude. He should be loved above all. We should love ourselves for the sake of this end that we may be joined to it; and we should love our neighbors for the sake of this end that we may be associated with them in this end. Since it is greater to be united to the end than to be associated with others in union with the end, we should love ourselves more than we love our neighbors.

We should love our bodies on account of this end and for the sake of this beatitude, because beatitude overflows to the body from beatitude in the soul. When someone is glad at heart, a more beautiful color reverberates to his body from the gladness in his heart. Such is the case in heaven, and much more so, where beauty and beatitude will overflow to the body from the beauty and beatitude in the soul. Thus our body is to be loved in the fourth place. But we ought to love the bodies of our neighbors as things that will be associated with our bodies in a sharing by the reverberation of beatitude. The bodies of our neighbors are to be loved lastly.

We have assigned five steps, as is clear from our discussion, in the category of things to be loved, insofar as they are things for which we desire good: first we desire divine good for God; second we desire that such good be united to us; third we desire our neighbors to be associated with us in that good; fourth we desire that good to somehow reverberate to our bodies; and fifth we desire the bodies of our neighbors to be associated with such reverberation in our bodies.

Just as we have assigned an order to the things we love insofar as they are things for which we desire good, so we may assign an order to those things we love insofar as they are certain goods which we desire for ourselves or for others. These are found in an order of three: first is love itself, or charity, which is the mother of all good; second are interior goods; and third external goods. All of these should be loved on account of the end and for the sake of beatitude. This love, then, and all these goods without which there is never love, and which are never without love, we should love as things apart from which beatitude cannot be enjoyed, and as things which, when possessed, we cannot lose. Interior goods we should love as things leading to our end, and as supports when present. And external goods we may love in ourselves and others as things that somehow help toward our end from afar. But we love all of these not properly as things for which we desire good, but as certain goods which we can love in ourselves and others. For we ought to desire and love charity in ourselves and others to such an extent that the words of the Canticles may be confirmed in us: *The king has brought me to the wine cellar, he has put love within me* (Sg 2:4). For whoever is inebriated by the wine of love is not separated from the right order of love; rather it holds him closer and envelops him. Inebriated in this way, we love all things to be loved in their proper order.

Chapter 15

In which it is shown what good effects divine love works within us.

Hoping to complete all the matters we have brought up concerning love, we wish to relate the good effects which love works within us. We intend to speak about this love according to Augustine in his *Confessions* XIII, 9 and in *The City of God* XI, 28: what a weight is in bodies, love is in spirits. Hence he says: My weight is my love; by it I am carried wherever I am carried. Understanding weight generally, as Augustine understands it, we may say that when bodies are carried to places that are proper to them, they attain five things by their weight: first bodies tend to their places through their weight; second they are united to their places; third the are made similar to their places; fourth they are conserved in them; fifth they rest in them. Heavy things tend to the center by their weight; they are united to the center; they are made like the center; thus they are conserved, and they rest in it. All these occur through their place in relation to the center. Things are said to be made similar to their places and to be conserved in them. Since they rest in their places, and since nothing rests in what is, simply speaking, unlike itself, when they are moved so as to rest in their places, they should have some likeness to their places, or take on some similitude, from the fact that they are in their places. It also follows that they are conserved in their places by reason of the conformity they have with them, or which they take on from the fact that they are in them.

These five things, then, concerning bodies with respect to their weight, are true also concerning spirits with respect to their love, especially since they are carried to God by love. This takes place through the virtues; and this motion is somehow natural or suitable to nature, for while it happens through grace, grace does not take away nature, but perfects it. To be carried by vices is to be carried against nature, for every vice is contrary to nature, as Augustine argues in *The City of God* XI, 17. Just as bodies do not rest in places contrary to their nature, so too a soul does not rest when it is carried somewhere through vice. Rather through this it incurs greater penalty, as Augustine says in the first book of his *Confessions*, chapter 12: You have ordained, O Lord, and so it is, that every inordinate soul is punishment unto itself.

Therefore when the mind is carried by love into what is according to nature, or into what is fitting to nature, or into what perfects natures, whereby it is brought to God, which is it love's role to accomplish in us, then we say that by such motion, and by such love, our spiritual nature attains five things that correspond to the five things bodies attain when they are brought by weight to a place that befits them: love causes us to tend toward God; it unites us with him; it transforms us into him; it makes us rejoice in God; and it causes us to rest in him.

First love causes us to tend toward God. Properly speaking, such love is divine; it causes us to have God as our end in everything, because it makes us love all things on account of him. Since a thing naturally tends toward its end, it follows from the nature of love, which makes us desire God above all, that love also makes us tend to him through desire.

Such love also unites us with God, for it is the definition of love that it is a certain unitive power between the lover and loved thing, as Augustine asserts in *The Trinity*, chapter ten. And Dionysius declares, in book four of *Divine Names*: We say that every love, whether divine, angelic, intellectual, animal, or natural, is a certain unitive power. This is why the apostle says that *whoever clings to God* (namely through love) *is one spirit with him* (1 Cor 6:17).

Third such love has the power to transform us into God. Love accomplishes more than wisdom because wisdom only makes us like God. It is enough for the likenesses of known things to be in the knower to the extent that they are known by him. Indeed somehow there is greater knowledge of a thing when it is known by likeness than by its essence. For an angel has knowledge of itself through its own essence, but God does not have knowledge of a created thing through its essence, but through his own essence, which is a likeness and exemplar of all creatures. Yet God has an incomparably fuller knowledge of the angels than the angels have of themselves. Hence Dionysius, in the sixth book of *The Angelic Hierarchy*, argues that only the principle, that is, God, knows the perfections of the heavenly spirits; and he adds that these angels are said to be ignorant of their own powers. This must be understood with respect to God, for the knowledge God has of the angels is so clear that, with respect to his knowledge, the angels are said to be ignorant of themselves. Therefore wisdom makes us like things, that is, a similitude is sufficient for knowing; but love transforms us. If there is perfect love, the lover wishes to be the same as the thing loved. Thus, in the fourth book of *Divine Names*, Dionysius says that love takes something outside of itself and places it with what is loved.

Fourth divine love makes us rejoice in God. When love transforms us into God and makes us divine forms of God, it follows that it causes us to rejoice in divine things. For delight and joy necessarily follow from the union of things fit for each other. This love, which transforms us and conforms us to divine things, makes divine things delightful to us. As the weight in bodies makes them tend to the place where they are conserved, so divine love makes us tend with delight unto God and to be in him. Therefore, of itself, this love causes us to remain in God, and it conserves us in him, for everyone freely remains in a delightful state. And because this is so, among other signs, this is the very great sign that a person is in the state of grace and has this love: when he delights in spiritual and divine things. We cannot know with certitude *whether we are worthy of love or hate* (Eccl 9:1), but we can know with strong probability through signs. Thus if we have no remorse of conscience, if we gladly listen to divine words, if we delight in them, then we should have confidence that we are in grace.

Fifth divine love causes us to rest in God. The mind that is delighted in something rests in it, and especially if it delights in it as a final end. And divine love works in us a final delight in God.

This, then, is the order of divine love: first it begins; second it perfects; third, once perfected, it makes the lover say with Paul: *I long to be dissolved* (in divine love) *and to be with Christ* (Phil 1:23), or to be in God and rest in him. According to this love, people begin with desire to tend toward God; they are perfected by being united to him; as perfect and complete forms of God, they are transformed into God; being transformed, nothing besides God is delightful to them; and delighting in God, they come to rest in him.

If you are still unsure about how we should love God, I say that we should love him without measure; that we should love him as much as we can extensively and intensively, as was discussed above; that we should love all things properly on account of him, whom we said is above the order of things loved; that we should love him in such a way that we tend to him, are united with him, are transformed into him, delight in him, and rest in him.

Chapter 16

In which it is shown from the fifth praise of divine wisdom, namely that it is near and closest to all things, how the fifth question is answered, how we ought to fear God and obey him in everything.

Having answered the first four questions and dealt with the first four praises of divine wisdom, we now wish to answer the fifth question, namely how we should fear God and obey him. And we shall answer it according to the fifth praise of divine wisdom, that it is near to all. This wisdom *reaches mightily from end to end and orders all things sweetly* (Wis 8:1); which would not be the case unless the divine works were more diffused than all else, and unless they were nearer and more intimate.

Three ways are commonly set down to explain how God is everywhere, and how he is close and intimate to everything: that he is everywhere by his presence, seeing and knowing all things; by his essence, conserving all things in being; and by his power, ruling over all things. We are able to adapt all of these very well to the divine wisdom. God knows all things by his wisdom, because whatever is known is known through wisdom, and thus the things known to God are known through God's wisdom. And just as God knows all by his wisdom, so he conserves them all in being. God is said to be the cause of things, and by his wisdom God is said to have caused things. Hence Augustine says in *The Trinity*, in book fifteen and the last chapter of book six: He knows all his creatures, both spiritual and corporeal, not because they exist, but they exist because he knows them. He demonstrates here that God's knowledge or wisdom is the cause of things. The philosopher asserts the same thing too, and thus the commentator says, in the *Metaphysics* 12.39, that God's wisdom causes things, while our knowledge is caused by things. If God causes things by his knowledge or wisdom, this means that he somehow causes them as he is the cause of all; but he is the cause of all things by making and conserving them, and thus he must bring things into being and conserve them in being through his wisdom.

All things are related to God as things made to their maker, because *he is the artisan of all, having all power* (Wis 7:21.23). It follows, then, that just as the will and wisdom of an artisan is the cause of all manufactured objects, so in God, his will and his wisdom are the cause of all things. Hence it is held in book six of the *Metaphysics* that the will is included in the definition of a manufactured object, that the thing made is willed, because no work is completed without a command of the will, but the artisan performs his art intentionally. This is why the causes of things are called God's speech, which pertains to wisdom: *He spoke and they were made* (Ps 33:9). And they are called God's will, which pertains to volition: *He has carried out all that he willed* (Ps 115:3). This means that the images, exemplars, designs, and ideas of all manufactured objects shine forth in the art and in the wisdom of the artisan. These designs and ideas are productive of things. The will of an artisan alone is unable to produce things because the ideas and designs which are productive of things are not present in the artisan's will, but are in his wisdom and understanding. Thus the will of the artisan, through the mediation of wisdom and understanding, advances to the production of manufactured objects. A hand impresses the form of the seal into wax, but the exemplar of the impressed form is not in the hand, so it is necessary that the hand act with a mediating seal, where the form exists. Thus, inasmuch as the hand directs the seal and moves it to make an impression, the hand may be called the cause of the impressed form; yet it will be a cause by the mediation of the seal, for we say that the form in the wax comes from the form in the seal. Likewise, closer to our purpose, a material house comes from a house that is in the soul, as the philosopher makes clear in book seven of his *Metaphysics*. As the builder's will is the cause of the building, yet the exemplar and image of the building to be constructed is not in his will (according to the will as such), the will cannot be the cause except through the mediation of the mind.

This argument holds for the matter in question. For the divine will is the first and highest cause of all, as Augustine declares in *The Trinity* III, 4. Nevertheless the divine will causes things through the mediation of the divine intellect and the divine wisdom, where reside the exemplars by which all things were created. As Augustine says about ideas in his *Miscellany of Eighty-three Questions*, we should not say that God created all things irrationally. And he declares: If this cannot be rightly said or believed, then it follows that all things are created by reason. And because a person and a horse are not created according to the same exemplar, but each is created according to its own exemplar, and because these exemplars are not to be thought to exist except in the mind of the creator, therefore the divine will or God himself is the cause of nothing which he does not cause through his wisdom. As God is the cause of things, he will cause them through his wisdom. And because God is a cause that produces and conserves things, nothing more fitting can be said than that by his wisdom he not only brings things into being, but also conserves them in being.

We should suppose that, just as a form, derived from a seal as from an exemplary cause, is much better and sturdier in certain matter, so too are things in their own nature derived from the exemplary ideas in the mind of God. And we should suppose that, without God's presence, things are more fluid in retaining the impression made by God, or in retaining the nature impressed on them by the divine exemplars, than is water in retaining the form of a seal. Just as it is necessary for a seal to be continually present in order for the water to keep the form impressed by the seal in it, so God, or the divine wisdom, or the exemplars of things that exist in the divine wisdom, must be present to things in order for them to be conserved in the nature impressed in them by those exemplars.

Therefore God by his wisdom, as we said above, sees all things, produces all things, and conserves all things. He also rules all things by his wisdom, for ruling is particularly ascribed to wisdom: *A wise servant will rule foolish sons* (Prv 17:2). In these three ways, namely by seeing all things, by ruling all things, and by producing and conserving all things, God is everywhere through his wisdom. But in a fourth way he is present to good and holy people, by granting them grace and gifts. And he is present in a fifth way to the wicked, by prosecuting justice in them according to their works, or being prepared to prosecute justice.

From these five ways, five reasons are drawn on account of which a person especially fears and obeys his Lord. The fact that someone does not fear his Lord, or does not obey his commands, can occur for five reasons, with respect to our present concern: first if he does not believe that his Lord sees all things; second if he does not believe that he rules all things; third if he does not believe that he rules easily. For if someone believes that his Lord knows all things, and rules everywhere, yet supposes that he does not rule easily, he may say within himself that he can safely get away with opposing his Lord; for even if his Lord may rule everywhere, and prosecute his justice everywhere, if it is difficult for him to do this, a person's wrong may go unpunished. Fourth a person sometimes will not obey the Lord if he believes that he is not gracious and generous. For people say, Why should we serve the Lord when we gain no reward from him? But because people readily desire rewards and remunerations, and have great fear of losing them, they willingly serve the Lord and fear offending him, whom they know is generous and gracious. Fifth a person may not care to obey the Lord and fear him if he believes that he does not punish the wicked or does not inflict punishments corresponding to the sins of wrongdoers.

Therefore, God first sees all things by his wisdom; second he rules all things; third he rules all things easily, because he so rules and conserves all things by his wisdom that they would perish as soon as he withdrew himself; fourth God is present by his wisdom to all good and just people, giving them his grace and gifts; and fifth he is present to all the wicked, prosecuting his justice in them, or being prepared to prosecute justice at the appointed time. All things, then, are very much under his dominion, since they could not exist for one moment without him. It is clear from this how we ought to fear God: we should fear him as one to whom no crime of ours can remain unknown; under whose rule all things are placed; who rules all things easily and at whose command all things came to be; and for whom no good goes unrewarded and no evil unpunished.

Chapter 17

In which it is shown from the sixth praise of divine wisdom, namely that it is fruitful in all it does, how the sixth question is answered, namely how we should thank God for blessings received.

Having treated the first five questions, we now wish to discuss the sixth praise of divine wisdom, namely its fruitfulness. It is so fruitful that it works all things in all ways. For the psalm declared: *I myself speak my works for the king* (Ps 45:1), as if to say: The king performed my works in me, or God worked within me. *I myself speak,* that is, I acknowledge, I confess that these belong to you, more as your works than mine. From this praise of divine wisdom, that it is so fruitful it works all things in all ways, we can answer the sixth question: How should we thank God for blessings received?

Dionysius states in his book *Divine Names*, chapter eight, and Damascene, in book two, chapter 23, that there exist three things in the universe: substance, power, and operation. According to these three we can discuss five things that divine wisdom, because of its fruitfulness, works in all things. By his wisdom God gives substance, power, and operation to all things; and he conserves all things in their substance, power, and operation.

Through his wisdom God grants substance or nature to all things. As Dionysius establishes in book four of *Divine Names*, the beginning is not duality, but unity. Thus, according to him, when any two things are presented, either one is caused by the other, or both are caused by a third; and that which is caused by none is necessarily the cause of all. If something were not caused by it, then these two would have to be caused by a third. But when one of them is uncaused, both cannot be caused by another. Therefore since God in himself is not caused by another, it follows that all things are caused by him, and that no nature exists which can be outside his causality. And we can not only show that he is the cause of all negatively, by denying what does not befit God, that he is something caused, but we can also determine this positively, according to what befits God, that he is being itself. And since he has supreme existence, he has brought all things into being, and there is no nature which is not produced by him.

We claim with the philosopher, in book two of the *Metaphysics*, that the greatest being is the cause of all others. Just as the hottest thing is the cause of all hot things, so the highest being is the cause of all beings. For we may judge being in itself in the way we approach other perfections: if heat is a certain perfection, the heat in matter does not have all the quality of heat, because it is limited to the capacity of the receiving matter. But if heat is separated, it would have the full quality of heat. Likewise the being in matter does not have all the quality of being, but if it is separated in itself, it is the entire quality of being. Nothing residing in matter or some material is the highest being. God, who is himself separated existence, is the highest being, contains all being within himself, and is the cause of all things that have being.

Created natures are brought into being inasmuch as existence is communicated to them, since every being is caused by the first being, God himself who exists supremely. Consequently God is the cause of all natures. And this is Augustine's view, in *The City of God* XII, 5 where he says: By God who exists supremely, the essences of all things that do not exist supremely are made. And the commentator, explaining the words of the philosopher in the *Metaphysics* 2, that the greatest being is the cause of all others, says: One is being in itself and truth in itself; but other things are beings and are true through his being and truth.

Every nature comes from God himself, and every power also comes from him. For it is proved in the *Book of Causes* that God needs no other medium in his action. All other natures or substances need a medium to act, for a created being does nothing immediately through its own substance. As the commentator proves in book seven of the *Metaphysics*, substantial forms are not immediate principles of their actions, but power, which is the immediate principle of action, must be added to created substances or natures. Thus, when a created being acts, that it might be united to its action, it needs a medium, that is, it needs some additional power which continues acting with the object acted upon; for since a created agent does not act through its own substance, it cannot itself continue in the object, nor can it advance in action, but it must act through another power added onto its own nature. Therefore nothing created is its own power, but it participates in power.

God, who immediately acts through his own substance, and who needs nothing additional to act, is necessarily his own power and not a participant in power. Since existence, which God is essentially, is the cause of all other beings that exist by participation, it follows that God is not only the highest being and the cause of all substances, but is also the cause of all powers, inasmuch as he is his own power essentially. In the *Book of Causes*, divine power is said to be the power of powers, for in proposition 16 it is written that all powers depend on the first infinite power, which is the power of powers.

The divine wisdom, then, is so fruitful in things that it is the cause of all their natures, all their powers, and all their operations. For operation in things always depends on the first mover, just as every motion here below, according to the course of nature we see, depends on a first motion, so that if the first motion ceases (unless God should change the order he has given to things), every other motion would cease. Hence the philosopher, in book eight of the *Physics*, labelled the first motion the life in beings, because, according to the commentator, this first motion, with respect to all other motions, acts as their life, since it behaves as a soul in living things. The motion of life in living things is from the soul in such a way that, when the soul is separated, no motion of life remains in bodies. Likewise every motion in all moving things is, simply speaking, from the first motion, so that if that motion ceased, every other motion would cease. Because God is the first mover, he is the cause of all other operations, and it belongs to him to bring about all operations. Hence the Lord says in the gospel: *Without me you can do nothing* (Jn 15:5); and Isaiah writes: *The Lord our God has worked all our works in us* (Is 26:12).

In the fourth place, the fruitfulness of divine wisdom is so great that it not only gives substance, power, and operation to all things, but it conserves all things in their substance and in their power. In his *Confessions* Augustine says: I desired to be without whom I would be unable to exist. Just as all substances are conserved in their being by God, so too all powers are conserved by him; otherwise he would not be the God of powers.

Fifthly the fruitfulness of divine wisdom is so great that he not only creates all other works, but also conserves all things in their works. We must distinguish this conservation from the conservation of substance and power. We did not distinguish the conservation of substance and of power from each other, because both the substance and power of creatures are in the category of things that follow one another, and especially if an operation or action is founded in motion. The author of *Principles* speaks about this kind of action in book six, chapter three, saying that every action is founded in motion. It is one thing to be successive and another to be permanent, since successiveness is a series of parts, not a simultaneity of parts. When a whole motion occurs, nothing more moves, which Augustine asserts in his *Confessions* XI, 13, where he shows that, because our years pass by, those years will all be complete when they will not all be. Successiveness, then, is not in simultaneity of parts, or in the connection of parts, or in complete existence, but in the order of part to part, so that the series lasts a long time and part follows part for a long time. And when the entire series is finished, there is no more. However it is not permanent, properly speaking, except when it is whole.

We must speak differently about the conservation of one being and the conservation of another when it comes to the conservation of things in their works, distinguishing this conservation from the conservation of things in their substances and powers. God not only gives things their ability to work, but also give them the ability to be conserved in their works. Thus Augustine, in his *Literal Commentary on Genesis* IX, 15, says: If God withdrew his hidden operation, the operation of nature would remain null. He argues from this that the operation of other agents cannot last, nor be conserved in being, without the operation of God.

Therefore, from this fruitfulness of divine wisdom, so fruitful that it produces substance, power, and operation in us, it is apparent how we ought to give thanks to God for blessings received. God is not only rich in himself, but as is said in the *Book of Causes*: We are rich in gifts, inasmuch as God desires to share with us and make us participants in his bounty. *We have nothing that we have not received* (1 Cor 4:7). Thus to God who dispenses and grants us all goods, namely our substance, power, and operation, and who conserves us in such goods, we ought to give thanks in everything, as it says: *In everything give thanks* (1 Thes 5:18).

Above, when we discussed how we ought to fear God and obey him, we treated certain things concerning the conservation of things through divine wisdom. Yet it should not be considered inappropriate if we are brought to God variously by one and the same perfection. Because God conserves us in being, we should both fear him and render him thanks.

Chapter 18

In which it is shown, from the seventh praise of divine wisdom, namely that it is so efficacious and prompt, how the seventh question is answered, namely how should God be served in all things.

Lastly we will look at the seventh praise of divine wisdom, by which we will answer the seventh question: How should we serve God? For to be fruitful and to be efficacious are not exactly the same. Fruitfulness pertains more to the multitude of results while efficacy pertains to the speed and ability of producing them. Thus we should serve God in everything because the divine wisdom is so efficacious that by it we are strengthened for every good. God has given us all things according to the order of his wisdom, and in everything he has been an effective giver. And so we should effectively serve him in everything.

All things can be distinguished into three parts, namely into soul, body, and external things. The soul, or powers of the soul, can be similarly divided into three: into intellect, will, and lower powers, which are the powers of the organs. Hence we should so serve God that we direct to him, obeying, honoring, and revering him, all five of these, namely our intellect, will, organic or bodily powers, the body itself, and external things.

In obedience, in honor, and in reverence to him, we should efficaciously order our mind or intellect, continually meditating on him. Thus it says in Deuteronomy: *The words I command you today shall be in your heart, and you shall tell them to your children, and you shall meditate on them as you sit at home* (Dt 6:6-7). And in the eleventh chapter it is written: *Set my words in your hearts and in your minds, and hang them on your hands for a sign, and place them between your eyes. Teach your children to meditate on them*, etc. (Dt 11:18-19). In obedience to God, then, we should order our heart, intellect, and mind in such a way that we always meditate on him, do not consent to sin, and do not transgress the commandments of God. As Tobit said to his son: *Keep God in your mind all the days of your life; and be careful never to consent to sin and transgress the commandments of God* (Tb 4:6).

Secondly we should serve God in obedience to him not only by directing our mind and intellect to him, continually meditating on him, but we should also direct our will and emotions in devotion to him. We should pray and sing to God; and we should be moved to praise him, not only in mind and intellect, but also in spirit, that is, with will, emotion, and spiritual devotion: *I will pray in the spirit, I will also pray in my mind; I will sing in the spirit, I will also sing in my mind* (1 Cor 14:15). And these two are connected, for if we loved and had devotion for God's law, we would meditate on it; indeed our love and devotion for God and his law is especially expressed and signified in this: when all day we continually meditate on it: *How I have loved your law, O Lord; all day it is my meditation* (Ps 119:97).

Thirdly we should serve God in obedience by ordering to him the lower powers of the soul and the bodily powers, which may be called our members because they are perfections of our members and organs: *I speak in a human fashion on account of the weakness of your flesh. As you have yielded your members to serve uncleanliness and iniquity upon iniquity, now yield your members to serve righteousness unto sanctification* (Rom 6:19). The apostle condescends to our weakness, for while he could command much more, he commands us to order to righteousness our members, that is, our organic powers and lower powers of the soul, and even our whole body, which we had ordered to iniquity. We owe much more in obedience to God than earthly service, but the apostle, speaking humanly and wishing to adapt himself to us, condescends to our weakness, and commands that we, having been converted to God, should serve him in righteousness, just as we had served iniquity when we were turned away from him.

Fourthly in obedience to God we should order our body to him, by worshiping God and showing him bodily reverence with genuflections and bows. We have received from God not only our soul, but also our body, and so we should direct both to him in obedience. Thus our whole poor body is used in his service, and we employ whatever is in our body for the sake of God. Hence it says: *Fear the Lord and give him honor. Adore him who made heaven and earth, the sea and all that is them* (Rv 14:7).

Fifthly in obedience to God we should order external goods to him, if we have any. Just as we have soul and body from God, so we have our external possessions from him. Thus it is written in Proverbs: *Honor God from your substance, and give to the poor from the first fruits of all your produce. Then your barns shall be filled with abundance and your presses shall overflow with wine* (Prv 3:9-10). It is indicated here that when we have temporal possessions, we must use them well, by ordering them in obedience to God and sharing them with the poor; and by so doing, God will multiply them. Thus all our offerings we make in the Church are brought for such service, and we order all temporal things in obedience to God.

And this applies to those of worse condition who make a vow of poverty, who are unable to make such offerings or to bestow temporal goods, having nothing of their own, no substance from which they can fulfill this command. For those who vow poverty, if they do so led by the divine Spirit and if they are poor in spirit, offer more temporal possessions to God than another offers, because they offer to him not only what they have, but also what they are able to have, in order to have more time to serve God. They offer themselves so completely to God that, for the rest, it is not allowed them to possess anything of their own.

When it is asked, then, how we ought to serve God, we say that we ought to serve him in all that we are and have. We should serve him by our intellect by continually meditating on him; by our affections by being devoted to him without interruption; by the lower powers of our soul by ordering them to the service of God; by our body by performing bodily worship, genuflections, and bows to him, and by bearing with bodily sufferings for his sake. We should also serve God out of our own substance, if we have possessions and as opportunities arise, by making offerings for churches and for alleviating the poor.

Here we draw this treatise to a close, which we have decided to call The Praises of Divine Wisdom. We have brought to completion all that you requested concerning the qualities of divine wisdom, and we have answered all your proposed questions. And because without you, O Lord Jesus Christ, we could not have done it, may honor and glory be yours forever. Amen.

Sermons

The Latin texts of the sermons on *The Washing of the Feet*, *The Assump-tion of Mary*, and *To the Students of Paris* can be found in *Aegidii Romani Opera Omnia I, 6*, ed. Concetta Luna (Florence, 1990) 404-416; 467-478; 506-512.

The sermons on *The Three Vices of the World* can be found in the same volume, pages 341-387.

The Washing of the Feet

Our task is to make clear how it is that God ought to have authority and power over our will and freedom of choice. This should in fact be quite obvious from the reference to *feet* — for if by feet we understand affections, and if affections arise from our will and freedom of choice, then no one can be said to wash our feet unless he has authority over our free will. Up to this point we have taken for granted that the feet represent affections, but now I wish to explain how this is a fitting interpretation.

We shall say that the feet are in a threefold relationship to the body as a whole. Firstly, they are the extremities of the body; secondly, they are that part of it by which the body moves; and thirdly, they support the body, preventing it from falling. In the same way our affections have a threefold relationship to our souls: they may be called the extremities of our souls; they are that by which our souls move along; and they also serve to support our souls.

Firstly, our affections are called the extremities of our souls because they are the last part of them to be cleansed. Thus, commenting on the verse Jn 13:10 of Saint John, *You are clean, but not all of you,* Saint Augustine says that since they had already been washed, that is, baptized, the disciples needed only to wash their feet; because as long as he lives in this world man treads on the earth with his affections, so to speak, and thereby sullies himself in some way. In the same place Augustine says that human affections are a necessary part of this mortal condition, and compares them to feet — they bring us into contact with human things. Now if we say we are without sin we deceive ourselves. Therefore, when all the rest of us has been cleansed our feet still remain to be washed, since it is impossible for us to avoid a certain impurity due to our continual involvement with things human and earthly, and the affections to which they give rise. The affections are the last part of the soul to be cleansed, and so are spoken of as in some way the extremities of the soul; thus it is fitting to call them feet, since feet are the extremities of the body.

From what we have just said it should be apparent that mystical theology does not proceed by strict arguments: such is the opinion of Dionysius, and Aristotle too tells us that there is no place for disputation in metaphysics. Now we have said before that the affections are the most intimate and deepest part of the soul, and we concluded from this that the action of God is perfect, since it is in his power to reach even the affections. However, now we are proposing that all these affections are the extremities of the soul, and this seems to contradict our former proposition. For to be an extremity is the opposite of being intimate and deep. Nonetheless, each proposition is true in different respects. The affections are certainly the most intimate and deepest part of the soul, since no mere creature can know them of its own nature. This is what Saint Paul means when he says that *The Spirit searches all things, even the depths of God*, and adds: *Who knows the things of man if not the spirit of man which is in him?* And he continues: *No one but the Spirit of God knows the things of God*. Therefore he calls the depths of God the things which God has arranged in himself, which no one but the Spirit of God knows. Likewise, the depths of man may be said to be his affections and the things he has arranged in himself. In this respect, the affections are the most intimate and deepest part of a man, since they are accessible to no one except to him whose affections they are. But when it comes to their cleansing, the affections may be called extremities, since they are the last part that must be purified: such is the purification Saint John has in mind when he says: If we say we are without sin we deceive ourselves, and the truth is not in us.

Secondly, affections of this sort are called feet not only because they are like the bodily extremities, but also because they are the means of the soul's advancement, just as the feet allow the body to advance. Thus, at many points in his *Confessions* Saint Augustine tells us that we do not draw near to God or move away from him by our bodily steps, but by the affections of our minds.

Thirdly, the affections are called feet because, just as the body stands by means of its feet and does not fall down, so by its affections the soul can stand and avoid collapse. By its affections the soul achieves union with God, and united to him it stands firm and steadfast and can in no way fall. Saint Augustine speaks of this union in his work *True Religion*, where he says that our union with another soul is greater than that which we may have with our friends or even with our fathers, but the greatest union of all is that which binds us to God, and this comes about when we love God himself with all our affection.

Thus we see that in addition to his other perfections God also has power over our affections, which are the feet of our souls: may he deign to wash and purify them so that we may be able to hold him face to face after this earthly life in all his power and glory. May the Word Jesus Christ himself deign to grant us this, who with the Father and the Holy Spirit is one God, blessed for all ages.

Amen.

The Assumption of Mary

Upon what throne does the Blessed Virgin sit? We may say that her throne is no less than the unmoved God himself.

God is the dwelling-place of the saints, as we read in Saint John: *In my Father's house there are many rooms* (Jn 14:2). Interpreting this passage Saint Augustine says that the many rooms in the one eternal life signify the various degrees of worthiness and merit. It follows that different saints are said to merit the possession of different dwelling-places in God according to their different degrees of worthiness. God, then, with respect to all the other saints may be called a dwelling-place, but with respect to the blessed Virgin he ought to be called a throne. Many people are to be found in a royal dwelling, but only one person sits on the throne. Likewise there are many people in the heavenly fatherland, and many are the citizens of that kingdom, but there is only one called Queen, namely the blessed Virgin. Compared to her all the other saints do not deserve to be spoken of as sitting on the throne, since they are neither higher than she nor even on the same level; but rather she, as exalted above all the rest, is said to sit upon the throne.

Let us now turn to today's gospel, which tells how Jesus *entered into a certain town and a certain woman . . . received him*. In historical terms the woman who received Christ as he entered the town was Martha, but by a mystical interpretation we may say that Christ entered a town when he came into the world: for compared to heaven, from where Christ descended, the whole world is like a little town. Thus we can interpret: As Christ was entering that town, that is, coming into the world, a certain woman, that is, Mary, received him into her house, that is, her womb. We know that there was no place in the whole world as worthy or as venerable as the Virgin's womb.

But if the blessed Virgin received Christ as he descended from heaven into the most worthy place to be found on earth, it follows that we must certainly believe that when the blessed Virgin ascended from the earth Christ received her into the most worthy place in the heavens. As Saint Bernard says, there was no place on earth more worthy then the temple which was the Virgin's womb, in which Mary received the Son of God, nor in heaven was there a place more worthy than the royal throne to which the Son of Mary exalted his Mother this day. If, then, the blessed Virgin occupies the most worthy place in the house of the heavenly King, and if there is no more worthy place in that house than the throne, then we must believe that Mary indeed occupies the throne.

To the Students at Paris

Peace to the brothers, and charity with faith (Eph 6:23). These are the words with which the apostle concludes his letter to the Ephesians, calling them brothers and wishing them peace, faith, and charity. They belong originally of course to Paul, yet we are able to make them our own. I can say that all Christians are my brothers, since one mother, that is, the Church, gave birth to us all. However, I can call brothers especially those who belong not only to the same Church but also to the same Order. Moreover, although I ought to call all the members of this Order my special brothers, you Parisian scholars, to whom I have a special mission, I ought to call my yet more special brothers. I shall put it thus. All Christians are my brothers in a special way, and all the members of this Order are my brothers in a more special way, but you, to whom I have been specially sent, are my brothers in a most special way.

Paul wanted to have a special care for the Ephesians, as if for his brothers, and so wished them the three blessings which we have mentioned. Likewise I want to care for you in a specially brotherly way, and so can wish you the same blessings. Therefore I say with the apostle: to my brothers, that is, to you, whom I hope to have as brothers, I wish peace, and charity, with faith.

In these words are expressed three qualities whose possession will give right order to the quality of life, and whose loss will utterly destroy it. Anyone who goes astray errs either in thought, by thinking what is not right, or in his affections, by desiring what is not right, or in his external actions, by doing what is not right. Therefore all our sins are due either to irregular thought, perverse affections, or a bad external lifestyle. Now, if we had peace in our outward doings, charity in our inner affections, and faith in our thought and understanding, then our life would be in right order. Peace sets right our external actions, charity inflames our will, and faith illumines our intellect.

We ought to wish that all would have peace in their outward actions, charity in their internal desires, and faith in their understanding, yet we ought to desire these qualities in a very special way for students and for those who are dedicated to study, for it is these who have a special need of them.

The first advice which students ought to receive relates to peace in their external dealings, since they are particularly inclined to its opposite. As we shall show, they who are given to study are especially prone to anger, and therefore must receive special advice about peace. Now we can say that students are particularly prone to anger for three reasons — their complexion, their constant reading, and their seclusion.

The first reason we have given concerns the complexion. A warm complexion seems to be more suited to study than a cold one. We see that in nature the elements are lighter and more refined when warm than when cold. Among the many types of complexion, the refined complexion is the most appropriate to study, since the more refined the complexion, the softer the skin, and we follow Aristotle in saying that the soft-skinned have good minds. It is true that if the softness of the skin is caused by an excess of rheum — such as is the case with women — then it does not imply a good intellect. If however the softness is due to a refined skin and a good complexion, then it is a sure sign of an agile mind. It seems then that a warm complexion is suited to study. Furthermore, as has been demonstrated elsewhere, anger is caused by an inflammation of the blood around the heart. We may conclude then that those who are suited to study are found to be rather prone to anger, since on account of that warmth which their complexion shows forth, their blood is more easily inflamed.

This sermon is aimed at you, my brothers, you who are the cream of the whole Order. In every province an inquiry is and ought to be made as to which members of the Order are more intelligent and mentally sharp, and then these are marked out for study. Their inner warmth shows itself in the warmth of their complexion. Now just as the warmer elements are generally more penetrating and subtle, in a like manner they who have a warm complexion are found to possess a sharper intellect and greater subtlety of mind. We all know that when something is warm it is more readily set alight, and for this reason the blood of such people as these is easily inflamed. As has been said, it is out of such an inflammation of the blood that anger arises — thus it is clear that such people are prone to anger.

Those whose complexion shows them to be prone to anger ought however to employ their reason to control it; and the warmer their complexion, the sharper their intellect and reason will be to control it. Young boys and women are also inclined to quarrels and disputes, yet in their case we readily forgive them, since their use of reason is defective. As we read in the first book of Aristotle's *Politics,* a woman's advice is invalid, and that of a boy is imperfect; they possess no restraint, that is, they do not have sufficiently clear reason and intelligence, to control their angry passions. But you who are dedicated to study, who excel all others in your seeking out the paths of reason and searching after the heights of wisdom, you indeed would be most blameworthy if despite your great powers of reason you did not know how to control your anger. The greater your intellectual powers, the nearer you ought to be to God and the more devoutly you ought to receive him as a guest in your heart. But if God loves unity, he also loves harmony; he will never be with you if you are unwilling to be at peace with one another. Rejoice then with a spiritual joy, be perfect in perfection of spirit, exhort one another to the way of peace, be of one mind, so that you may all follow the way of perfection, each one being of the same opinion as the other. If you are at peace in this way, the God of peace will be with you, just as Paul says in his second letter to the Corinthians: *Finally brothers, rejoice, be perfect, take exhortation, be of one mind, have peace, and the God of peace and of love will be with you* (13:11). This then is the first advice which I must give you concerning peace: you must overcome by your reason that proneness to anger which your complexion shows you to have.

We have seen now how students must be exhorted to be peaceful on account of that proneness to anger which is due to their complexion. Next we must consider the proneness to anger which is caused by constant reading. Constant reading by its very nature tends to inflame the blood, and so we see that men who are forever reading are generally hot-headed. Even wise men have fiery blood on account of their constant reading, and are easily made indignant. This leads them on to anger, since the man who readily becomes indignant is always prone to anger. That the pursuit of study renders a man's nature indignant is clear from this text of Ecclesiastes: *I thought in my heart to withdraw my flesh from wine, that I might turn my mind to wisdom; but I saw that in this also there was toil and vexation of the spirit, because in much wisdom there is much indignation* (Eccl 2:3; 1:17).

So we see that constant reading leads to inflammation of the blood and a tendency to anger. This tendency also must be overcome by peace, and this peace will come through grace. In this we follow the teaching of Paul, who often wishes the faithful these two blessings at the same time. For example, writing to the Romans he says: *Grace be to you and peace, from God our Father and from our Lord Jesus Christ* (1:7). Likewise to the Philippians: *Grace to you and peace, from God our Father*, etc. (1:2). Indeed, in nearly all his letters Paul wishes the faithful these two blessings, grace and peace. In the letter to the Colossians: *Grace be to you and peace, from God our Father*, etc. (1:3). And again in both letters to Timothy he joins these two greetings. It seems that peace always goes hand in hand with grace, and so among you the greatest peace and concord should be found, since you ought to be especially aglow with grace.

So far we have shown that you must be exhorted to be peaceful because your tendency is to be angry. One cause of this tendency is your complexion, and this cause must be controlled by reason. Another is constant reading, and divine grace is needed to control this. It remains to show how your tendency to anger is caused by excessive seclusion — and this you must combat by your holiness.

Seclusion of its very nature seems to lead to a certain crudeness and inhumanity, and engenders a tendency to anger. We know that anyone who gives himself to study ought to abstain from the company and conversation of men. However, association with other people makes us courteous and sociable, while the absence of it has the opposite effect: we become crude, inhuman, and unsociable.

We may doubt whether this is truly a rule of our nature, that seclusion from the company of others makes us crude and prone to anger. Let us consider the wild beasts, since in them the natural instincts have free range and they always follow their native impulses. We notice that those beasts which have no contact with men are cruder, fiercer, and more prone to anger. Even dogs, which are usually so friendly to men, become violent, wild, and angry if shut up or tied or in any other way removed from the company of men. We conclude then that by their very seclusion from the company and conversation of others, those who are given to study become cruder and more prone to anger.

Nonetheless, although your dedication to study may inevitably lead to a tendency to anger, you ought to fight against this by your holiness. The whole purpose of your devotion to study is to contemplate God and arrive at a vision of him. No one however can see God if he is not holy. Therefore you must be holy in a very special way. Through this holiness you ought to be at peace, avoiding anger, and restraining other evil impulses when they arise.

Paul speaks of this peace and this holiness in his letter to the Hebrews: *Follow peace with all, and guard your holiness, without which no one shall see God* (12:14). This is your whole purpose here: by doing the will of God to gain a worthy desert and receive the promise due to you. To this end you will need peace and patience, as we read in Hebrews: *Patience is necessary for you so that, doing the will of God, you may receive the promise* (10:36).

Having now shown why all Christians, and especially students, must be exhorted to be peaceful, it remains to explain why they must be exhorted to be charitable: for in our opening quotation the brothers were wished not only peace but also charity.

Charity is necessary for all Christians, and without it we are nothing. Even if we had that faith which the Lord speaks of in the gospel, a faith great enough to move mountains, yet without charity we would be nothing. Charity is necessary in all Christians, but more so in clerics, and more so again in religious, and especially in those religious who devote themselves wholeheartedly to study. This is the reason you have come here — to study theology, to devote yourselves to the sacred scriptures; therefore you must especially be led toward charity.

We can give three reasons why there must be great charity and great love among you who are devoted to the sacred writings. (Indeed this is the reason I was sent to you, to promote peace and harmony and to increase your charity and love.) The first reason then why charity is necessary for you who study the scriptures we find in the source of the scriptures themselves. The second reason is derived from their end. The third reason comes from the means by which we come to know them.

Firstly then, God is love, and so the scriptures have as their author the source of love himself: he dwells in them. Who would doubt then that the man who is joined to the author of the scriptures would not have a better understanding of them? Therefore you ought to be charitable so that, thus joined to the author of the scriptures, you may be better able to understand them. On every page of the holy writings charity shines forth, and so you ought to be charitable if you wish to devote yourselves to their study. For this reason Saint Augustine in his work *In Praise of Charity* says: "Of what use are so many books? Be charitable. For in the case of the sacred writings, when you truly understand them charity becomes obvious, when you do not, it lies hidden. He who lives charitably possesses both what is obvious and what lies hidden in the sacred scriptures" (Sermon 350, 2).

Having now seen how charity is necessary for students of scripture because of its author, we must now show how they need it because of the end to which scripture is ordained. All of scripture is ordained toward one thing — charity. It would be terrible if someone wished to labor over the sacred writings without any desire for that to which they are directed. We can be sure that charity is the end and fullness of the law, and therefore of the scriptures, from the words of Paul: *The fullness of the law is love* (Rom 13:10). Just as all things which have a particular end are fulfilled when they reach that end, so the scriptures find fulfillment in charity and love. Do you wish then to fulfill the law? Love one another. As Paul says: *Owe no one anything, but to love one another; for whoever loves one's neighbor has fulfilled the law* (Rom 13:8).

Thirdly, students of the scriptures have need of charity because of the means by which they are learned. The most effective way we can come to understand the scriptures is through purity of heart. Just as matter must be disposed to receive its form, so must the mind be disposed to receive sacred learning. Furthermore, just as the disposing of the matter is the means by which it acquires a form, so the disposing of the mind is the means by which it arrives at knowledge. The best way to dispose our minds so as to receive knowledge is through purity. And since charity purifies us, it follows that we are best disposed to receive the sacred scriptures by means of charity. We read in the book of Wisdom that *wisdom will not enter into a malicious soul, nor dwell in a body subject to sins* (1:4). This implies then that wisdom will enter into a good soul, and will dwell in a soul which through brotherly love has joined itself to God, a soul which, leaving sin behind, has separated itself from the world.

You have seen now why I must wish you peace, which tempers one's external conduct, and charity, which inflames the will. It remains finally to show why I ought to wish you faith, which illumines the understanding. For our quotation had three wishes for the brothers: *Peace to the brothers, and charity with faith.* Peace is necessary in one's outward behavior, and charity in one's inner affections. We must now show how faith is necessary in one's mental knowledge.

As we often have said before, you have come here to study sacred scripture. Now the scriptures did not come about by human ingenuity, but by divine revelation. Thus Saint Augustine in the second book of *The Trinity* says that God is known in two ways:

through the creatures which he has created, and through the scripture which he has inspired. Because sacred scripture, that is, divine wisdom, is God's revelation, because it is inspired by him, it follows that these writings direct our attention to God and make us know him in a special way.

Therefore, for our present purposes we can say that our approach to divine wisdom should be threefold. Firstly we ought to receive this wisdom devoutly into our minds. Secondly, in receiving it we ought to understand God in it. Thirdly, by understanding God we ought to direct our attention as much as possible toward him. Now we can go on to say that the effect of faith is also threefold: it prepares, elevates, and purifies the mind. It prepares it to receive divine wisdom, elevates it to know God through the wisdom received, and purifies it that, knowing God, it can keep its attention fixed on him. Since faith has these effects, it is obviously very necessary for those who wish to study the scriptures.

That faith is what makes us receive divine wisdom is clear from what Saint James says: *If any of you want wisdom, let him ask of God who gives to all abundantly and without reproach, and it shall be given to him.* And immediately he goes on: *But let him ask in faith, without wavering* (1:5-6). Therefore if we ask in faith, we shall receive divine wisdom from God. It follows that faith disposes us to receive divine wisdom.

Faith also elevates, allowing us to understand the things of God, as we learn from a variant reading in the seventh chapter of Isaiah: *Unless you believe you shall not understand* (7:9).

Thirdly, faith purifies us, allowing us to fix our attention on God. We ought to conceive of our human powers of attention as so weak and infirm as to be incapable of focusing on the dazzling light of God, unless cleansed, converted, and purified through the righteousness of faith. Thus Saint Augustine in the first book of *The Trinity*: "The attention of the human mind is powerless to fix itself on such excellent light, unless through the righteousness of faith it be changed, that is, cleansed and purified and made as white as snow."

May God himself, whose works are perfect, grant to you my brothers peace in your outward dealings, charity in your affections, and faith in your understanding, so that believing in him and clinging to him you may be led to eternal life. And may Jesus Christ be our guide, he who with the Father and the Holy Spirit is one God, blessed forever and ever. Amen.

The Three Vices of the World

Introductory Letter

Reverend father, lord in Durham:

Greetings from brother Giles, archbishop of Bourges. It has entered my mind, lord of Durham, to send you three sermons on the three things that are in the world. For *all that is in the world*, as John says in his first letter (2:16), *is the desire of the flesh, the desire of the eyes, and the haughtiness of life.* Three vices are connected with these: gluttony, greed, and pride. Gluttony corresponds to the desire of the flesh, greed to the desire of the eyes, and pride to the haughtiness of life. All our temptations arise from them because by these three vices our first parents were tempted, Christ was tempted, and we are daily tempted.

When our first parents were tempted by the forbidden fruit, they were tempted by the desire of the flesh. When they were told, *you will be like gods* (Gn 3:5), they were tempted by the pride of life. And from what was added, *knowing good and evil*, they were tempted by greed, taking greed generally as the desire for having any desirable thing. This includes knowledge, insofar as it is a desirable good, so that anyone is called greedy for knowledge who desires it inordinately.

Likewise Christ himself was tempted by these three: by gluttony or the desire of the flesh, by greed or the desire of the eyes, and by haughtiness or the pride of life. He was tempted by gluttony or the desire of the flesh when the devil said to him, *If you are the Son of God, tell these stones to become bread* (Mt 4:3). He was tempted by greed or the desire of the eyes when the devil led him onto a very high mountain, showing him all the kingdoms of the world and all their glory, and said, *All of these I will give to you if you fall down and worship me.* And he was tempted by the pride of life when the devil led him onto a pinnacle of the temple and said, *If you are the Son of God, throw yourself down* (Mt 4:5-6), in order that Christ might rise up in pride since, by the guardianship of the angels, he could do this without injury.

In like manner we ourselves are tempted daily either by the desire of the flesh in regard to a pleasurable good, or by the desire of the eyes in regard to a utilitarian good, or by the pride of life in regard to an honorable good. For according to the understanding of the wise, good is only threefold: pleasurable, utilitarian, and honorable. And since no one desires anything but an apparent or real good, no one is tempted, no one sins, except from an inordinate appetite for some good.

According to Dionysius, *The Divine Names,*[1] no one does what he does looking to evil, and evil is outside the will and outside intention. In the same place he says further that no one does evil except in virtue of the good, for since evil is essentially a certain privation, and privation is of itself non-existent, then it is impossible that anyone do evil under the aspect of evil; or if he does evil, either it will be on account of an apprehended good or on account of a good in which it is rooted. And because good is only threefold, as is clear from what has been presented, all our temptations can be reduced to these three types, which are said to be in the world because by them worldly people fall into sins.

Therefore, I have taken up the present work briefly that I might compose three sermons according to these three vices, by which the three mentioned goods are desired inordinately, and which correspond to the three things said to be in the world. According to the order which John lays down in his letter, the desire of the flesh or gluttony, whose offspring is lust, should be handled first, and afterward the desire of the eyes or greed, and third the pride of life. We, however, intend to arrange these three sermons in the opposite order, treating firstly the third vice, namely the pride of life, secondly the second vice, namely the desire of the eyes or greed, and thirdly the first vice, namely the desire of the flesh.

Viewing it from our perspective, the desire of the flesh is first, since a child, before he has the use of reason, finds pleasure in nursing; later comes desire of the eyes, since a boy, when he sees something lovely, such as a golden apple, is attracted by it and desires it; and lastly he is proud and becomes haughty in life. Yet among themselves these have another order, for the honorable is more excellent than the utilitarian good since a person may give away all his possessions in order to have honor and avoid shame. And the utilitarian seems more excellent than the pleasurable good since people commonly abstain from many pleasurable things in order to acquire utilitarian goods. According to this order pride, which considers the honorable good, must be discussed first, then greed, which considers the utilitarian, and finally gluttony, whose offspring is lust, which considers the pleasurable.

There are, moreover, other reasons why these vices have this order. For pride and greed taken in one way are general sins because pride is in every sin insofar it is a turning away from an unchangeable good. And likewise with greed because it is a turning toward a changeable good. For he is surely proud who does not wish to be subject to God; and he is surely greedy who forsakes God on account of a changeable good. Therefore pride and greed should be discussed before gluttony since they are more general; and pride should be discussed before greed because it is more constitutive of sin, for although both are in sin (pride by the turning away from God and greed by the turning toward the world), pride, that is, the turning away, is therein more constitutive of sin than greed, that is, the turning toward; and sin has more of the nature of sin in that the sinner turns away from God than that he turns toward the world. I will present, therefore, first a sermon on pride, second a sermon on greed, and third a sermon on gluttony.

Sermon 1

Beginning and taking up for our theme that text in Sirach 10:15, *Pride is the beginning of all sin and he who has it will be filled with curses,* let us say with Ptolemy, as it is recounted in the beginning of the *Almagest:* One is wiser among human beings who is less concerned about who wields worldly power. People who are concerned about human pomp and seek vain glory gladly involve themselves in worldly matters. Therefore, if we wish to avoid pride, we ought to spurn completely worldly things so that, even when riches are abundant, we do not place our hearts there.

It is great wisdom, therefore, to remain unconcerned about earthly things because from such concern, or from such pomp, we are brought into pride, and from pride all sins take their origin. Indeed, he who would bring himself into pride and desires to mix himself with worldly things not only stains himself with vices in guilt, but also fills himself with curses in punishment.

Every preacher and proclaimer of God's word ought to lead hearers to become wise enough not to bring themselves into pride; wise enough not to be concerned about who rules in this world; wise enough not to turn themselves toward changeable goods, because every sin arises from this. If we can lead you to this, we hope that when you leave behind pride, which is the beginning of all sin in guilt, you might never again embrace it lest you be filled with curses in punishment.

It is the greatest foolishness to cling to pride, from which follows so much guilt and punishment. And in the opposite way, it is the greatest wisdom to embrace humility, according to Proverbs 11:2:

Where there is humility there is wisdom. Of ourselves we are unable to lead you to avoid pride and foolishness and to cling to humility and wisdom, and therefore we rely on God, the enlightener of minds, to whom be glory forever.

Sermon 1

Pride is the beginning of all sin, etc. Although the prologue was based upon this text, we can still build the body of the sermon on the same text. Since this text leads us to state some things against the proud, it must be seen first how pride relates to the other capital vices and how it is understood to be a member of the capital vices. Rather, because we intend to create sermons on the three capital vices that correspond to the three things that are in the world, the capital vices must be enumerated first and their number assigned, and then we can approach the particular matter of those three capital vices.

A Delineation of the Vices

The seven capital vices are designated pride, greed, gluttony, lust, laziness, envy, and anger. These are called capital vices because many vices have their origin from each of these vices. For just as the head is that to which many members are ordered, and as the father is metaphorically called the head of his children and the king the head of those in his kingdom, so by a certain metaphor each of these is called a head of vices since from each, as from a head, many vices arise.

Their number is reached in the following manner: Sin comes about from a disorder of the soul. Our soul, moreover, is able to act inordinately in two ways: first if it tends toward a good inordinately, second if it inordinately and improperly shrinks from a good on account of something connected with it. I say "on account of something connected with it" because everyone desires the good as far as it is good. But if someone rejects a good, this will not be because of itself, but because of some difficulty or something inconvenient connected with it. For example, if it is good to be healthy, then everyone will cherish health, speaking of health in itself. But if someone does not wish to be healthy, this will be either because he does not want to take medicine or because of another inconvenience that he perceives as threatening to himself if he should have health. Every sin, therefore, will be unable to exist except in one of these ways: either because we desire a good improperly and inordinately, or because we improperly and inordinately reject a good on account of something connected with it.

The good is threefold, as is clear from Aristotle's *Ethics*,[2] namely, honest or honorable, pleasurable, and utilitarian. And pleasure consists especially in two things, namely in food, which is ordained for the sustenance of the body and the good of the individual, and in sex, which nature ordains for the procreation of children and the good of the species. Therefore we can inordinately desire the good in four ways: either because we inordinately desire an honorable good, such as to rule or to be superior and other such things, and pride comes from this; or secondly because we can inordinately desire a utilitarian good, such as wealth and all coins and whatever can be measured in money, and greed comes from this; or thirdly because we can inordinately desire a pleasurable good, in regard to food, which is ordained for the conservation of the body and the good of the individual, and gluttony comes from this inordinate desire; or fourthly we can inordinately desire a pleasurable good in regard to sex, which, as was said, nature ordains for the procreation of children and the good of the species, and lust comes from this inordinate desire. Therefore, there are four capital vices insofar as we inordinately desire good, namely pride in regard to honorable good, greed in regard to utilitarian good, gluttony and lust in regard to pleasurable good; and it is clear in what way these are distinguished by what has been presented.

The remaining three capital vices are included because we inordinately draw back from a good or inordinately resist a good on account of something connected with it. Laziness draws us back from a spiritual good on account of the effort involved. For he is called lazy who is so weighed down in his soul that he wants to do nothing good because of the effort involved. Envy also resists good and opposes itself to good on account of something connected with it. Thus when someone sees that the good of another is able to diminish his own stature, by reason then of something connected — lest his own stature be diminished — he envies the other's good. Anger also opposes itself to another's good and intends his harm because of something connected. Thus if someone perceives himself being ridiculed or despised, on account of such offense he opposes himself to another's good and intends his harm. Wherefore in *The Rhetoric*, book two, it says that anger is the desire to punish arising from a perceived offense.[3]

Anger and envy, then, are seen to agree, because each desires another's harm on account of something connected, namely, that he not be despised. Thus it says in Job 5:2 that *envy kills the little person*, because in order that he might not be despised, and that his stature might not be overshadowed, he envies another's good and desires his overthrow and harm. And likewise with anger on account of an offense, because when someone is despised he wishes to rise up in vengeance, desiring another's punishment and harm.

This does not happen, however, in the same way. That someone appears despised and that someone does not appear superior can happen in two ways, namely by overshadowing and by the opposite operation. For we see that the brightness of a candle is taken away either by the sun or by the wind. The sun takes it away by overshadowing because the lesser light is overshadowed when overtaken by a greater light. But wind takes away such brightness by an opposite operation when it extinguishes it. The envious person, then, lies in wait for another's good so that he himself might not appear small; for he wants to be superior. But the angry person opposes himself to another's good and desires another's punishment. For he felt despised when he was offended by another or when another did something harmful to him.

Just as the former four vices, namely pride, greed, gluttony, and lust, arise when someone inordinately desires good, so the latter three vices, namely laziness, envy and anger, arise when someone opposes himself to good on account of something connected with it. These three vices are further distinguished in this way, that a man avoids or resists on account of something connected with either his own good or with another's good. If with his own then it is laziness, which opposes itself to the man's own good on account of the effort or tediousness involved. Thus the one who is presently lazy does not wish to do anything good. But if, on account of something connected to a good not his own, he opposes himself to another and desires his harm, this will be either because he wishes not to appear small but wishes to be superior, and then it is envy, or because he wishes not to be despised when he is offended and harmed by another, and then it is anger.

It seems from this that the preceding four vices are prior to the subsequent three because what is sought for itself is prior to what is sought accidentally. Since tending toward good is tending toward good in itself but resisting good cannot be resisting good in itself, but accidentally, then these four vices that arise when we desire good inordinately are prior to the other three that come about when we reject good inordinately. Further, among those four, pride is said to have first place because honorable good, to which pride inordinately tends, is more excellent and worthier than, and thus prior to, utilitarian good and pleasurable good, to which the other vices inordinately tend.

Two Reasons for Detesting Pride

Speaking of pride, then, we should say first that in the proposed text, taken from Sirach 10:6-18, we are brought to detest pride in two ways: first by the vileness of the sin, second by the bitterness of the punishment. There are two general ways of stopping vices: Some people are so good that from simply seeing the vileness of the vices and the goodness of the virtues they are sufficiently brought to abandon the vices and to be filled with the virtues. But others are so perverse that unless fear of punishment restrains them, they would never refrain from evil. Pride stains us in such a way that we dispose ourselves to all of the vices, because it is the beginning of all sins. In addition pride ordains us to the greatest punishment: that if we cling to it we will be filled with curses. Therefore we are brought sufficiently to detest pride both by the infection of sin and by the obligation of punishment.

In the proposed text, then, two things are noted: First it is shown that we should detest pride because of the sin by which we are infected; second it is suggested that we should detest pride because of the punishment which we incur and to which we are obligated. The first is noted when it says, *pride is the beginning of all sin*; the second is touched when it adds, *and he who has it will be filled with curses.* For if any sin infects and corrupts the soul, that sin should be shunned; yet we should especially shun that sin which corrupts the soul in itself and is even the way, the beginning and the reason why the soul is corrupted by other sins. Wherefore if we can show that pride is not only vice and sin in itself, but also is the beginning of all sins, it will appear that it should be especially detested.

That pride is the greatest sin is clear by the gloss on Psalm 19:14. *I will be cleansed from the greatest sin*, that is, from pride, says the gloss. But one need not insist much on this point since almost all the Scriptures proclaim how great a sin pride is.

It should be known that in the beginning of the *Metaphysics*, book five, where the different ways of speaking of "beginning" are distinguished, it is said that in as many ways as "cause" is used, so many are the ways that "beginning" is used, for every cause has the character of a beginning.[4] Wherefore also in the same place it is held that all causes are principles. Since, then, there are four causes, namely material, formal, efficient and final, we can say that in all these four ways pride is somehow the beginning of all sin. For it can be said first that pride is the beginning of all sin materially, second it is the beginning formally, third finally and fourth efficiently.

Pride Is the Material Cause of All Sin

Pride is said to be the beginning of all sin materially because pride was the sin of our first parents, according to Sirach 10:14: *the beginning of man's pride is to apostatize from God.* For our parents, wishing to be like gods who know good and evil and believing the serpent's temptations, ate the forbidden fruit. Although it was in one sense a sin of gluttony, nevertheless it was principally a sin of pride because their desire to be like gods was an inordinate desire for their own superiority.

From this first sin of the parents, then, a rebellion of powers arose in us that is the spark of all sin. For we should consider that a certain original justice was granted to Adam by which the body was subject to the soul and the inferior powers were subject to reason. This justice and this good would have been passed on to all their posterity if Adam had not sinned. But when he sinned, at once a rebellion of powers came about, at once flesh desired contrary to the spirit and the spirit contrary to the flesh, at once he saw another law in his members fighting against the law of his mind and leading him captive to a law of sin. We not only see this rebellion of powers and this contrary law in ourselves, but the apostle even discerned it in himself, as he says in Romans 7:23. Thus from pride, which was the first sin of our first parents, arose a rebellion of powers; sin entered into us and the spark of sin entered into us, according to Romans 5:12: *through one man sin entered into the world and death through sin.*

So if a rebellion of powers arose in Adam by pride, which is called the spark of sin, and if such a rebellion and such a spark is handed down to us all, we can say that in this way pride is the beginning of sin. For the beginning of every sin comes into being through this spark of sinning. The spark of sin and the rebellion of powers are, as it were, the material of sinning, for that is called matter which is in potency to form. And to the extent that its aptitude for receiving a form is greater, so far is its matter more suitable, just as copper is more suitable matter for a statue than clay. For a statue cannot be made from clay except by many transformations, but it can be made more easily and suitably from copper since it does not require so many transformations. To be prone to something and to have an aptitude for it is regarded as the material cause. Since, then, from the rebellion of powers and from the spark of sin a certain aptitude and a certain propensity for sinning is in us, the rebellion of powers or the spark of sin is materially the beginning of all sin and fault.

By our first parents' first sin, which was pride, as has been said often, the rebellion of powers and the spark of sin arose in us, which are in us materially as the beginning of all sin. We can say, then, that pride is materially the beginning of all sin. And because the corruption of this sin is so great, because its perversity is so enormous, by which, in the way it has been said, every sin has its beginning, it must therefore be especially avoided. Knowing this, Tobit instructed his son, as it is found in Tobit 4:14, to be especially on guard against pride, saying, *Never allow pride to rule in your mind or in your speech,* for every evil takes its beginning in pride. And because all evil and all sin take their beginning materially, as it were, from pride, it is rightly said that it should be especially avoided.

Pride Is the Formal Cause of All Sin

Having seen how pride is the beginning of all sin materially, as it were, because the spark of sin or the rebellion of powers took its origin from it, it remains to show how pride is the beginning of all sin formally. It should be known that in all sin are two things, namely a turning away from the unchangeable good and the turning toward a changeable good. For turning away alone cannot suffice for sin because every sin is voluntary; indeed it is voluntary to such an extent that if it were not voluntary it would not be sin, as Augustine says in his book *Free Will.*[5] Moreover evil for the sake of evil cannot be willed and so the turning away from God, speaking of it in itself, cannot be willed. Every sinner, therefore, wills some changeable good by reason of which he turns away from the unchangeable good. The turning away alone does not suffice to account for sin because, as was said, turning away *per se* cannot be willed. Further, neither does the turning toward a changeable good suffice to account for sin since, if someone turns toward a changeable good in such a way that he does not turn away from the unchangeable good, then strictly speaking it would not be sin. Therefore both turning away and turning toward occur together, yet the turning away is related to sin formally, as it were, and principally, while the turning toward is related to sin materially. For it must be said that the changeable good toward which the sinner turns is like the material of sin, while the reality of sin is completed formally when someone turns toward a changeable good to such a degree that he turns away from the unchangeable good.

In all sin, then, there are two things: covetousness and pride. Covetousness is involved in the turning toward because he is very greedy for whom God is not enough; he is extremely covetous who, having rejected God, turns toward some temporal good. Therefore when the sinner turns to a changeable good he is thereby covetous. When, however, he turns away from the unchangeable good he is thereby proud. For he is very proud who wishes to turn away from God and wishes not to be subject to him. If covetousness, then, is noted in the turning toward, and pride in the turning away (since these two occur in all sin, namely the turning toward the changeable and the turning away from the unchangeable) then in every sin will be both covetousness and pride. But because, as was said, in sin the turning away is like a certain principle and a certain formal cause, while covetousness is like a material cause, then pride is more formally in sin than covetousness. And because this is so, it was well said what had been said previously that the beginning of all sin is pride. For in sin the turning away or pride is more important and more formal than the turning toward or covetousness.

It should be kept in mind, however, lest my hearers vacillate and lest they believe we speak contradictions in our words, that when we said above that pride is the beginning of all sin materially, this does not contradict what we say now, namely that pride is the beginning of all sin, formally, because pride is not understood in the same way here and there.

In one way pride is a particular sin and has a particular matter and a particular object. Taken in this way it is nothing but a certain inordinate appetite for one's own superiority. According to this way of speaking, not every sin is pride since all sins do not directly and properly desire such superiority and such an honorable good. Rather, some people detest honors and do not wish to be famous nor to be held in high esteem only so that they might more freely pursue their lusts and other pleasures. For we see that many leave their own country, where they are known and held in honor, and go to strange and foreign places in order to satisfy their pleasures without reproach. Not all sinners sin through pride, as far as it is a particular sin, because all are not proud nor do all, when they sin, desire an honorable good. Rather, some desire a pleasurable good, and such people are lustful or gluttonous; others desire a utilitarian good, like outward possessions or money, and such people are greedy. And this is true for each sin, for every particular vice has a particular matter toward which it tends inordinately.

In another way pride is understood not as a particular sin, nor as is it has a particular matter, but as it overflows into all sins and is a certain formal condition of all sins. In this way the turning from God, in which every sin consists formally and principally, is a certain pride. And as was said, every sinner is proud since he does not wish to obey God and does not wish to be subject to him, but wishes rather to turn away from God.

Therefore in the things we have said, the latter do not contradict the former, because pride understood particularly, such as the first sin of our first parents, from which arose the rebellion of powers and the spark of sin, was the beginning of all sin and fault materially, since the spark of sin is connected to sin materially. For no one sins because the spark of sin is in him, but from it he has the ability and possibility to sin. This ability and possibility to take on some form or condition is understood as a material cause. But pride understood generally, and as it overflows into all sins, is the beginning of all sin formally.

Let the sinner consider that in every sin he turns away from God and lifts himself up in pride against him. But he cannot resist God, for if a sinner is able to reach up to the stars, he will be pulled down and completely destroyed, according to the words of Obadiah 1:4: *If you are exalted like an eagle and set your nest among the stars, I will pull you down from there, says the Lord.* And we read in Psalm 37:35-36, *I saw a wicked,* that is, a proud, *man highly exalted and lifted up like the cedars of Lebanon; and I passed by and behold he was not, nor was his place found.* For the time will come when the wicked shall see that pride profited them nothing, that the boasting of riches gave them nothing. For all these will pass away like a shadow. All are transitory like the waves upon which a passing ship leaves not a trace behind. Thus the wicked and the proud quickly run through their time and leave not a trace behind them, since memory of them soon vanishes. Many tyrants accomplished many things that people rarely or never speak of. Such tyrants speak for themselves in Wisdom 5:6, *We have wandered from the way of truth and the light of justice has not shined upon us.* They continue in verses 8-10: *How has pride profited us and what has the boasting of riches given us? All these pass away like a shadow, like a running herald, like a ship that passes through the waves and the trace of it, when it has sailed past, is not to be found.*

Pride Is the Final Cause of All Sin

Having shown how pride is the beginning of every sin both materially and formally, it remains to show how pride is such a beginning also as a final cause. For this it should be known that, just as pride and covetousness are general sins and are the conditions for all sins, they are each in their own way the beginning of all sin. For covetousness, which consists of turning toward some good, is connected materially to fault and sin while pride, which consists of turning away from God, is connected formally to fault and sin. In addition we can say that covetousness and pride, as they are understood particularly, are in a manner of speaking the beginning of every sin and every fault. But they are so in different ways, for covetousness is such a beginning and cause efficiently and pride is such a beginning by final causality.

For proof of this it must be carefully noted that, as is commonly said and as the philosophers have handed down, there are two orders in things that proceed from the intellect and the will: one according to intention, another according to execution. Thus things that are earlier in intention are later in execution and vice versa. For example, the physician first of all intends health, but seeing that he cannot bring about health except by medication, he then intends to apply medicine. First health and later medicine occur in the physician's intention. But in execution it is the reverse, for he gives medicine and by medication he later brings health. Things that are prior, then, have the character of a beginning or a cause with respect to later things. Thus it is right that things earlier according to intention and things earlier according to execution both have the character of causality. Yet they have it differently because things prior according to intention have the character of cause in the category of final cause, since the end is that which first occurs in intention; but things prior according to execution have the character of a cause in the category of efficient cause, since execution, action and motion pertain properly to efficient causality. To perform or to move something applies to efficient causality. Therefore, when the philosopher wishes to name the efficient cause, he always, or almost always, calls it the beginning of motion.[6]

That things prior in intention would be final causes while those prior in execution would be efficient causes is manifestly clear. For we see that health, which is prior to medicine according to the order of intention, is its final cause, but medicine, which is prior to health according to the order of execution, is the efficient cause of health. Every sinner intends to follow his own will. And everyone wishing to follow his own will does not wish to be subject to another, but wishes rather to surpass and be superior. Therefore pride, by which someone inordinately seeks his own superiority, occurs in the intention of each sinner. That which first occurs in the intention has the character of final cause, and thus pride is the beginning of every sin in the category of final causality. Anyone sinning in any sin intends to follow his own will. And as he intends not to be subject, but to surpass, so he in some way intends to be proud.

Covetousness, according to that way already discussed, is the root of every sin, not in the order of intention or in the category of final cause, but in the order of execution or in the category of efficient cause. For just as anyone who sins in any way intends his own superiority, so anyone who wishes to do or perform any sin can carry it out especially through money, since it is said in Ecclesiastes 10:19, *all things obey money.* Money, by which we especially carry out or are able to carry out our desires and sins, is the matter of covetousness, and thus covetousness is the beginning and root of all sins in the order of execution and in the category of efficient cause. But superiority, which we especially intend in our actions and in our sins, is the matter of pride, and thus pride is said to be the beginning and cause of all sins in the order of intention and in the category of final cause.

Yet if we want to properly understand superiority as the particular matter of pride, when we understand pride particularly as an individual sin, then it must be kept in mind that, by a certain manner of speaking, pride is the beginning of every sin and we fall into sins through pride. For wishing to subject all things to ourselves and wishing to be superior and famous, we seek delicate foods and fall into the vice of gluttony. For the same reason we also seek money and fall into greed. Furthermore, because a proud man, according to the nature of pride, does not deign to refrain himself, he pursues his passions and pleasures and rushes into lusts. All vices, then, seem by a certain manner of speaking to take their origin from pride.

If we wish, however, to extend the name of superiority by saying that by it someone wants to follow his own will, just as he wishes not to be subject but wishes to be superior, then pride is actually intended in every sin, since in every sin the attainment of one's own will is intended

According to this way, then, in the order of intention and in the category of final cause, pride is the beginning of all sin, not only by a certain manner of speaking, but also in actuality. And since this vice is so great, and the ruin from this sin so enormous, we ought to avoid it completely. God rightly resists them, that is, the proud, because such people do not strive to attain God's will, but their own will, according to the words of James 4:6, *God resists the proud, but gives grace to the humble.* By this vice we justly lose God since we do not wish to be subject to him. Thus Hugh of Saint Victor says: "Pride takes God from me, envy takes my neighbor from me, anger takes me away from myself."[7]

Pride Is the Efficient Cause of All Sin

Having discussed how pride is the beginning of all sin by material, formal and final causality, it remains to show fourthly how it is the beginning of all sin efficiently. Therefore it must be known that every sin is either toward oneself, or toward one's neighbor, or toward God. Through pride, then, we sin efficiently in every kind of sin because by it we act against ourselves, against our neighbor and against God.

We act against ourselves in three ways, because by pride we are wounded in our natural virtues, we are robbed of spiritual virtues and we persevere in vices. We are wounded in natural virtues since our heart is puffed up with pride, our mind is darkened and our natural diligence is lost. For the proud person, as if he were drunk, loses his natural diligence and does not know what he is doing, according to Habakkuk 2:5, *Just as wine deceives the one who drinks it, so will be the proud man.* Therefore the proud man is deceived by pride as is the drinker by wine.

Secondly the proud person acts against himself not only because he is wounded in natural virtues, losing his natural diligence, but also because he is robbed of spiritual virtues, losing divine grace. For the proud person is made detestable to God and so divine grace is stripped away, according to Sirach 10:7, *Pride is detestable before God and men.*

Thirdly the proud person acts against himself because by pride he perseveres in sins. Pride in man is like a certain tower that defends all vices. For the person who is puffed up and elevated by pride and placed on high does not deign to stop or repent, and thus because of his hardness of heart he perseveres in vices. What is said, then, in Romans 2:5-6 can be applied to the proud and hardened person: *According to your hardness and unrepentant heart you are storing up for yourself wrath in the day of wrath and of revelation of the just judgment of God, who will render to each one according to his works.* For the works of the proud will be abundantly paid back to the proud, according to Psalm 31:24, *It will be abundantly paid back to those who act proudly.*

Because of these three evils that it produces, pride is rightly compared to the wind, and proud people are rightly called puffed up and full of wind. For wind extinguishes light, dries up the dew, and throws down and lays low lofty places. So through pride the light of wisdom is extinguished in the proud, because they are wounded in their natural virtues and cannot fully use their natural diligence. The dew of grace is dried up within them because they are stripped of supernatural virtues and lose divine grace. They are thrown down from their high place because those persevering in vices are plunged into hell. The proud person, then, sins against himself.

He also sins against his neighbor and against God. We are able to distinguish six types of pride, of which we can assign three against God and three against neighbor. The proud person, as far as he is considered at present, is deceived in four ways in the mind and is disordered in two ways in the will.

He is deceived firstly in the mind when he believes that everything he has from God he has from himself. It should not be understood that this deception is directly in him, because any learned person knows that all things are from God. Yet it happens indirectly in those who believe they are wise. Those who are proud believe they have from themselves what they have from God. For in one way proud people act as though they do not recognize anyone superior to them, and in another way they act as though they believed that the good things they have they possess from themselves. The apostle speaks against these in 1 Corinthians 4:7: *What do you have that you did not receive? But if you have received it, why do you boast as if you had not received it?* Therefore the proud are deceived firstly because they act as though they have from themselves what they possess from God.

Secondly they are deceived because, although they believe that what they have they have from God, they nevertheless believe they have by their own merit what they have through divine grace. Such people do not believe that God is a giver and bestower, but rather a vendor. For what is given for merits is no longer grace, but is owed; it is not bestowed but bought. When such people seek the oil of mercy, they are told in Matthew 25:9, *Go rather to the vendors and buy for yourselves.* Thus the wise and humble virgins responded, in the voice of the Lord, to the proud and foolish virgins: *Go rather to the vendors and buy for yourselves.* This is would be like saying, You think that God is a vendor, for up to now you wished to have good things by your own merits and by your own abilities; but you should know that God does not sell, but bestows, and thus you will not be able to have the oil of mercy. So Christ says to them sarcastically, *Go to the vendors,* that is, seek if you can find vendors from whom to obtain the oil of mercy.

Thirdly the proud person is deceived in the mind because he believes he has what he does not have. Such are those who are wise in their own eyes. Against them it is said in Isaiah 5:21, *Woe to you who are wise in your own eyes and are prudent in the sight of yourselves.*

Fourthly the proud person is deceived in the mind because in his own estimation he thinks he should be preferred to all. But while considering himself greater than everyone else, he is actually considered inferior by everyone else. Thus it often happens that the one wishing to place himself above others is thrown down to a lower place, so that he who exalts himself will be humbled; and the one wishing to place himself below others is often pulled up to a higher place, so that he who humbles himself will be exalted. Thus the Lord says in Luke 14:8-9, *When you are invited to a wedding feast, do not take the first place at the table, lest it be said to you, Give the place to him, and you must go with shame to take the lowest seat.* And in the same chapter, verse 11, it says that *everyone who exalts himself will be humbled and everyone who humbles himself will be exalted.*

In these four ways, then, the proud are deceived in their mind. Moreover they are disordered in two ways in their will. For they do not only believe that they should be preferred to others, but by inordinate will they desire and wish to be superior to all others. The Lord restrained this desire in Luke 22:24-26 when an argument began among his disciples as to which of them was greater. The Lord said, *He who is greater among you shall become like a lesser, and he who is a leader shall become a servant.*

Secondly, the proud are not only disordered in their will because they wish to be superior to others, but they also have an inordinate will because they wish to attempt what they cannot complete and undertake what they cannot bring to completion. Such people should be rebuked because no one ought to rely on his own strength, but on divine strength. For those who rely on God's strength are not forsaken while those who rely on themselves are humbled and cast down, according to Judith 6:15, *Lord of heaven and earth, look upon their pride and consider our humility, and show that you do not forsake those who rely on you, and that you humble those who rely on themselves and boast in their own strength.*

Six types of pride, then, can be distinguished, and the first three seem to be especially against God. For the proud person does not think that what he has he has from God, or he believes that what he possesses he possesses by his own merits, or, believing he has what he does not have, he extols himself more that he should and contradicts the divine example. Such a person is turned especially against God because if you have some things that you do not believe you have from God, you particularly oppose God in not believing that he is the universal cause. Or if you believe that you have all from him, but through your own merits, then you are opposed to him because you believe he is ungenerous. Or thirdly if you believe that you have something from God, and not by your own merits but by his grace, when you in fact do not have it, you are still opposed to God because it follows from this that God is empty and insufficient when he does not satisfy his creatures with his goodness, but with emptiness.

Therefore these three types of pride are especially against God because the first type denies that God is the universal cause, the second says that he is ungenerous, the third claims that he is empty and insufficient. But the other three types are against one's neighbor because no one believes he should be preferred to all, or wishes to be superior to all others, or in his regard of others relies on himself, without sinning against others or being a burden to others.

Pride, then, is the beginning of all sin, not only materially, formally and finally, but it is also the beginning of all sin efficiently. For every sin is against oneself or against God or against one's neighbor. And by pride, as was shown, one may become as much against oneself as against God as against one's neighbor. Therefore we do well to detest pride on account of the infection of evil that is the beginning of all sin. But we ought to detest it further because of the obligation of punishment. For he who holds onto it will be filled with curses, that is, he will be filled with evil and abuse. But, on the other hand, humility is the beginning of all good and he who holds onto it will be filled with blessings. May we be brought to these blessings by the Lord Jesus Christ, who with the Father and Holy Spirit is one God blessed forever. Amen.

Sermon 2

Covetousness is the root of all evil, and some who desire wealth have strayed from the faith and have brought themselves into many sorrows (1 Tm 6:10). According to Gregory, sin that is not washed away through repentance soon drags one, by its weight, to another sin.[8] Therefore through one sin man falls and is dragged into another. But this fall and this dragging are not the same in all cases. Since we distinguish two kinds of sins, some against faith and others against morals, some people are dragged from sins against the faith into sins against morals, others are dragged in the opposite direction.

Pagans and unbelievers, ignorant of the way of truth, fall into many sins against morals because of their sins against faith. Concerning these the words in Romans 1:25 can be understood, *They have changed the truth of God into a lie, and they worship and serve the creature rather than the creator.* And the next verse continues, *Therefore God has handed them over to passions of shame.* Pagans and infidels, then, are handed over to passions of shame, that is, to sins against good morals, because they worshiped and served the creature rather than the creator, that is, because they sinned against faith.

But among Christians it seems to be the opposite. For most of these stray from faith and fall into sins against faith because of covetousness and other sins against morals. The sinner hurries on even if he comes to the worst of sins. Therefore when covetousness flourishes greatly, and when sins against morals overflow, evil Christians begin to doubt the truth of faith and deviate from correct faith. Among them, then, this order occurs often: first they sin against morals, second they stray from faith, third, and because of the first two, they make themselves liable for punishment.

The preacher and proclaimer of God's word should persuade his hearers not to sin against morals, not to err against the faith, and not to make themselves liable for punishment through these two sins. Therefore in the proposed text, found in 1 Timothy 6, these three are described in order. First it is shown how great a sin is covetousness, which is against good morals; second it is declared how those desiring it stray from faith and sin against the faith; third it is shown how those who practice these make themselves liable for punishment and entangle themselves in many sorrows. The first, namely covetousness, a terrible sin against good morals, is recorded when it says, *for covetousness is the root of all evil*; the second, namely how some desiring it stray from the faith and sin against faith, is considered when it adds, *and some who desire it have strayed from the faith*; the third, namely how those who practice these make themselves liable for punishment and entangle themselves in various sorrows, is considered when it adds, *and they have brought themselves into many sorrows.*

First we would persuade you not to sin against morals, by showing you how great a sin is covetousness; secondly we would persuade you not to err against the faith through covetousness; thirdly we would persuade you not to make yourselves liable for punishment and not to entangle yourselves in many sorrows by sinning against morals and erring against faith through covetousness. But we are unable to accomplish this of ourselves, and therefore we rely on God who gives grace, to whom be glory forever.

Sermon 2

Covetousness is the root of all evil, etc. (1 Tm 6:10). Although the prologue was based upon this text, we can still build our sermon on the same text approached in a different way. For we intended, after the sermon on pride, to write a sermon on covetousness or greed. And it seems that these two sins are in a certain sense more general because, as was said above, pride is the beginning of all sin, and as it says here, covetousness is the root of all evils. Because these two vices are general in this way, it is well to speak of them first. Therefore, having spoken of pride, it remains next to write a sermon on covetousness or greed.

Covetousness Is Very Detestable

To manifest its nature, it must be known that covetousness or greed is not simply an evil of any kind but is an evil of a certain overabundance or excess. For evil has usually been distinguished in two ways, namely of guilt and of punishment. And these two evils are connected to each other since there is no evil of guilt without the evil of punishment. For there is no guilt that some punishment does not follow at some time, and no guilt that remains unpunished in the end. And just as there is no evil of guilt without an evil of punishment following, so there is no evil of punishment without an evil of guilt preceding. For if no guilt preceded, no punishment would have followed. For God created human nature innocent and upright in its origin, not deserving any sorrow or penalty, but death and penalty resulted from the sin of our first parents because *by one man sin entered into the world, and death through sin,* as it says in Romans 5:12. Therefore from the evil of guilt results the evil of punishment.

Yet it should be diligently noted that not only an evil of punishment follows upon an evil of guilt, but also many other evils of guilt may follow upon an evil of guilt. For sin, if it is not removed by repentance, drags one into many sins by its weight. One sin may be more serious and more detestable than another in three ways, namely causally, formally and in terms of punishment. For we say that one sin is more serious and more detestable than another causally when many evils are caused and result from it. Accordingly covetousness or greed, from which other evils flow, is a very serious sin because it is the root of all evils.

Secondly one sin may be more detestable than another formally. Every sin consists of this, that by it someone inordinately despises one good and inordinately subjects himself to another good, as was said above. And there is no turning away from one good unless there is turning toward another good, nor can there be the despising of one good unless there is the desire for another good. For to despise good and to turn away from good cannot be willed in themselves, but only secondarily. By desiring one good in itself, someone may despise another secondarily or consequently; and by turning toward one good he may turn away from another. Therefore one sin is more detestable than another formally and in itself when it despises a greater good or when it subjects one to a lesser good.

According to this, idolatry is a very detestable sin. We see that an external good, such as money and whatever can be measured in money, is not as great a good as one's neighbor; and one's neighbor is not as great a good as God himself. Therefore robbery, which acts against the external good of a neighbor, is not as great a sin as murder, which acts against a neighbor's person. And murder, which acts against a neighbor's person, is not as great a sin as blasphemy or idolatry, which acts directly against God. Idolatry, then, is a very detestable sin considered in itself because therein the greatest good is despised. For by it one despises and thinks little of God himself. Rather, idolatry is not only a very detestable sin because by it someone despises the greatest good, namely God, but it is also a very detestable sin because by it someone subjects himself to the least good, like an idol that is a corporal, inanimate and insensible good. Greed is a kind of idolatry, according to Ephesians 5:5, *for the greedy person, who is the servant of idols, has no inheritance in the kingdom of Christ.* If we consider rightly the way of idolatry and the way of greed, we will say that just as the idolater sins gravely because he subjects himself to an idol (which is the least good because it is a corporal, inanimate and insensible good), so the greedy person sins gravely because he subjects himself to money (which is the least good since it is corporal, inanimate and insensible). Therefore greed is very detestable not only because it is a terrible evil causally, since it is the root of all evil, but also is very detestable because it is a terrible evil formally, since it is a kind of idolatry and deviation from the faith.

Thirdly greed is very detestable because it is a terrible evil in terms of punishment. For greedy people expose themselves to many punishments and various sorrows

In the proposed text that is taken from 1 Timothy 6, greed is described as very detestable. It is described as being very detestable in the first place because it is a terrible evil causally; secondly because it is a terrible evil formally; it is described as detestable in the third place because it is a terrible evil in terms of punishment. The first is recorded when it says, *for covetousness is the root of all evils;* the second is considered when it adds, *some who desire money have strayed from the faith;* the third is manifested when it adds, *and they have brought themselves into many sorrows.*

Covetousness Is a Terrible Evil Causally

Firstly covetousness is a terrible evil causally and is the root of all evil in four ways. Thus covetousness can be understood in four ways, generally in two ways and particularly in two ways. Again, as it is understood generally with respect to every sin, it may be taken in two ways. First covetousness can be called a universal spark of sinning; secondly covetousness can be understood generally with respect to sin and with respect to changeable good and refer to any inordinate turning toward good.

That covetousness or concupiscence may be called a spark is clear from the master in his gloss. While explaining the words of Romans 6:12, *Therefore do not let sin reign in your mortal bodies so that you obey its concupiscence,* he says that he sometimes calls concupiscence by the name of spark, that is, by the name of innate corruption. Because of concupiscence we are born without original righteousness. Because of it we have inordinate powers from birth. Because of it our flesh is not fully subject to the soul and the inferior powers are not fully subject to reason. Within us there is a certain aptitude for coveting and a certain propensity for sinning. And this aptitude for coveting, called a spark of sin, may be named concupiscence or covetousness and is the root of all sins.

Secondly covetousness is understood generally as the turning toward changeable good. In the previous sermon we said that he is very greedy for whom God is not enough. For whoever rejects God, who is the unchangeable good, and turns toward a temporal and changeable good, ought to be called greedy and covetous. Just as in every sin there is pride on the side of turning away, so also there is covetousness on the side of turning toward. Covetousness, then, is understood generally in these two ways, because it is both a spark of sin and a turning toward changeable good, which cover all vices universally.

But just as covetousness is understood in two ways generally with respect to every sin, so it may be understood in two ways particularly with respect to money or with respect to what can be measured in money. For in one way covetousness can be called that act of coveting money or the coveting of money itself. In a second way covetousness can be called the money itself that is coveted. For if covetousness is a kind of idolatry or deviation from faith, as will be clear in what follows, then just as one calls faith sometimes the act of believing but at other times the thing itself that is believed, so also covetousness can be called the act of coveting or the money itself that is coveted. Covetousness, then, is taken in four ways: first as the spark of sinning, second as the turning toward changeable good, third as the act of coveting money, and fourth as the money itself that is coveted. The first two of these ways are general, but the two subsequent ones are particular. Firstly covetousness is the root of all evils as the spark of sin; secondly covetousness is a root of this kind as the turning toward changeable good or turning toward sinning; thirdly covetousness is a root of this kind as the inordinate love of money; fourthly covetousness is a root of this kind as money unjustly coveted.

And thus covetousness is the root of all evils, that is, the spark of sin that, as was said, can be called covetousness. For from such a spark of sin arise all sins as branches arise from a root. Just as branches have their vitality from the root and immediately dry up if they are not connected to the root, so vices have their vitality from the spark and from the rebellion of powers, and they are preserved in vitality by such a spark. Thus this spark is sometimes called concupiscence because by it we are prone to covet. Sometimes it is called the old man because by that spark we are inclined to sin and are old. The apostle speaks of this spark in Romans 6:6, *Our old man*, that is, the spark of sin, as the gloss interprets it, *has been crucified with Christ that the body of sin might be destroyed*, that is, that all sins might be destroyed or that the whole mass of sins might be destroyed. For just as anyone is said to have the body of law when he has all the legal books, because by the name of body we understand all members, so by the body of sin we should understand all sins or should understand the whole mass of sins. Therefore if the body of sin is destroyed, that is, all sins are destroyed, by the crucifixion of the spark, then all vices take their origin from this spark. For branches never dry up from the drying up of a root unless they take their origin from it. Likewise all sins are not destroyed or dried up by the crucifixion, that is, the disabling, of the spark unless the other vices took their origin from this spark as from a root. And because this is so, it is rightly said above that covetousness is the root of all evils, that is, the spark of sin that may be called covetousness.

Secondly covetousness is the root of all evils because it is concupiscence for a changeable good or turning toward a changeable and temporal good. Although, according to Augustine in *Free Will*,[9] every sin is voluntary to such an extent that if it is not voluntary it is not sin, yet, since there are two things in sin, namely turning away and turning toward, one is more important in guilt while the other is more important in volition. Turning away is principally in guilt because every sin principally has the character of guilt from the fact that one turns away from God. But turning toward is more principally in the one willing or in the intention of the one sinning because, although the sinner sins principally from the fact that he turns away from God, he does not however principally intend to turn away from God, but rather principally intends to turn inordinately toward a changeable good.

Since what is a root or a beginning always has the character of a principle, and since covetousness, on the side of turning toward, and pride, on the side of turning away, are both in some way principles in every sin, then each may be called the principle or beginning of all sins, but each in a different way, for since every sin includes guilt and the object willed, pride or turning away will be the beginning of all sins from the fact that it is a principle in the category of guilt. Covetousness, on the other hand, and turning toward a changeable good will be such a beginning because they are principles in the intention of the sinner and in the reason of the person willing.

There is nevertheless a particular reason why covetousness or the turning toward a changeable good is more correctly called the root of all evil rather than the beginning of all sin. For one does not call any cause or principle a root, but only that which is found in a lower place. Although a root may hold a higher position in a sprout, it holds a lower position in the whole tree. For with respect to the whole, nothing in a tree is as low as the root. But the principle from a higher part can also be called a beginning. Therefore, while in sin the turning toward or covetousness is found in the lower place because it involves a changeable good that is lowest, the turning away or pride is found in the higher place because it involves an unchangeable good that is highest. Covetousness, then, will be called the root of all evils since it holds a place as a lower cause, but pride will be the beginning of all sin because it holds a place as a higher cause.

Therefore concupiscence or covetousness of this kind was prohibited in the law, and by this prohibition all sins were prohibited because it is the root of all sins. Thus, in commenting upon those words of the apostle in Romans 7:7, *I would not have known concupiscence if the law had not said, You shall not covet,* Augustine says that the law is good, which, when it prohibits concupiscence, prohibits all sins.[10] Therefore we can understand every sin by the word concupiscence, which means the turning toward a changeable good. And on the following verse, the gloss explains this word in this way: *But taking occasion by the commandment, sin worked in me every concupiscence,* that is, every sin; for by the phrase "every concupiscence" is understood "every sin," as is clear from the cited gloss.

Thirdly covetousness is the root of all evils because of the desire for having money. The person who is very covetous to have money and who is excessively greedy the philosopher calls petty. For he never attempts great things but always performs petty things in order to devour petty money. The greedy person has six qualities, elaborated in his *Ethics,* from which we can argue that such covetousness is the root of all evils.[11]

The first quality of the greedy person is that he fails in everything. He is so afraid to empty his purse that he does everything with misery and failure.

His second quality is that he always spends money with sadness. The greedy person clings to money with such love that it seems to him that his own limbs are cut off when money is separated from him. For just as the cutting off of limbs cannot happen without sadness and pain, so he is unable to make payments without being violently afflicted. Indeed, on account of the excessive love he has for coins, money is, as it were, joined and incorporated into him. And just as pain comes about from the division of something conjoined, so great pain is caused in him from the separation of money.

His third quality is that he always delays expenditure. He holds himself reluctantly to the way prescribed by the doctor for the health of his body, namely that he should endure the amputation of his foot. He always delays, he always avoids this amputation, because, as was said, it seems to the greedy man that, when money is separated from him, the limbs of his own body are amputated. So he not only spends money with sadness, but also delays expenditures for as long as he can.

The fourth quality of the greedy or petty person is that, even when he spends nothing, he always believes that he spends more than he should. Just as no one can bear anything in his eye, however small, that does not seem large to him, so the greedy person, because he loves money as the apple of his eye, cannot bear a loss of money, however slight, that does not seem great to him. So it is that when he spends a little, he considers that slight amount to be so great that it seems to him he has spent more than he should. Or we can say that, because the greedy person values money more than the honor that follows the spending of money, he cannot spend anything so little that it does not seem to him that he has spent more than he should. For he cannot pursue so great an honor for however little money that it does not appear to him that the cost towers above what he gained and that he has spent more than he should.

The fifth quality of the greedy person is that he thinks more about how to save money than about how to behave properly or how to accomplish beautiful work. Since he loves money more than all else, he does not have as much concern about other things as he does about how he can save money.

His sixth quality is that he loses what is great on account of what is small. Thus it is said proverbially that for one grain of pepper the miser loses a marriage partner. It is said that the greedy person is more concerned about how to save money than about how to do things properly. On account of the slight amount of money that he saves, he gives a banquet, or whatever else, improperly.

Therefore if the greedy person is such a failure at everything, and loves money so much, he will be unconcerned about how much evil he commits, as long as he is able to accumulate money. Therefore covetousness, that is, the desire for money and the inordinate love of it, is the root of all evils. Thus it is said in Sirach 10:9-10 that *nothing is more wicked than the greedy person.* And it continues that *he,* that is, the greedy person, *holds his soul for sale.* Money is so dear to the greedy person that he is unconcerned about losing his soul and committing all sorts of evil, as long as he can possess money. Thus it is rightly said that nothing is more wicked than the greedy person, that is, no substance is so defiled as the covetous person.

Fourthly covetousness is the root of all evils because money is coveted. As was said in the previous sermon, just as the beginning of all sin is pride in terms of intention, since everyone who sins intends some excellence for himself, so covetousness is the root of all evils in execution. For money, around which our concupiscence turns, is that by which we especially perform an evil desire of any kind or obtain a perverse wish of any kind. According to the common proverb, all things are done through money, and, as is said in Ecclesiastes 10:19, *all things obey money.*

Covetousness Is a Terrible Evil Formally

Having seen how greed is detestable causally, which is recorded when it says, *for covetousness is the root of all evils,* it remains to show just how detestable is covetousness or greed formally, which is recorded when it adds, *and some who desire wealth have strayed from the faith.* Greed is called a kind of idolatry and a kind of deviation from the faith by a certain similitude, since just as the idolater subjects himself to an external creature, an idol, so the greedy person subjects himself to an external creature, money. Yet each does so differently. For the idolater or the one who departs from the faith subjects himself to an external creature, an idol, by giving divine worship to it, but the greedy person subjects himself to an external creature, money, by loving it immoderately.

If we wish, we can discuss four things that we owe to God which the greedy person renders to money. Firstly God must be supremely loved since he is the highest good. For just as truth is the object of the intellect, so good is the object of the will. Therefore, just as the greatest truth is the greatest thing to know, so the highest good is the highest good to love.

Secondly God must be supremely trusted since he is the highest power. For everything is placed in his control and he does whatever he wills. We should trust in him who can fulfill our desires.

Thirdly God must be supremely honored since he is the universal Father. For children ought to honor their father, as it is asked in Malachi 1:6, *If I am your father, where is my honor?*

Fourthly he must be supremely feared and he must be obeyed in everything. We should show fear and obedience to our lords, as it is asked in the same verse from Malachi, *If I am your lord, where is my fear?*

Now the greedy person renders all these to money. He loves money more than the goodness of God; he trusts in money more than in the power of God; he gives more honor to coins than to the divine fatherhood; he is more obedient to money and fears more to lose money than the divine governance; he wishes to serve money more than God. Therefore just as the stomach of gluttons is their god, about whom the apostle speaks in Philippians 3:19, *whose god is their stomach,* so also money is the god of the greedy. Thus on that verse in Ephesians 5:5, *or the greedy, who is the servant of idols,* the gloss says that money is the god of the greedy.

Firstly, then, the greedy person loves money more than God. That is loved more in which one's final intention is placed. And one's final intention is placed in that which is loved without limit. For according to the philosopher in the *Politics,* book one, this is the difference between the end and those things that are for the end: the end is that which is loved without limit while those things that are for the end are not loved without limit, but are loved according to the rule and measure of this end.[12] Therefore the greedy person who never has enough money loves money without limit. He places his final intention in money since no one can erect two ultimate ends for himself. If the greedy person places his final intention in the good of money, his final intention truly pulls back and turns away from the divine good. Therefore he loves money more than God since he places his final intention in money and not in God. It is rightly said, then, that those who follow covetousness and desire money deviate from the faith. They are like infidels since they love the creature, that is, money, more than God. Therefore those who are such people should wail and mourn because they love goods that can rot, which can be ruined by moths and destroyed by rust, according to the words of James 5:1-3, *Therefore listen now, you rich, and weep, wailing in the miseries that come upon you. You riches have rotted, your clothes have been eaten by moths and your gold and silver have rusted.*

Secondly greed is very detestable as it is in itself and as it is considered formally. For it is like idolatry and so like a deviation from the faith because the greedy trust in money more than in God. For if they trusted in God more than in money, they would give all their money to the poor in order to attain divine love. Since they do not do this, but trust completely in coins, the gods of the greedy are the coins in which they put their trust. You do not believe, miserable ones, that such gods are impotent, yet they cannot help you in the throes of death. Only the true God is he in whom you should trust, because he alone is able to kill and to make alive, to wound and to heal.

Therefore the words of Deuteronomy 32:37 that are spoken against idolaters may be directed against the greedy: *Where are their gods in whom they trust?* If we wish to rephrase this concerning the greedy we would say, Where are the coins, the gods of the greedy, in which they trust? Arise and help us and protect us in our need. It is as if he should say: Idols or coins or whatever other creatures you say are your gods, these gods are impotent; you ought not to trust in them because they cannot help you. And thus it continues in verse 39, *Understand that I alone exist and there is no other God besides me*, as if to say, The idol is not God, money is not God, nothing else besides me is God; one should trust in me alone because I can do all things. And so it continues, *I will kill and I will make alive, I will wound and I will heal, and no one can deliver you from my hand.*

Thirdly greed is compared to idolatry and is very detestable because the greedy person honors money more than God and the creature more than creator. For the greedy and covetous receive persons of power and they honor the rich, seeing that they can obtain profit and advantage from them. But they despise the poor. And because God loves the poor, by honoring the rich and not the poor, the greedy and covetous despise God in the poor and honor wealth. For if they only show honor to the wealthy because of the money they possess, it is certain that they honor money and not God.

This is also the judgment of James 2:3-6: *If you attend to him who is dressed in fancy robes and say to him, Sit here in this fine place; but to a poor person you say, Stand over there, or Sit on the stool at my feet, you have become judges with wicked thoughts.* And he adds that *God has chosen the poor of this world, but you have dishonored the poor.* Therefore, because the covetous do not honor the poor whom God has chosen and among whom God dwells, it follows that they do not honor God. And since they honor the wealthy possessors of money, they honor money more than God.

Fourthly greed is compared to idolatry because the greedy obey money more than God, and money rather than God rules them. Thus in Psalm 76:6 it is expressly stated of the greedy that they are *men of riches.* It does not say "riches of men" because it is more true that the greedy are held by riches than that riches are held by them; they are owned rather than being owners. And since they are servants of money, they are more obedient to money than to God. Therefore the greedy who are men of riches and are those who serve riches must be severely rebuked. They love money but cannot receive any profit from it, according to Ecclesiastes 5:9, *They who love riches will receive no profit from them.*

Covetousness Is a Terrible Evil Penally

Having shown how greed is very detestable causally since it is the cause of all evils, which is recorded when it says, *For covetousness is the root of all evils,* and having manifested how covetousness is very detestable in itself or formally since it is a kind of idolatry and deviation from the faith, which is considered when it adds, *for some who desired money have strayed from the faith,* it remains to show how covetousness is very detestable in terms of penalties, which is considered when it adds, *and they have brought themselves into many sorrows.*

To make this evident, it must be shown that any guilt or any sin can be harmful and can be detestable because of penalties in four ways: 1) in the soul, 2) in the body, 3) in time, 4) in one's neighbor. Firstly any sin is harmful to the soul if it has anxiety of the soul connected with it; secondly it is harmful to the body if it has any lack of the bodily needs connected with it; thirdly it is harmful in time if it has durability of time connected with it; fourthly any sin is harmful with regard to one's neighbors when it takes away from them any advantage or usefulness. In all these ways greed is very detestable because of penalties; and those who desire riches bring themselves into many sorrows.

Firstly, then, greed is a harmful vice and covetous people bring themselves into many sorrows of the soul because the soul of the greedy is always full of anxiety. For money cannot satisfy the soul of the greedy and so their soul is always anxious since it is never satisfied with money. This can be discussed in a fourfold manner: First it can be understood in regard to the soul that has money; second in regard to the money possessed; third in regard to the way of possessing; fourth in regard to both the soul and the money.

The first way is clear because something that is capable of great good can never be satisfied and fulfilled by a small good, just as the chest that is capable of containing much money is not able to be filled up by a little money. A soul is capable of great good because it is capable of receiving God and is God's temple in which God ought to dwell. Temporal things, then, which are very small goods with respect to the divine good are unable to satisfy or fulfill the soul capable of God. Thus Augustine say that the soul capable of God cannot be fulfilled by anything less than God. And expressing the same thought to God, he says, "You have made us for yourself, Lord, and our hearts are restless until they rest in you."[13] Therefore greed is a harmful vice with regard to the soul itself because the soul laboring under this vice is full of anxiety and is never satisfied by money.

The second way that money does not satisfy can be understood with regard to the money possessed. For possessed money, as with all other sensible objects, has being mentally in the soul. The mind does not receive into itself the things themselves but the images of things. For the stone is not in the soul but a likeness or image of the stone and likewise silver is not in the soul but a likeness or image of silver. Such likenesses and images of things are defective and, as it were, empty beings. They do not, then, fill the soul but make it empty. Thus it is said in Luke 1:53, *He filled the hungry with good things and the rich he sent away empty.* Literally the rich are empty because, since riches do not fill the soul, they leave it empty.

The third way that the soul is not satisfied by money is understood with regard to the manner of possessing. The greedy person keeps his money in a chest or in a purse, and because he has it outside his soul, his soul will never be satisfied by it. For he would be a person of great stupidity if he had a large abundance of grain and wished to fill some sack with the grain but put none of the grain into the sack, because when he received the grain he always put it outside the sack and never filled the sack with it. This would be like someone who had a great abundance of food in front of him but always placed the food outside his mouth and none of the food ever entered his stomach, and his stomach was never satisfied with food. It is the same in the case of the greedy person because money cannot enter the soul and he puts no money into his soul. He accumulates all outside his soul and so his soul is never satisfied by it.

Thus it is rightly said in Habakkuk 2:6, *Woe to him who multiplies things that are not his; he accumulates thick mud against himself.* Coins and all that can be measured by coins are not our goods because they are not internal goods that can enter our soul, but are external goods. Such goods, like silver, gold and other metals, are a kind of thick mud because they are born of the earth, have their origin in the veins of the earth, are discovered and mined among the minerals of the earth. Woe to the greedy one, then, because he accumulates goods that are not his own and thus accumulates thick mud against himself, that is, against his soul. By so doing his soul will always be in need and never be satisfied with goods.

It has been customary to employ a familiar example to show that such goods are not ours but are goods of the world.[14] We see that if some dog walks along with two men, which of the two is the dog's master remains unknown as long as the men continue on together. But if they separate from each other, the dog will turn away from one to follow his master. Because of this it appears clearly that the other man was not the dog's master, but only the one whom the dog followed. So it is in our case, for as long we are in the world it seems to us that riches are ours. But this is not true; rather the riches are the world's. For when we are separated from the world we do not take them with us, but they remain in the world, according to 1 Timothy 6:7, *for we have brought nothing into this world, nor can we take anything from it,* and Job 1:21, *I came forth naked from my mother's womb, and naked I will return there.*

The fourth way that money does not satisfy is understood with regard to both, namely as much with regard to the money possessed as to the soul possessing. For what fills and what is filled ought to be of the same kind since it is right that a corporal entity be filled by corporal things and a spiritual entity by spiritual things. A corporal entity can never be filled by spiritual things because all spirits of the world do not even fill up one chest. In the same way, just as spiritual things do not fill corporeal things, so corporeal things will not fill up spiritual things. Therefore such corporeal things will not be able to fill up or satisfy the soul, which is something spiritual. Thus it is rightly said in Ecclesiastes 5:9, *The greedy person will not be satisfied with money.*

Having discussed how greed is a harmful vice and how the greedy bring themselves into many sorrows (because their soul is always full of anxiety and can never be satisfied with money, which is clear with regard to the soul of the possessor, to the money possessed, to the way of possessing, and with regard to both the soul and money together), it remains secondly to show how greed is a harmful vice and how the greedy bring themselves into many sorrows, not simply with regard to the soul, in that their soul is always full of anxiety, but also with regard to the body, in that their body is always in want.

Greed may be described as a cruel mistress. For that mistress would be cruel who determined that her servants should never eat well, never drink well, never dress themselves well, and never sleep well, but that they should be continually at her disposal. Thus greed acts against the greedy when it causes them to be always thinking about how to accumulate money, when it does not allow them to spend money to eat or drink or clothe themselves, but causes them to remain always in want.

Solomon speaks against these in Ecclesiastes 6:1-2, *And there is another evil that I have seen under the sun, and it occurs often among men: a man to whom God has given riches, substance and honor, and whose soul lacks nothing of all that he desires, but God does not grant him the ability to eat of it, but a stranger will consume it.*

Thirdly greed is a harmful vice and the greedy bring themselves into many sorrows not only with respect to the soul, as far as anxiety, and with respect to the body, as far as want, but also with respect to time, as far as durability. For greed is a certain incurable vice. Thus the philosopher proves in his *Ethics*[15] that greed is worse than prodigality since, as he says, prodigality can be cured by poverty. For some first live as prodigals, but when they experience what it is like to be in want, and how many miseries the poor are exposed to, they stop being prodigals. Prodigality can also be cured by age. For youths, since they are of a warm constitution and it is the character of warmth to diffuse itself, naturally diffuse themselves and are naturally generous. But when they come to an older age they learn better how to save money and how not to dissipate their own substance. Greed however is never cured. For as much as someone has more, he desires to have still more; and the older he gets the more greedy he becomes. For old people are of a cold constitution and it is the character of cold to constrict and compress. Old people are therefore naturally greedy and stingy. Further, the soul of the greedy follows the constitution of the body, and just as the humors are lacking in them and their body fails, so it appears to their soul that they lack the whole world. Therefore they are terrified and afraid to spend money and are naturally stingy.

Isaiah 5:8 is spoken against those who always want to accumulate and, because of their covetousness, never want to stop: *Woe to you who join house to house and connect field to field up the limit of the place. Will you alone dwell in the midst of the earth?*

Fourthly greed is a harmful vice not only with respect to the soul as far as anxiety, to the body as far as need, and to time as far as durability, since it is very harmful to be ill with a incurable ailment, but such a vice is also harmful with respect to neighbors because it takes away from them any advantage or usefulness. Thus the philosopher also assigned this cause as a reason why greed is worse than prodigality.[16] For prodigality is advantageous for many people. When he disperses his goods, the prodigal is useful to many, many receive a portion from him and many have an advantage from him. But the greedy person is advantageous neither to himself nor to others, according the words of Sirach 14:5, *He who is evil to himself, to whom will he be good?* For if the greedy person does not do well to himself, how will he do well to others? Rather, he does not only not do well to others, he actually lies in wait for the money of others that he might somehow take it and defraud them.

Therefore may God grant us to avoid and detest that which is so great a vice, that which is so great an evil causally because it is the root of all evils, that which is so detestable formally because those who follow greed stray from the faith, that which is so afflicted and so full of grief in terms of punishments because those behaving this way bring themselves into many sorrows. Thus avoiding this vice and also fleeing the other vices, let us follow the straight path so that by following it we might enjoy eternal happiness. May we be brought to this happiness by the Lord Jesus Christ, who with the Father and the Holy Spirit is one God blessed forever. Amen.

Sermon 3

Whose end is destruction, whose god is their stomach, whose glory is in shame, and who are wise about earthly things (Phil 3:19). Every preacher should be especially concerned that his hearers not be wise about earthly things, that is, that they not have a taste for the earthly, but have a taste for the heavenly. May they say with the apostle in Philippians 3.20, *But our meditation is upon heaven.* The tastes for earthly and for heavenly things seem to occupy opposite poles. And it is the law of opposites that if someone stretches himself away from one pole he must approach its opposite. Therefore if our hearers will pull back from the taste of the earthly they will be brought to a taste of the heavenly. But among other things that pull someone back from something there are evils that follow from it. For it seems that people are commonly more afraid of falling into evils than of not obtaining goods. For example thieves refrain from stealing more because of punishment they incur by stealing than because of the good reputation they lose by stealing. Although a good reputation is a great good, yet we refrain from acting wickedly not so much because we fear the loss of our good reputation as because of the obligation of punishment. Therefore, in order that our hearers not become wise in earthly things, that is, lest they develop a taste for them, they must be told about the evils that accompany those who wish to experience the taste of such things.

Our entire position, and also the position of any being, is distinguished in three ways, namely at the beginning, middle and end (or entrance, progress and departure). Those who have a taste for the earthly, such as gluttonous people who are devoted to the pleasures of the flesh, experience evils in departure, in exiting, or in the end, because their end is destruction. This means either a corporal death, since those who wish to pursue such pleasures die sooner than others, or an eternal death, since they descend to hell.

Secondly they do not only have an evil end or evil departure because their end is destruction, but they also have an evil beginning or evil entrance because when they fall away from God they no longer have the true God for their lord, but their god is their stomach.

Thirdly, since they are wise about the earthly and are devoted to carnal pleasures and have a taste for earthly things, they do not only have an evil end or an evil departure because their end is destruction, and they do not only have an evil beginning or evil entrance because their god is their stomach, but they also have an evil middle or evil progress because their glory is in shame. Thus in Philippians 3, from which our text is taken, the apostle describes, in the way just mentioned, the evils that accompany gluttons.

By this sermon we intend for gluttons who are wise in earthly things to pull back from their vices because of the evils that accompany them. But we cannot bring this about by ourselves, and therefore we rely on [God who enlightens our hearts, to whom be glory forever].

Sermon 3

Whose end is destruction, etc. (Phil 3:19). Although this text was interpreted in one way and the prologue was built on it, we are able to interpret it in a different way and build the body of the sermon on it. And since we intend to admonish gluttons, it will show how detestable a vice is gluttony. A vice seems to be detestable to the extent that it opposes love, for love is that virtue which never ends, as is said in 1 Corinthians 13. In the same chapter, verse 13, it is also asserted: *now these three remain, faith, hope and love, but the greatest of these is love.* Since love is so great a virtue, to the extent that something is opposed to love in many ways, it seems to be more detestable. Because gluttony, as will be clear, is opposed to love in many ways it deserves to be detested. For it is not improper that some vice be detestable on account of something else.

In the first book of *Teaching Christianity,* Augustine lists four things that must be loved: one thing that is above us, God; another that is below us, our body; third, what is next to us, our neighbor; and fourth, what we are.[17] And because these four must be loved, namely God, neighbor, ourselves, and our body, then that seems to be very detestable and seems to be very contrary to love which contradicts all four of these. And since gluttony is a vice that harms our body, that is contrary to God, that injures our neighbor, and that offends our own selves, then to be gluttonous is very detestable.

In expounding our proposed text against the gluttonous, we will speak of that which is described for the detestation of gluttony. First it is shown that gluttony is a vice that harms the body; second that it offends God; third that it is contrary to our neighbor; and fourth that it harms ourselves or that it harms our soul. For no one sins unless he acts against his own body or against his own soul or against God or against his neighbor.

As will become clear, gluttony has five species and five offspring and five injuries with respect to one's own person and five injuries with respect to one's neighbor. It is against the body because of the five injuries with respect to one's own person; it is against God because of the five species, as will be clear; it is against neighbor because of the five injuries with respect to one's neighbor; and it is against the soul because of its five offspring. Gluttony is not only a vice against our body, but also against ourselves or our soul. Thus in the proposed words that are read in Philippians 3:19 these four are described in order. For it is shown first that gluttony is against the body when it says, *Whose end is destruction*; secondly it is revealed that it is against God when it adds, *whose god is their stomach*; thirdly it is manifested that it is against one's neighbor when it adds, *whose glory is in their shame*; fourthly it is shown that gluttony is against ourselves or against our soul when it adds, *who are wise about earthly things*.

Gluttony Harms the Body

Firstly the vice of gluttony is against our body because the end of the gluttonous is destruction, that is, death, according to the words of Sirach 37:34, *Many have died because of drunkenness.* Literally, the intemperate and immoderate die sooner than others. Not without reason do physicians who discuss the treatment of the body praise especially abstinence among the virtues.

Yet it must be carefully noted that, since death is the last of all frightful things, then that which is against the body because it brings on death seems also to bring on other evils. For our body seems to have five things against which intemperance acts and operates. First our body has the tongue; second it has limbs; third it has bodily faculties, such as the senses and memory, which are corporal powers connected with organs; fourth it has humors, for since it is composed of the four elements, it has four humors that correspond to the four elements; and fifth it has life. Intemperance harms the body in all of these ways, because it corrupts the humors, it weakens the limbs, it dissipates the powers, it ties up the tongue, and finally it destroys and takes away life. Thus let us say with the apostle, *the end of the gluttonous is destruction.* Although this is true of the death that is sin because gluttony is a capital and mortal sin, and although it is also true of the death that is hell because gluttons will go into hell unless they repent and stop, it is also true of bodily death because intemperance in the end takes away corporal life and kills the body.

Firstly intemperance corrupts the humors. Intemperance seems to be like a raw meal. Our natural heat is not sufficient to digest too much food and drink, just as a small fire is not sufficient to burn up a lot of green wood. Therefore it happens that both food and drink remain undigested and so it is really like a raw meal since it is not boiled by natural heat. And because this undigested fluid is drawn into the limbs, the humors that are generated from such food are corrupted. From this arise bodily infirmities, because just as health is the balance of humors as the required constitution demands, so infirmity is the corruption and imbalance of the humors. Therefore we should very much avoid the vice of gluttony since not only is the soul wounded by it, but also the humors are corrupted and the body weakened. This is what is said in Sirach 37:33, *for there will be infirmity in many foods*; literally, an abundance of foods ruins and corrupts the body.

Secondly intemperance not only corrupts the humors, but also weakens the limbs. This happens in two ways. First from the exhaustion of natural heat, for when a lot of food is eaten the natural heat labors too hard to digest it. The natural heat becomes exhausted and weakened from this labor. And when it is exhausted and weakened, the muscles are made weak and powerless. And with weak muscles, the limbs become weak and feeble.

This happens from the corruption of the humors in a second way when there is a continual loss due to the natural heat's consumption of moisture. Just as a burning lantern continually nourishes itself with oil because of the heat of fire, so every animal body nourishes itself with moisture, which is from the composition of the limbs, because of natural heat. And since this is a continual loss, it is right that a continual restoration comes about through nourishment. Thus in *On the Soul* the philosopher determined that so long as animals can do this they will live.[18] Therefore if the restoration of what is lost in all limbs comes about through nourishment, but in intemperance and in excess of food the fluid transmitted to the limbs remains undigested and corrupts, then the required restoration is not made. And since the required restoration of what is lost does not come about in the limbs, the limbs become feeble and weak through intemperance.

Even if someone is doubtful about this account, anyone can experience in himself that this is so. By denying that the humors are corrupted and weakened through intemperance, one denies his senses and denies what he experiences in himself. Therefore the vice of gluttony, by which so many evils arise in the body, is very detestable.

Thus it is written in Sirach 37:33 that *greediness for food leads to bile*. Literally, when a person consumes food very greedily, as gluttons do, he becomes hot in his liver and bile is increased in him, and thus gluttons usually have yellow eyes and yellow face. And because those who behave in this way have a sickly body and have feeble limbs, it is rightly said that intemperance not only corrupts the humors but weakens the limbs.

Thirdly intemperance dissipates the bodily powers because it takes away memory and dissipates the senses. The senses and memory are faculties connected with organs, and whatever is founded in an organ is a corporal faculty that functions in regard to the body. The senses and memory, then, are bodily faculties. Thus drunkenness and intemperance must dissipate the senses since it weakens the limbs and causes the organs of the body to be feeble. When these are made feeble the sensitive powers are weakened because the senses are each founded in an organ as in a subject.

That drunkenness and intemperance dissipate all the senses is clear from what is said in Proverbs 23:35, where the wise man speaks in the voice of drunkards and those who practice intemperance, saying, *They beat me and I did not feel pain, they dragged me and I did not sense it*. Literally, the brain is so inflated from the fumes of intemperance and wine that one is made insensible and does not feel whatever happens around him. Thus the senses are so dissipated from wine that a person does not perceive wounds and does not feel pain from blows.

Rather, because of intemperance and because of wine drunk to excess not only is the sense of touch destroyed so that a person does not feel blows and wounds, but the sense of vision is also destroyed. Thus drunkards commonly have dissipated eyes, as it is written in Proverbs 23:29-30, *Who has a spreading of their eyes?* that is, Who has diffused eyes and in whom is there the spreading out of eyes? *Is it not they who linger in wine and are eager for drinking cups?* Drinkers, then, have diffused eyes because they lose the sense of vision. More-over, when they are drunk they do not feel blows because the sense of touch is dissipated within them.

That we might briefly pass over every sense, let us simply say that drunkenness and intemperance destroy all the senses. And if they destroy all the senses then they take away memory since memory arises from the senses. Memory is made from many sensations, as is said at the end of book two of the *Posterior Analytic*,[19] and many senses give birth to memory, as is said in book one of the *Metaphys-ics*.[20] Memory is also the storehouse of sensible images, as Avicenna says in *On Natural Things* 6.[21] And because this is true, then when the senses are destroyed the memory is naturally injured. There-fore intemperance must be strictly avoided, drunkenness must be strongly detested, for the bodily faculties are injured by them, the senses are destroyed and the memory dissipated.

Fourthly intemperance does not only corrupt the humors and weaken the limbs and dissipate the bodily faculties, it also ties up the tongue. For intoxicated men and those who practice intemper-ance speak perversely and cannot untangle their words. Unless it has some external impediment, the tongue has continual saliva, which suffices for moistening the muscles so that the tongue can be moved properly to form words. But when the external moisture of wine is added, the tongue is enlarged and the muscles immobilized in such a way that the drunkard cannot move his tongue properly nor can he form words correctly.

Thus it is said in Proverbs 23:33-34 that if you are eager for drink-ing cups, *your eyes will see strange things, your heart will utter perverse things, and you will be like one who sleeps in the midst of the sea*. For wine that is drunk to excess makes a person speak perversely; it impedes the tongue so that he does not speak correctly. It takes away the un-derstanding so that he does not think correctly. It makes the eyes see strange things because fumes are increased to the nerves of the eyes by drunkenness and intemperance. Thus from the increase of fumes comes a darkening of the nerves by which vision is made, and visible images are received improperly by these nerves so that they present strange sights. Therefore the drunkard's tongue speaks perversely and his eyes see strange things. Further, drunkards are like those put to sleep in the midst of the sea. They are put to sleep because they have dazed and stunned senses. They are said to be in the midst of the sea because it seems to the drunkard that his house is like a ship. For as a ship is lifted at one instant and pressed down at the next, it appears to the drunk that his house is spinning around and that it is pressed down and lifted up. Even granting that intemperance causes no spiritual evil, people should still be on guard against it because it harms the body.

Fifthly intemperance kills and takes away life. Since by drunkenness and intemperance the tongue is rendered stammering and tied up, the bodily faculties are dissipated, the limbs weakened, and the humors corrupted, it is only natural that in the end it kills and destroys the body. For the acts of activating forms are in something receptive and well-disposed, and the form has existence in proportionate and fitting matter. Therefore any wrong disposition of matter causes the expulsion of form. But by drunkenness and intemperance the entire body is rendered unsuitable and ill-disposed to the soul, since every passion rather casts away forms from substance. So it is natural that intemperance and drunkenness, if they are practiced too often, weaken the body and finally kill it. Therefore drunkenness and intemperance bring about death more quickly while abstinence and temperance extend life. Thus it is said in Sirach 37:34, *Many have perished on account of intemperance, but he who is temperate extends his life.*

Therefore it is rightly stated that the end of the gluttons and drunkards is death because, as is clear from our discussion, they have a stuttering and tied-up tongue, they have a dissipated memory and sensitive power, they have weakened and feeble limbs, they have corrupted humors, and finally they are destroyed and killed so that their end is destruction.

Gluttony Offends God

Having seen how many evils intemperance brings into its own subject, and how it is contrary to the body because the end of the gluttonous is death, it remains to show how many species of gluttony there are, and how God is offended because the god of the gluttonous is their stomach. Gluttons offend God according to Augustine in Prosper's commentary of the *Sentences*,[22] and as it is determined in the gloss to Philippians 3:19, because gluttons make their stomach a god, for they labor in eating as if their salvation were in food and as if their stomach were God.

In order for it to be better seen how the stomach of the gluttonous is a god and how God is offended by this vice, it must be understood that five species of this vice are commonly distinguished. According to these five species gluttons fall into five divine offenses. With regard to those who are engaged in this vice, just as we assigned five modes and five injuries by which they act against their own body, so we distinguish five species of this vice by which they act against God. The species of gluttony that are discussed by the doctors and saints are contained in this verse: "over-hastily, elegantly, too much, eagerly, diligently." Some sin in this vice as far as hastiness because they want to eat before the hour and want to greatly hasten their eating. Secondly some sin in this vice as far as elegance because they desire elegant, that is, delicate, foods. Thirdly some sin as far as excessiveness because they take food beyond a proper measure and gorge themselves with too much food. Fourthly some sin as far as eagerness because they consume their food with too much devotion and too much eagerness. Fifthly some sin as far as diligence because the gluttonous do not only want to anticipate the dinner hour, not only desire delicate foods, not only eat too much and eat with eagerness, but they also desire food that is prepared seriously and diligently. Now this fifth species, which is named diligently, differs from the second, which is named elegantly, because one is to wish for delicate foods while the other is to wish for foods prepared with care.

The number of these species is accounted for in this way. Three things are to be considered in everything that we do, namely the thing done, the way it is done, and the time of action. So also there are three things to be considered concerning eating, namely, the time of eating, the thing eaten, and the manner of eating. As far as the time of eating, one species is designated, which is called over-hastily because the person anticipates the time and desires the hour to come earlier. As far as the thing eaten, two species are understood since someone is able to sin in two ways concerning the thing eaten, namely as to the quality and as to the quantity. As to quality a person sins by elegance when he desires too delicious and delicate foods. As to quantity a person sins by excessiveness when he noticeably eats more than he should of the food placed before him. So also one may sin doubly in the manner of eating something because there is a double mode in it: one in preparing the food and the other in consuming it. As to the manner of preparing a person sins by diligence when he desires that foods be prepared for him with seriousness and great diligence. As to the manner of consuming a person sins by eagerness when he eats too ardently and too eagerly.

Therefore, that it might appear how gluttons offend God in five ways by these five species of gluttony, we will note five things about divine love. In God's love there are three things to consider according to the pattern of discussion we have been observing, namely the time of loving, the thing loved and the mode of loving. As far as the time of loving, God is to be loved before everything, as the Lord teaches us in the gospel (Mt 6:33), *Seek first the kingdom of God and later all these things will be given to you.* As far as the thing loved, God is to be loved more purely and more fully. He must be loved before all else because he is a greater good, and he must be loved more purely because he is a more absolute and purer good. As for the mode of loving, there are also two things to be observed, for he is to be loved more ardently and more diligently. But gluttons sin in all of these. Thus it is rightly said that their god is their food or their stomach since they worship their stomach rather than God and offer to their stomach what should be given to God.

We can also distinguish how God should be loved in a different way: first principally, because nothing is to be loved before him; second he should be loved finally because all things are to be loved on account of him; third he should be loved totally because nothing is to be loved above him; fourth he should be loved intensely and ardently because nothing contrary to him should be loved; fifth he should be loved with perseverance because nothing is to be loved that might bring to an end or take away the love that we have for him.

Gluttons also sin against all these, for they offer to their stomach or to their food everything that should be given to God. By wishing to hasten the time of eating, they love food principally because they seek nothing before food. Secondly, by desiring elegant and delicate foods, they love food finally since they love everything on account of food. Thirdly, by wanting food, too much food in great quantities, they love food totally because they love nothing beyond food or more than food. Fourthly, by consuming food ardently and with eagerness, they love food not only extensively and totally, but also intensively and ardently, so that they love nothing contrary to food. Fifthly, by loving food that is diligently prepared, they love food with perseverance because they are so attentive to it that they love nothing that could take away the love they have for food. Therefore gluttons sin in five ways against God according to these five species. And since they offer things to their stomach which should be offered to God, it is rightly said that gluttons are those whose god is their stomach, for they consider food or stomach as a god and worship it as God.

Firstly, then, by wanting to hasten the time of eating, gluttons seek food principally when they ought first to seek God. Thus it is said against them in Isaiah 5:11, *Woe to you who rise up early in the morning to pursue drunkenness, and to drink until sundown, so that you are inflamed with wine.* They rise early in the morning to pursue drunkenness who are seeking first how they might fill up their stomach rather than seeking how they might worship God.

Secondly, by seeking delicate foods, the gluttonous fail to love God finally because they do not love all things on account of God, but rather love everything on account of food. The gloss to Philippians 3:19 speaks against these when it says that gluttons do whatever they do for their stomach as if they were worshipping the stomach itself.

Thirdly, by loving food too much and in great quantities, they fail to love God finally because they do not love God more than food, but love food more than God. Although God is greater and better than all things and should be loved more than everything and worshipped above everything, gluttons nevertheless love their stomach or food more and worship it more than God. Thus Augustine, in Prosper's commentary on the *Sentences*,[23] speaks against gluttons because what people love before all else is that which they worship. And he adds that, since God is greater than all things, he is to be loved more than everything so that he might be worshipped. But they, that is, the gluttonous, make their stomach a god since they worship it and love it more than God.

Fourthly, by consuming food eagerly and ardently, they fail to love God intensely and fervently because they love something contrary to God. Rather, they love food more intensely and fervently because they love nothing contrary to food. Indeed they would rather lose God than food. Against those who are very delighted with the sweetness of wine and those who consume their meals too eagerly, it is said in Joel 1:5, *Wake up, you drunkards! Weep and mourn, all you who drink wine in its sweetness, for it is taken away from your mouth!* They should be ridiculed because they trusted in something transitory and in something that is taken away.

Fifthly, by loving foods diligently prepared, gluttons fail to love God with perseverance because they love something that causes them to separate from God and to fall away from him. For wine and all feasting cause even the wise to fall away from God. Just as women corrupt lustful men, even those who are wise and sensible, so wine and feasting cause the gluttonous to fall away from God, even those who are wise and sensible. Thus in Sirach 19:2 it is written that wine and women cause the wise and compel the sensible to fall away from God.

Gluttony Harms One's Neighbor

Having discussed how gluttons are those whose end is destruction because in five ways they act against their own body and ultimately destroy it, and having shown how they are those whose god is their stomach because they offend God in five ways and worship their stomach, it now remains to show how their glory is in shame because they offend their neighbor and injure him in five ways.

Five injuries of neighbor accompany gluttony, and on account of these five injuries the glutton's glory is not in respect but in shame. Gluttons, as far as our present concern, offend their neighbors in five ways and behave in such a way to them that they should be shamed and blamed. It is rightly said, then, that the glory of gluttons is in shame because they glory in things of which they should be ashamed.

The five injuries of neighbor that gluttons practice, and on account of which they should be ashamed, are the following: fraud, envy, abuse, lust and savage cruelty. For five things can be noted concerning a neighbor, namely his own person, a person in his family, his possessions, his good reputation and kindness that should be shown to a neighbor in his time of need. If the glutton will not refrain from his gluttony, he is unmerciful when he withholds the kindness owed to his neighbor. Secondly he is fraudulent when he defrauds his possessions. Thirdly he is lustful when he acts indecently against a person of his neighbor's family. Fourthly he is abusive when he says improper things and denigrates the reputation of his neighbor. Fifthly he is cruel and savage when he harms and sometimes kills his neighbor's own person.

First, then, the glutton is unmerciful when he withholds the kindness that necessity requires. A person who is completely gluttonous is so concerned about his own skin and body that he does not care about others, nor is he led to show them compassion. We have the example of the rich feaster who, although he was wealthy and feasted in splendor daily, was so unmerciful and cared so little about the poor that he denied Lazarus a crumb of bread. Therefore, concerning such a gluttonous person, the words of Ecclesiastes 6:7 can be presented: *All the labor of man is for his mouth*; literally, the entire aspiration of gluttons, and all of their labor, is to find some way to satisfy their appetite. Because they do not care about their neighbors, they refuse to show them mercy. Of them also apply the words of Amos 6:6, *drinking wine from bowls and being anointed with the best ointment, they are not concerned about the distress of Joseph.* For when they drink wine, when they are involved in their own pleasures, gluttons refuse to show mercy because they do not care about the affliction and distress of their neighbors.

Fraud is the second injury of neighbor that accompanies gluttony. Feasting and splendid foods reduce a person to a state of want and poverty. For if a person is diligent and hard-working, but loves wine and feasts, he is unable to grow rich; according to Sirach 19:1, *the drunk workman will not grow rich.* Rather, not only do they not grow rich, but they are in want and poverty. And because they were used to living in splendor, when they descend into poverty and are no longer able to lead the life of splendor from their own substance, they attempt to defraud their neighbors' possessions in order to substitute with another's goods what they are unable to draw from their own. That feasting in this way leads to poverty is clear from what is said in Proverbs 21:17, *The one who loves feasts will be in want, and he who loves wine and rich foods will not be rich.*

Lust is the third injury of neighbor that accompanies gluttony. We are inclined to lust on account of three things, namely an overabundance of matter, an excess of heat or a defect of reason. It occurs from an overabunduce of matter because semen is an overflow of nourishment. Therefore he who is very gluttonous and eats a lot has much of this overflow and so is easily aroused to lust. Secondly we are inclined to lust from an excess of heat. For it is the nature of cold to constrict and immobilize and the nature of heat to extend and move. Therefore when the flesh is warmed, which happens through an abundance of food and drink, it easily extends itself to sexual pleasures. Thirdly it comes about from a defect of reason because, as is said in the *Ethics*, reason always intercedes for the best choices.[24] Therefore reason is like a bridle that holds back sensuality. But when this restraint is broken or weakened, we are easily inclined to indecencies. And since intemperance inflates the brain, dissipates the senses and takes away memory, it is natural that it should stun the reason, for our understanding does not work without images and consequently not without the senses. With the understanding and reason stunned and weakened, as was said, we easily rush forth into shameful acts. Gluttons incited by lust, then, harm their neighbor as far as it regards a person of his family by doing injury to his wife or sister or daughter or another person connected and joined to him. That wine incites to lust in this way is clear from what is said in Ephesians 5:18, *Be not drunk with wine, in which is lust, but be filled with the Holy Spirit.* For intemperance and overeating provokes adultery according to Jeremiah 5:7, *I fed them to the fill and they committed adultery.*

Abuse is the fourth injury that accompanies gluttony. From wine and drunkenness arise fights and quarrels in which someone speaks insults to another and denigrates his reputation. Therefore just as the gluttonous sin by being unmerciful when they do not show the required kindness to their neighbor, and just as they sin by fraud when they steal the possessions of their neighbor, and just as they sin by lust when they offend their neighbor by doing injury to a person connected to him, so they also sin by abuse when, provoked to fight and quarrel by drunkenness, they denigrate their neighbor's reputation. That drunkenness causes quarrels and provokes fights is clear from what is said in Proverbs 20:1, *Wine causes lust and drunkenness quarrels, and whoever is delighted in them will not be wise.*

Savage cruelty is the fifth injury of neighbor that accompanies gluttony. People warmed by wine are enkindled in their blood and easily provoked to anger; When they are provoked to anger they proceed to blows, and fighting cruelly against each other they wound their own persons with blows. Thus it is said in Proverbs 23:29-30, *Who has fights? Who has wounds without cause? Is it not those who pass their time with wine and are diligent with their drinking cups?* For people of this kind wound each other and fight cruelly against each other without cause. Therefore if someone is wholly worthy of shame who is unmerciful when he denies the required kindness to his neighbor, who is fraudulent when he usurps his neighbor's possessions, who is lustful when he offends his neighbor with regard to a person connected with him, who is abusive when he denigrates his neighbor's reputation, so he is also worthy of shame who is cruel and savage when he does injury to his neighbor's own person. And because all these evils accompany gluttony, it is well said that the glory of the gluttonous will be in shame. For they glory in feasts and drinking cups, out of which so many shameful and indecent acts arise.

Gluttony Harms One's Own Soul

Having shown how gluttons are those whose end is destruction because in five ways they do injury to their own body and ultimately destroy it, and having shown how gluttons are those whose god is their stomach because in five ways they do injury to God and worship their own stomach, and having discussed how their glory is in shame because in five ways they do injury to their neighbor, for which they are worthy of shame, it remains in the fourth and final place to show how gluttons are those who are wise about earthly things because in five ways they do wrong to their own soul and their own selves.

It should be carefully noted that gluttony does not only have five evils by which it harms the body, and not only has five species by which it offends God, and not only has five accompanying evils or five consequences by which neighbors are injured, but it also has five offspring by which the soul is injured. Five offspring, then, are assigned to gluttony, namely silliness, buffoonery, impurity, talkativeness, and dullness of mind.

For by knowing earthly things, that is, by having a taste for earthly things such as gluttons have, we fall into five evils against the soul corresponding to the five offspring of gluttony. An evil against the soul is an evil that resists virtue; and, as far as our present concern, an evil against virtue can be understood in two ways: first with regard to the subject in whom it exists, and second with regard to the act which is performed. For the subject of virtue is twofold: the intellect and the appetite. And the appetite is twofold: the intellective, which is called the will, and the sensitive. Further, the sensitive appetite is divided into two: the irascible and the concupiscible. Therefore the subject of virtue will be fourfold: the intellect, the will, the irascible appetite and the concupiscible appetite. By its five offspring, then, gluttony brings evils into the soul because it corrupts the intellect, disorders the will, pollutes the concupiscible appetite, perverts the irascible appetite, and dissipates external actions. These five evils correspond to the five offspring of gluttony because it corrupts the intellect through a dullness of mind, it disorders the will through silliness, it pollutes the concupiscible appetite through impurity, it perverts the irascible appetite through talkativeness, it dissipates external actions through buffoonery.

Firstly gluttony corrupts the intellect through a dullness of mind. Gluttonous people fill themselves to such an extent that fumes ascend to their head so that nothing is able to appear clearly to the imaginative faculty. And when the imaginative faculty is darkened, the intellect is immediately darkened and made dull. Since this is so, dullness of mind is called an offspring of gluttony. For whatever arises from another has a filial relation with respect to it. And because dullness of mind or thickness of understanding arises from gluttony it is considered its offspring. By this offspring of gluttony the intellect is corrupted because the person in such a condition cannot understand well, for *wisdom,* according to Job 28:13, *is not found in the land of those who live pleasantly.* People who wish to live pleasantly and luxuriously are thick of mind and cannot attain to wisdom. Thus it is said in Hosea 4:11, *Wine and drunkenness take away the understanding,* that is, they corrupt the mind and destroy the intellect. Therefore gluttony, by its offspring dullness of mind, destroys the intellect.

Secondly gluttony disorders the will by another offspring, which is silliness. People filled with wine and drunkenness rejoice pointlessly. Since they have lost the restraint of reason on account of their dullness of mind, and since reason is what restrains silliness, people in this condition immediately begin to rejoice pointlessly and be glad without cause. The will is disordered through this silliness or pointless joy. Warning about this, the wise man says in Sirach 37:32, *Be not greedy for every feast nor abandon yourself to every food.* For the person who is greedy for feasts and who abandons himself to every food achieves silliness and pointless joy, from which the will becomes very disordered.

Thirdly gluttony pollutes the concupiscible appetite through impurity. Impurity is every purposeless emission of semen through which we are intemperate and our concupiscible appetite is corrupted. This impurity is an offspring of gluttony because it is born from it. For, as is clear by what was discussed, gluttons consume so much nourishment that, after the restoration of what was lost in each limb is accomplished, an excess of nourishment overflows. Thus there is in them a great abundance of semen and they are easily inclined to impurity, by which the concupiscible appetite is corrupted. On account of this, the apostle forbids and prohibits impurity, which is an offspring of gluttony, saying in Ephesians 5:3, *But as is fitting for saints, let not fornication nor any impurity nor lust be known among you.*

Fourthly gluttony perverts the irascible appetite through talkativeness. Wine and intemperance cause a person to talk too much. This happens in two ways: first by an attempt to do what is prohibited, second by a defect of reason. Wine twists the tongue and causes it to stutter. And because a person attempts what is prohibited, he tries to speak more, the more he is hindered. For we see that cripples want to walk more than others since nature has prevented them from walking; and stutterers and those with a speech impediment want to talk more than others because nature has inhibited them in speech. We commonly see that we try to do what is prohibited and always desire what is forbidden. Therefore the more drunkards are hindered from speaking because of their speech impediment due to the moisture of wine, the more they try to speak. In intemperance and drunkenness, then, this attempt to do what is prohibited causes a profusion of words.

A defect of reason causes this profusion of words in a second way. On account of drunkenness and intemperance people have a dullness of mind and rejoice for no reason, and thus they easily rush into talkativeness. And by rushing into talkativeness and pointless speech, their irascible appetite is perverted and provoked to anger or elation from pointless speech. Therefore, just as intellect is corrupted from the offspring of gluttony that is called dullness of mind, and just as the will is disordered from the offspring of gluttony that is called silliness, and just as the concupiscible appetite is polluted by impurity, so the irascible appetite is perverted from talkativeness. This talkativeness that is born of intemperance and wine is discussed in 2 Ezra 3:21, where it is said that the one who drinks wine does not remember the king nor the magistrate. And it adds that wine makes a person say everything repeatedly, for it causes a person to multiply words and speak inordinately.

Fifthly and lastly gluttony disorders external actions by the offspring called buffoonery. Any disorder of external gestures is called buffoonery. Not only are drunk and intemperate people unable to restrain inordinate words, they also cannot restrain improper gestures and inordinate movements of their limbs. Such disorder is called buffoonery. The apostle prohibits this buffoonery and this inordinate playfulness and these inordinate gestures in Ephesians 5:3-4, when he says, *Let not obscenity, nor foolish talk, nor buffoonery which is to no purpose be known among you.* For such lasciviousness and such senseless playfulness, which may be called buffoonery, arises from intemperance and drunkenness, according to Exodus 32:6, *The people sat down to eat and drink, and the men rose up to play.*

Therefore gluttons who are wise about earthly things offend their own soul first through dullness of mind that disorders the intellect, second through silliness that disorders the will, third through impurity that corrupts the concupiscible appetite, fourth through talkativeness that perverts the irascible appetite, and fifth through buffoonery that disorders external actions.

Since gluttony causes so many evils, so injures the body, so offends God, so harms neighbors, so corrupts the souls, then with the utmost effort we should be zealous to do all we can to detest this vice. And may this be granted to us by our Lord Jesus, who with the Father and the Holy Spirit is one God blessed forever. Amen.

Notes

1. Dionysius, *The Divine Names* 4: PG 3, 716.
2. Aristotle, *Nicomachean Ethics* VIII, 2, 1155b.
3. Aristotle, *Rhetoric* II, 2, 1378a.
4. Aristotle, *Metaphysics* V, 1, 1013a.
5. Augustine, *Free Will* III, 18, 50.
6. See Aristotle, *Metaphysics* 1, 3, 983a.
7. Not found in the works of Hugh of Saint Victor.
8. Not found in the works of Gregory the Great.
9. Augustine, *Free Will* III, 18, 50.
10. Not found in the writings of Augustine.
11. Aristotle, *Nicomachean Ethics* IV, 6, 1123a.
12. Aristotle, *Politics* I, 8, 1257b 25-28.
13. Augustine, *Confessions* I, 1.
14. See Giles of Rome, *Sentences* II, dist. 12, 9.2, a.3.
15. Aristotle, *Nicomachean Ethics* IV, 3, 1121a 20-21.
16. *Ibid.*
17. Augustine, *Teaching Christianity* I, 23.
18. Aristotle, *On the Soul* II, 4, 416b.
19. Aristotle, *Posterior Analytics* II, 19, 100a.
20. Aristotle, *Metaphysics* I, 1, 980a 28-29.
21. Avicenna, *On Nature* IV, 1.
22. Citation not found.
23. Citation not found.
24. Aristotle, *Nicomachean Ethics* I, 13, 1102b 15-16.

I Bow Before You, Face of Our Redeemer

I bow before you,
face of our Redeemer,
reflecting the splendor
of God's beauty.

You have left your image
on snow-white linen,
a gift to Veronica
in token of love.

I bow before you,
glory of this world,
mirror of the saints,
joy of the angels
as they contemplate you in heaven.

Remove from our hearts
every stain of sin,
and bring us into the joyful company
of the citizens of heaven.

I bow before you,
our inspiration in this life,
a life that is so difficult,
so uncertain, so fragile,
and will pass away so soon.

Source of God's blessing,
lead us home to heaven,
to see you as you are,
the very face of Christ in glory.

Be our sure help, we pray,
refresh our spirit,
be our strength,
keep us unscathed by the evil one,
so that we may rejoice with the saints
in the everlasting happiness of heaven.

Giles of Rome, O.S.A.

A Prayer to God the Father
before Communion

Almighty and merciful God,
I am about to receive the sacrament
of the Body and Blood of your Son,
our Lord Jesus Christ.

I come as one who is sick to the healer of body and soul,
as one who is unclean to the fountain of mercy and grace,
as one who is blind to the brightness of eternal light,
as one who is poor to the Lord of heaven and earth,
as one who is naked to the King of glory.

Eternal Father,
in your boundless and overflowing generosity
be pleased to heal my sickness,
to wash my uncleanness,
to give sight to my blindness,
to enrich my poverty,
and to clothe my nakedness,
so that I may receive Jesus, your Son,
the Bread of angels,
the Lord of lords and King of kings,
with the reverence,
the fear and trembling,
the faith and purity,
the contrition and devotion,
the purpose of amendment and spirit of humility,
that I should have for my soul's salvation.

Father, I beg you,
grant that I may not only receive this sacrament
of the Body and Blood of the Lord
but also its saving power.
God of all gentleness,
grant that in receiving
the Body and blood of your only Son,
our Lord Jesus Christ,
I may be one with his mystical Body
and take my place among its members.

God of all grace,
may the sacred Body of Jesus Christ, your son,
be the delight and joy of my spirit,
my salvation and protection in all temptation,
my peace and happiness in every sorrow,
my light and strength in all I say or do,
my consolation and safeguard in my dying hour.

Loving Father,
as I look forward to receiving your Son,
now veiled by sacramental signs,
grant that I may at last see his face unveiled in heaven,
where he lives and reigns with you
in the unity of the Holy Spirit,
God, for ever and ever. Amen.

The Works of Giles of Rome

Philosophical Works

Super Posteriora Analytica
Super libros Elenchorum
Super Physicam
Super De generatione et corruptione
Super De anima
Quaestiones Metaphysicales
Super libros Rhetoricorum
Super De physiognomia
Super De bona fortuna
Super De causis
Quaestiones de esse et essentia
Theoremata de esse et essentia
Contra gradus et pluralitatem formarum
De gradibus formarum accidentalium
De gradibus formarum in ordine ad Christi opera
De formatione corporis humani in utero
Quaestio de medio demonstrationis
De plurificatione intellectus possibilis
De materia caeli contra averroistas
De intentionibus in medio
De partibus philosophiae essentialibus
De differentia ethicae, politicae et rethoricae
De erroribus philosophorum
De regimine principum

Theological Works

Apologia
Super librum primum Sententiarum
Super librum secundum Sententiarum
Super librum tertium Sententiarum
Theoremata de Corpore Christi
Tractatus de Corpore Christi
Quodlibeta
Quaestiones de mensura angelorum
Quaestiones de cognitione angelorum
Quaestiones de compositione angelorum
Quaestiones de motu angelorum
De praedestinatione et praescientia
De divina influentia in beatos
De peccato originali
De defectu et deviatione malorum culpae et peccatorum a Verbo
Quaestiones de resurrectione mortuorum
Quaestiones disputatae in capitulo generali Paduae
De subiecto theologiae
De distinctione articulorum fidei
De laudibus divinae sapientiae
Quaestiones de charactere
Hexaemeron
Super epistulam Pauli ad Romanos
Super epistulam Pauli ad Corinthios
Super Cantica Canticorum
Super prologis Bibliae
Sententiae super Lucam

Various Works

De renuntiatione papae
De ecclesiastica potestate
Super bullam *Unam Sanctam*
Super decretalem *Firmiter*
Super decretalem *Cum Marthae*
Capitula fidei christianae ad Tartarum maiorem
Contra exemptos
Quaestio quomodo reges et principes possint possessiones et bona
    regni pecularia ecclesiis elargiri
Oratio in die coronationis Philippi regis
Sermones de Corpore Christi
Sermones de tribus vitiis mundi

Sermones de tempore
Horae canonicae Salvatoris
Hymnus ad faciem Salvatoris

Index

Compiled by Joseph Sprug